The Complete Book

of

Contemporary Business Letters

Written by Strategic Communications

Edited by Stephen P. Elliott

Round Lake Publishing
Ridgefield, Co

Fourth edition

Round Lake Publishing Co.
31 Bailey Avenue
Ridgefield, CT 06877

Printed in the United States of America

20 19 18 17 16 15 14 13 12 11 10 9 8 7 6 5 4

ISBN 0-929543-07-6

Other Helpful Books from Round Lake Publishing

If your bookstore doesn't have these books, you may order directly from Round Lake Publishing.

The Complete Book of Contemporary Business Letters
400 model letters for all areas of business, including customer relations, handling customer complaints, credit and collections, personnel relations, memos and reports, job search, personal letters and much more. 470 pages, soft cover, 6" x 8 3/4" $19.95

Encyclopedia of Money Making Sales Letters
Over 300 letters covering all phases of selling, from prospecting for new customers to closing sales. Includes responses to objections, keeping the customer buying, selling yourself, plus much more. *"Helps sell anything"*—The New York Times. 370 pages, soft cover, 6" x 8 3/4" $19.95

The Only Personal Letter Book You'll Ever Need
Over 400 letters cover all areas of personal correspondence, including apologies and thank you's, complaints to companies and individuals, congratulations and invitations, saying no, sympathy and condolences, and much more. 460 pages, soft cover, 6" x 8 3/4" $19.95

Hiring, Firing (and everything in between) Personnel Forms Book
160 forms covering all aspects of personnel management, including job applications, interviewing guides, personnel policies, performance appraisals, orientation, attendance, salary, discipline, benefits, termination, federal regulations, and more. 370 pages, soft cover, 6" x 8 3/4" $19.95

The Complete Book of Consulting
150 forms—plus expert advice— for starting and running a successful consulting practice. Includes business plans, fee calculation worksheets, sales letters, brochures and cover letters, proposals, contracts, invoices, plus much more. Maximize your income with this extremely unusual and helpful consulting resource. 300 pages, soft cover, 6" x 8 3/4" $19.95

Step-By-Step Legal Forms and Agreements
165 legal forms for business and personal use. Includes wills, living will, power of attorney, forms for buying and selling real estate, starting a company, corporate forms, and much more. The most comprehensive book of its kind. *"Could hardly be easier to use"*—The New York Times. 440 pages, soft cover, 6" x 8 3/4" $19.95

Ads Plus
260 ready-to-use ads, brochures, business cards, direct mail, flyers, press releases, plus much more. Over 900 pieces of custom art! Created by award-winning copywriters and graphics designers, this unique book is a treasure trove of sales-generating devices. 450 pages, soft cover, 6" x 8 3/4" $19.95

Order Form

Please rush me the following books: cbcbl
☐ Complete Book of Contemporary Business Letters $19.95
☐ Encyclopedia of Money Making Sales Letters $19.95
☐ The Only Personal Letter Book You'll Ever Need $19.95
☐ Hiring, Firing (and everything in between) Personnel Forms Book $19.95
☐ The Complete Book of Consulting $19.95
☐ Step-By-Step Legal Forms and Agreements $19.95
☐ Ads Plus $19.95
Add $3.95 to the total order for shipping. Sorry, no orders shipped outside of North America.

I have enclosed ☐ Check   Bill my credit card   ☐ Am Ex   ☐ Visa   ☐ MasterCard

Credit card # _____ Exp. Date _____

Signature (required for credit card) _____

Name _____
          Please print
Company _____

Address _____

City _____ State _____ Zip _____

Round Lake Publishing   **Phone (203) 438-6303**
31 Bailey Avenue, Ridgefield, CT 06877   **Fax (203) 431-6811**

Contents

Preface .... *xix*

How to Use this Book .... *xxiii*

Chapter 1 SALES AND MARKETING

Introduction 1

Dealing with the Customer
Welcome to the Area (1-01) 3
Welcome to the Family (1-02) 4
Welcome, Brochure with Company Terms (1-03) 5
Welcome, Catalog Enclosed (1-04) 6

Sales Call Follow-ups
Follow-up to Sales Call: First Follow-up to New Client/Customer (1-05) 7
Follow-up to Sales Call: Inactive Customer (1-06) 8
Solicitation of Additional Business to Current Customer (1-07) 9
Solicitation of Former Customer (1-08) 10

Requests and Responses
Response to Request for Information (1-09) 11
Request to Use Name As Reference (1-10) 12
Thank You for Permission to Use Name As Reference (1-11) 13

Lead Generation
Lead Generation, Consumer Services (1-12) 14
Lead Generation, Industrial Products (1-13) 15

Promotional Announcements
Flyer (1-14) 16
Contest (1-15) 17
Discount Offer (1-16) 18
Premium Incentive (1-17) 19
Trade Show Announcement (1-18) 20

Store Opening, Special Offer (1-19) 21
Workshop Promotion (1-20) 22
Announcement of Sales Program, Consumer Goods (1-21) 23
Announcement of Sales Program, Industrial Products (1-22) 24
Announcement of Advertising Campaign, Consumer Goods (1-23) 25
Announcement of Advertising Campaign, Industrial Products (1-24) 26
Announcement of New Product/Service to Former Customer (1-25) 27

Communicating with the Sales Force
Explanation of Changes in Prices to Sales Force (1-26) 28
Update on Product Specifications (1-27) 29
Introduction of New Salesperson to Sales Force (1-28) 30
Explanation of Changes in Territory Assignments (1-29) 31
Explanation of Bonus/Commission Program (1-30) 32
Request for Meeting to Review Sales Performance (1-31) 33

Research
Cover Letter for Questionnaire (1-32) 34
Thank You for Answering Questionnaire (1-33) 35
Questionnaire about Salespeople (1-34) 36
Questionnaire to Inactive Client (1-35) 38
Consumer Expo Questionnaire (1-36) 40

Orders
Order Received, Being Processed (1-37) 42
Order Received, Being Shipped (1-38) 43
Order Received, Delivery Delayed (1-39) 44
Order Received, Merchandise Not Available (1-40) 45
Order Received, Unable to Process (1-41) 46

Shipping
Merchandise Being Shipped (1-42) 47
Backorder Arrived, Being Shipped (1-43) 48
Merchandise Ready for Customer Pick-up (1-44) 49

Statements
Statement for Services (1-45) 50
Statement for Goods Delivered (1-46) 51

Quotations and Proposals
Request for Opportunity to Quote (1-47) 52
Thank You for Opportunity to Quote, Proposal Enclosed (1-48) 53
Quotation Cover Letter (1-49) 54
Proposal (1-50) 55

Follow-up to Proposal (1-51) 56
Revised Proposal Cover Letter (1-52) 57
Response to Request for Bid, with Questions (1-53) 58
Request to Extend Decision Deadline (1-54) 59
Confirmation of Deadline Extension (1-55) 60
Confirmation Letter, Terms Accepted (1-56) 61
Confirmation Letter, Terms Accepted, Invoice Enclosed (1-57) 62
Confirmation Letter, Exception to Original Terms (1-58) 63
Confirmation Letter, Changes in Specifications (1-59) 64
Confirmation Letter, Acceptance of Changes in Terms/Specifications (1-60) 65
Consignment Terms (1-61) 66

Contracts and Government Regulations
Contract Enclosed for Signature (1-62) 67
Approval of Drawings (1-63) 68
Request for Verification of EEOC Compliance (1-64) 69

Chapter 2 ADVERTISING AND PUBLIC RELATIONS

Introduction 71

Dealing with Advertising Agencies and Rate Requests
Hiring Advertising Agency (2-01) 73
Request for Meeting on Agency Fees (2-02) 74
Notification to Advertising Agency of Impending Review (2-03) 75
Termination of Relationship with Advertising Agency (2-04) 76
Request for Newspaper Advertising Rates (2-05) 77
Request for Magazine Advertising Rates (2-06) 78
Request for Broadcast/Television Advertising Rates (2-07) 79
Work Agreement with Freelancer (2-08) 80

Announcements to Customers
Announcement of Change of Address (2-09) 81
Announcement of New Subsidiary (2-10) 82
Announcement of New Business, Professional (2-11) 83
Announcement of New Employee (2-12) 84
Announcement of New Product Line (2-13) 85
Announcement of New Business Name (2-14) 86
Announcement of Branch Office/Store (2-15) 87

Public Relations Companies and Fees
Hiring Public Relations Firm (2-16) 88
Request for Meeting on Public Relations Firm's Services (2-17) 89

Acceptance of Request for TV Interview (2-18) 90

Press Releases
Announcement of New Product (2-19) 91
Announcement of New Product Line (2-20) 92
Announcement of New Employee (2-21) 93
Announcement of Employee Promotion (2-22) 94
Announcement of Award/Achievement by Employee/Principal (2-23) 95
Announcement of Merger (2-24) 96
Announcement of New Partner (2-25)..97
Company Press Release, Short Version (2-26)..98
Company Press Release, Long Version (2-27) 99
Thank You for Printing Article (2-28)...100

Chapter 3 CUSTOMER RELATIONS

Introduction 101

Changes in Business
Announcement of New Product to Current Customer (3-01)...............................103
Notification of Price Increase (3-02) 104
Notification of Price Decrease (3-03) 105
Notification of Change in Services (3-04) 106
Notification of Change in Policy (3-05) 107
Notification of New Salesperson in Territory (3-06) 108
Notification of Change in Administrative Arrangements (3-07).........................109

Compliments
Congratulations on Promotion (3-08) 110
Congratulations on New Job (3-09) 111
Congratulations on Being Quoted (3-10) 112
Congratulations on New Office (3-11) 113
Congratulations on Expansion of Business (3-12) 114
Enjoyed Your Article/Speech (3-13) 115
Appreciation of Business Suggestion (3-14) 116
Acknowledgment of Compliment to Company/Employee (3-15) 117

Meetings and Appointments
Setting Up Meeting (3-16) 118
Confirmation of Meeting (3-17) 119
Request for Associate to Attend Meeting (3-18) 120
Setting Up Appointment (3-19) 121
Confirmation of Appointment (3-20) 122

Thank You for Meeting (3-21) 123
Thank You for Setting Up Sales Call (3-22) 124
Apology to Customer for Missing Meeting (3-23) 125
Apology to Business Associate for Missing Appointment (3-24) 126

Returned Checks

Check Returned, Polite Request for Payment (3-25) 127
Check Returned, Firm Request for Payment (3-26) 128
Check Returned, Warning of Collection Agency (3-27) 129

Payments and Returns by Customer

Thank You for Prompt Payment (3-28) 130
Thank You for Prompt Payment, Other Products/Services of Interest (3-29) 131
Discount for Early Payment (3-30) 132
Payment Received, Pre-Payment Required in the Future (3-31) 133
Payment Incorrect, Will Credit Next Statement (3-32) 134
Payment Incorrect, Will Debit Account (3-33) 135
Payment Incorrect, Send Balance (3-34) 136
Overpayment, Check Enclosed (3-35) 137
Duplicate Invoice Provided as Requested (3-36) 138
Acknowledgment of Return for Exchange (3-37) 139
Acknowledgment of Return for Credit (3-38) 140
Acknowledgment of Refund for Damaged Goods (3-39) 141
No Record of Returned Goods (3-40) 142

Chapter 4 HANDLING CUSTOMER COMPLAINTS

Introduction 143

Complaint Justified

Clarification of Billing (4-01) 145
Apology for Billing Error (4-02) 146
Apology for Computer Error (4-03) 147
Apology for Delay in Shipment (4-04) 148
Apology for Error in Shipment (4-05) 149
Apology for Damaged Shipment (4-06) 150
Apology for Employee Rudeness (4-07) 151
Apology for Missing Documentation (4-08) 152

Complaint Unjustified

Company Not at Fault (4-09) 153
Company Not Responsible for Delay in Shipment (4-10) 154
Company Not Responsible for Rudeness (4-11) 155

Customer Misunderstood Delivery Time (4-12) 156
Customer Misunderstood Terms of Sale (4-13) 157
Customer Misunderstood Terms of Sale, Special Order (4-14) 158
Customer Misunderstood Product Specifications, Features Explained (4-15) 159
Customer Misunderstood Product Specifications, Return Authorized (4-16) 160
Customer Misunderstood Product Specifications, Return Not Possible (4-17) ... 161
Customer Misunderstood Delivery Terms (4-18) 162
Response to Customer Who Is Threatening Legal Action (4-19) 163

Chapter 5 CREDIT AND COLLECTIONS

Introduction 165

Extending and Refusing Credit
Request to Customer to Complete Credit Application (5-01) 167
Request to Customer for Financial Information (5-02) 168
Request for Credit Report on Individual (5-03) 169
Request for Credit Report on Company (5-04) 170
Approval of Credit, Retail (5-05) 171
Refusal of Credit, Commercial (5-06) 172
Refusal of Credit, Retail (5-07) 173

Collection Sequence (moderate tone)
Collection Letter, Moderate Tone, Letter #1 (5-08) 174
Collection Letter, Moderate Tone, Letter #2 (5-09) 175
Collection Letter, Moderate Tone, Letter #3 (5-10) 176
Collection Letter, Moderate Tone, Final Notice (5-11) 177

Collection Sequence (stern tone)
Collection Letter, Stern Tone, Letter #1 (5-12) 178
Collection Letter, Stern Tone, Letter #2 (5-13) 179
Collection Letter, Stern Tone, Letter #3 (5-14) 180
Collection Letter, Stern Tone, Letter #4 (5-15) 181
Collection Letter, Stern Tone, Letter #5 (5-16) 182

Credit Reports
Response to Credit Report, Misleading Report (5-17) 183
Response to Credit Report, False Report (5-18) 184

Chapter 6 DEALING WITH SUPPLIERS

Introduction 185

Requests and Inquiries

Inquiry about Product (6-01) 187

Request for Credit (6-02) 188

Inquiry about Credit Terms (6-03) 189

Inquiry about Discounts (6-04) 190

Bids and Proposals

Request for Bid (6-05) 191

Rejection of Bid (6-06) 192

Declining to Do Business at This Time (6-07) 193

Rejection of Proposal (6-08) 194

Dissatisfaction with Shipment or Service

Return of Item after Trial (6-09) 195

Request for Repair under Warranty (6-10) 196

Request for Service under Warranty (6-11) 197

Confirmation of Offer to Repair under Warranty (6-12) 198

Shipment Refused on Quality Grounds (6-13) 199

Payment to Be Made When Work Is Completed (6-14) 200

Invoice Cannot Be Processed, Shipment Incomplete (6-15) 201

Invoice Cannot Be Processed, Charges Incorrect (6-16) 202

Documentation Missing (6-17) 203

Cancellation of Order (6-18) 204

Performance Unsatisfactory, Temporary Employment Agency (6-19) 205

Performance Unsatisfactory, Service Company (6-20) 206

Refusal to Accept Proposed Remedy (6-21) 207

Compliments and Suggestions

Thank You for Cooperation During Difficult Project (6-22) 208

Suggestion to Supplier (6-23) 209

Compliment to Supplier (6-24) 210

Compliment for Supplier's Employee (6-25) 211

Payment

Payment Enclosed (6-26) 212

Authorization to Transfer Funds (6-27) 213

Apology for Incorrect Payment (6-28) 214

Apology for Late Payment (6-29) 215

Explanation of Late Payment (6-30) 216

Payment Stopped on Check (6-31) 217

Check Has Been Sent (6-32) 218

Return of Item for Credit (6-33) 219

Request Permission to Return Item/Shipment

Request Permission to Return Item in Shipment, Damaged (6-34) 220
Request Permission to Return Item in Shipment, Not Ordered (6-35) 221
Request Permission to Return Shipment, Not Ordered (6-36) 222
Request Permission to Return Shipment, Arrived Too Late (6-37) 223
Request Permission to Return Shipment, Damaged (6-38) 224
Request Permission to Return Shipment, No Longer Needed (6-39) 225

Chapter 7 PERSONNEL RELATIONS

Introduction 227

Hiring

Announcement of Job Opening (7-01) 229
Request for Help in Recruiting New Employees (7-02) 230
Response to Resume, Unsolicited (7-03) 231
Response to Resume, with Referral (7-04) 232
Thank You for Application, Will Keep on File (7-05) 233
Invitation to Interview (7-06) 234
Interview Outline (7-07) 235
Confirmation of Job Offer, with Terms (7-08) 236
Revised Job Offer (7-09) 237
Follow-up to Interview, Rejection (7-10) 238
Termination of Job Offer (7-11) 239

Problems

Warning about Excessive Lateness (7-12) 240
Warning about Excessive Sick Days (7-13) 241
Termination of Employee (7-14) 242

References

Reference for Departing Employee, Good Employee (7-15) 243
Reference for Departing Employee, Unsolicited (7-16) 244
Reference for Former Employee, Average Employee (7-17) 245
Request for Reference, to Company (7-18) 246
Request for Verification of Employment (7-19) 247
Response to Request for Employment Verification (7-20) 248

Employee Benefits

Description of Employee Benefits (7-21) 249

Job Descriptions and Evaluations

Job Description, Entry Level (7-22) 250

Job Description, Middle Level (7-23) 251
Performance Appraisal, Written Evaluation (7-24) 252
Performance Appraisal, Rating Form (7-25) 254
Notification of Promotion (7-26) 256
Notification of Salary Increase (7-27) 257
Motivation of Employee (7-28) 258

Chapter 8 MANAGING YOUR BUSINESS

Introduction 259

Business Logistics
Inquiry about Office Lease (8-01) 261
Inquiry to Bank about Outstanding Credit Application (8-02) 262
Inquiry about Business Credit Card (8-03) 263
Inquiry about Insurance Coverage (8-04) 264
Inquiry about Accounting Service (8-05) 265
Inquiry about Office Equipment (8-06) 266
Inquiry about Car Leasing (8-07) 267
Inquiry about Consulting Services (8-08) 268
Inquiry to Franchisor (8-09) 269
Inquiry about Phone Equipment (8-10) 270
Inquiry about Utilities Service (8-11) 271
Inquiry to Planning and Zoning Commission (8-12) 272
Inquiry about Event Planning Services (8-13) 273
Inquiry about Supplies (8-14) 274
Inquiry about Medical Plans (8-15) 275
Inquiry about Banking Services (8-16) 276
Inquiry about Legal Services (8-17) 277
Inquiry to Business Association (8-18) 278
Inquiry to Venture Capital Firm (8-19) 279
Inquiry to Federal Government, New Business (8-20) 280
Inquiry to State Government, New Business (8-21) 281
Request for Help from Elected Representative (8-22) 282
Request for Action to Local Town Government (8-23) 283
Request to Employment Agency for Information (8-24) 284
Request to Executive Search Firm for Information (8-25) 285
Request to Temporary Agency for Information and Rates (8-26) 286
Dealing with Local Government (8-27) 287
Dealing with Tenants (8-28) 288
Dealing with Your Landlord (8-29) 289
Request to Excuse Employee from Jury Duty (8-30) 290

Business Plans, Help, and Housekeeping

Business Plan, Executive Summary (8-31) 291
Business Plan, Executive Summary Cover Letter (8-32) 292
Request for Help (8-33) 293
Thank You for Help (8-34) 294
SBA Loan Application Cover Letter (8-35) 295
Announcement of Annual Meeting (8-36) 296
Announcement of Board Meeting (8-37)..297

Reservations and Rentals

Request for Hotel Rates (8-38) 298
Reservation of Hotel/Meeting Facility (8-39) 299
Confirmation of Equipment Rental (8-40) 300
Appreciation to Hotel/Facility for Help/Good Service (8-41)..............301
Complaint to Hotel/Facility about Poor Service (8-42).......................302
Special Travel Requirements for Company Employees (8-43) 303

Chapter 9 INTERNAL COMMUNICATIONS

Introduction 305

Meetings and Planning

Notification of Meeting (9-01) 307
Agenda (9-02) 308
Agenda, Background Meeting (9-03) 309
Follow-up to Meeting, Assignments (9-04)...310
Planning Memo (9-05) 311
Recap of Meeting (9-06) 312

Suggestions, Reports, and Recommendations

Thank You for Employee Suggestion, Accepted (9-07) 314
Thank You for Employee Suggestion, Cannot Use (9-08)....................315
Request for Change in Project (9-09) 316
Request for Employee Participation in Charity Drive (9-10) 317
Progress Report, Executive Summary (9-11) 318
Final Report, Executive Summary (9-12) 319
Explanation for Lateness of Work/Report (9-13) 320
Recommendation to Purchase Equipment (9-14) 321
Recommendation to Adopt a Course of Action (9-15)..........................322
Recommendation to Adopt a Strategy (9-16) 324

Procedures and Policies

Procedure for Dealing with the Media (9-17) 325

Clarification of Existing Policy (9-18) 326
Recommendation to Change a Policy (9-19) 327

Announcements

Announcement of New Procedures, Developed within Company (9-20) 328
Announcement of New Procedures, Imposed from Outside (9-21) 329
Announcement of Promotion (9-22) 330
Announcement of New Company Policy, Travel Expenses (9-23) 331
Announcement of New Company Policy, No Smoking (9-24) 332
Announcement of Motivational Award (9-25) 333
Announcement of Resignation of Employee (9-26) 334

Difficult Times

Announcement of Bad News (9-27) 335
Request for Cooperation in Difficult Times (9-28) 336
Procedure for Dealing with the Media, Company Problem (9-29) 337

Chapter 10 COMMUNITY SERVICE

Introduction 339

Fund Raising Requests and Responses

Approach Letter (10-01) 341
Direct Solicitation, Cash Donation (10-02) 342
Direct Solicitation, Fund Raiser (10-03) 343
Thank You for Cash Pledge (10-04) 344
Thank You for Item Pledge (10-05) 345
Thank You for Cash Donation (10-06) 346
Thank You for Item Donation (10-07) 347
Understanding of Inability to Give (10-08) 348
Acceptance to Donate (10-09) 349
Refusal to Donate (10-10) 350

Serving or Speaking Requests and Responses

Asking Individual to Serve as Program Chairperson (10-11) 351
Asking Individual to Serve as Development Chairperson (10-12) 352
Asking Individual to Serve as Board Member (10-13) 353
Welcome to the Board (10-14) 354
Refusal to Serve on Board (10-15) 355
Solicitation of Votes for Election to Board (10-16) 356
Acceptance to Serve in Trade Association (10-17) 357
Declining to Join Organization (10-18) 358
Inability to Attend Function (10-19) 359
Offer to Write Article (10-20) 360

Request to Company/Organization to Provide Speaker (10-21) 361
Acceptance of Invitation to Speak (10-22) 362
Confirmation of Individual's Agreement to Speak (10-23) 363
Declining Request to Speak (10-24) 364
Acceptance to Attend Function by Award Recipient (10-25) 365
Resignation from Organization (10-26) 366
Invitation to Dinner/Luncheon (10-27) 367
Response Card (10-28) 368
Thank You for Company Hospitality (10-29) 369

Chapter 11 JOB SEARCH

Introduction 371

Resignation and Agencies
Resignation from Current Job (11-01) 373
Approach to Executive Search Firm (11-02) 374
Request for Information from Outplacement Agency (11-03) 375

Resumes
Resume: Chronological, Entry Level (11-04) 376
Resume: Chronological, Early Career (11-05) 378
Resume: Chronological, Mid-Career (11-06) 380
Resume: Achievement, Early Career (11-07) 382
Resume: Achievement, Mid-Career (11-08) 384
Resume: Functional, Entry Level (11-09) 386
Resume: Career Change (11-10) 388
Resume: Curriculum Vitae (11-11) 390

Letters to Companies and Individuals
Job Approach, "Cold" (11-12) 391
Job Approach, with Referral (11-13) 392
Thank You for Referral (11-14) 393
Request for Information (11-15) 394
Thank You for Information (11-16) 395
Request for Interview (11-17) 396
Thank You for Interview (11-18) 397
Thank You for Interview, Not Interested in Job (11-19) 398
Thank You for Interview, Second Interview (11-20) 399
Acceptance of Job Offer (11-21) 400
Interest in Job Offer, with Questions (11-22) 401
Interest in Job Offer, with Conditions (11-23) 402
Negotiation of Job Offer (11-24) 403

Rejection of Job Offer (11-25) 404
Request for Information Interview (11-26) 405
Thank You for Information Interview (11-27) 406
Update after Information Interview (11-28) 407
Thank You for Help (11-29) 408
Request for Reference, to Business Associate (11-30) 409

Chapter 12 PERSONAL LETTERS

Introduction 411

Sympathy, Congratulations, and Thank Yous

Get Well (12-01) 413
Sympathy to Business Associate and Friend (12-02) 414
Sympathy to Business Associate's Family (12-03) 415
Sympathy to Employee's Family (12-04) 416
Sympathy to Employee (12-05) 417
Congratulations on a Birth (12-06) 418
Congratulations on an Adoption (12-07) 419
Congratulations on a Marriage (12-08) 420
Congratulations on Child's Honor (12-09) 421
Thank You for Hospitality (12-10) 422
Thank You for Gift (12-11) 423
Thank You for Flowers (12-12) 424
Thank You for Favor (12-13) 425

Personal Reference

Character Reference (12-14) 426

Putting Issues before Public Officials

Letter to the Editor (12-15) 427
Putting Issues before Public Officials (12-16) 428

Chapter 13 FAXES

Introduction 429

Cover sheets

Master Cover Sheet (13-01) 431
Resume Cover Sheet (13-02) 432

Sales

Response to Request for Information (13-03) 433
Quotation (13-04) 434

Correction of Pricing Information (13-05)...435
Confirmation of Order by Fax or Phone (13-06) 436

Customer Service
Notification of Shipment (13-07)...437
Apology for Shipment Error (13-08) 438

Supplier Relations
Request for Price Quotation (13-09) 439
Order (13-10) 440
Request Permission to Return Shipment, Damaged (13-11) 441
Cancellation of Order (13-12)..442
Complaint to Supplier, Cannot Reach by Phone (13-13)....................443

Urgent Matters
Communication of Urgent Data (13-14) 444
Decision Required (13-15) 445
Request for Immediate Approval (13-16) 446
Conveying Client Information to Colleague (13-17) 447

Telephone Confirmations
Confirmation of Phone Conversation (13-18) 448
Setting Time for Telephone Conversation (13-19) 449

Chapter 14 NETWORKING

Introduction 451

Announcements and feedback requests
Announcement of Start-Up Business (14-01) 453
Request for Feedback on Article (14-02)...454
Request for Feedback on New Product (14-03) 455

Requests for referrals
Thanks You for Input, Request for Referrals (14-04)..........................456
Thank You for Input, Free Gift (14-05) 457
Offer to Exchange Referrals (14-06) 458

Chapter 15 BUSINESS FORMS

Introduction 459

FORMS
Letter. Full Block (15-01) 460
Letter, Modified Block (15-02)...462
Memo (15-03) 464
Report Format (15-04) 465
Outline (15-05)..466
Invoice for Services (15-06) 467
Invoice for Goods (15-07)...468

INDEX *469*

Preface

Many bright people, perhaps you're one of them, go to great lengths to avoid writing letters. Even when it means losing sales, alienating customers, or missing opportunities to present themselves in the best light, the threat of facing a blank page or a bare computer screen can be more powerful than the need to write a letter.

Just the thought of getting started can strike terror! "How should I open the letter?" "Just what information do I need to include?" "Am I communicating in the best tone for the situation and is my approach the most effective one?" "What closing will bring the action or reaction I want?" Sometimes the challenge of all these factors so overwhelms the writer that no letter at all is ever sent, or the letter that is finally composed misses the mark completely or subverts the writer's purpose.

All of this is most unfortunate because, in fact, armed with some simple guidelines to follow, and some excellent models from which to learn, business letter writing can be a relatively easy, extremely rewarding task.

Every piece of business correspondence is a sales tool. When you write to a customer, even about such a simple matter as confirming a delivery date, your correspondence is telling him about you and your company—about your professionalism, your interest in serving him, the style with which you conduct business. The same is true of an internal memo. Here your market is your associate, your boss, your subordinate. A weak or confusing communication represents you poorly, sending the message that you are inept or that you exercise poor judgment.

This book gives you your very own "file" of concise, crisp letters, memos, proposals and other business documents covering all of the major areas of business. Each one is designed to provide a model for effective communication. Of equal significance are the comments accompanying each document, which highlight the important features and help you to customize it.

Before you begin, decide whether you should be writing at all. This might seem like a foolish point, but it isn't. Writing is too time-consuming to engage in frivolously. The key question is "What do I want the reader to do after he or she reads this?" If you can't answer this question, you might reconsider whether you should write at all.

Don't **write** under the following conditions:

- When a quick phone call will do the job just as well as a letter, *and* a written record is *not* required.
- When you want to congratulate yourself. If your sole reason for writing is to let people know how great you are, think again. It's always better to *show* people you're competent than to tell them.
- When you're emotionally upset. If you're in a rage because someone on your staff failed to do what he was supposed to do, take some time to cool down before you begin to write. The letter will be better thought out, and you'll avoid saying things you may regret later on.

Do **write**, however, if any of the following apply:

- When the reader needs time to understand and absorb the message—for example, the material is complex and technical.
- When a permanent record is necessary to guard against misinterpretation or to protect the writer and the reader from the memory lapses that come with the passage of time.
- When you need a polite way to get someone's attention. For example, when you've been trying to reach a potential customer by phone, to no avail.
- When writing a letter can demonstrate that you've made a special effort.

Be prepared! It is impossible to write a well-reasoned letter or memo without preliminary thought. You need to focus on the decision maker, the person who will take action on what you are writing, and write with that person's needs in mind. Whether that person is a customer, a supplier, a creditor, a member of your staff, or your boss, aim your letter at the intended reader. The best way to achieve this is to picture the person in your mind as you write.

Get to the point. Establish what the main point of the letter is to be by asking yourself, "What is the one thing I want the reader to remember?" Start with a sentence that compels the reader to continue reading, and then quickly make the main point or points. Don't save important information for late in the document. Many readers will never get that far.

Be brief. If your letter is well organized, you won't be tempted to run on.

Most readers are just as busy as you are. They won't read pages and pages of explanation or analysis. Keep your letters, memos, and executive summaries to one page, if possible. Keep your paragraphs short.

Say what you mean. Hedging fools absolutely no one. Many people fall into the habit of qualifying their sentences in order to avoid categorical statements that may later be proven false. As a result, their documents are loaded with sentences starting with "There is a possibility that" or "There is some potential that." Lopping off these phrases will improve most prose. Use the active voice (he completed the project) rather than the passive voice (the project was completed by him) for the same reasons—it's shorter and more forthright.

Be positive. If you can state something positively, do so. Saying "We can't fill your order" is honest enough, but saying "We'd like to substitute Product X, a superior version of the product you ordered" is much better. People are much more receptive to the positive approach.

Be natural. Letter writing doesn't have the stilted, formal sound it once did. Don't use slang, but do write in a conversational style, similar to the way you speak. Even contractions like "I've" and "let's" accurately reflect the way people converse, and are perfectly acceptable in written communications today. People have been so used to Victorian phrasing in business correspondence that they find it hard to resist phrases like "Per your letter of August twenty-first" or "Enclosed herewith please find." Read your letter or memo aloud. If it sounds stiff, it probably is! Change it so that it sounds more natural.

How to Use This Book

This book provides an easy-to-access file of model letters for every category of business. Using the chapter openers as background and the comments accompanying the letters as a guide, you should find it easy to customize any document to suit your particular needs.

Accessing the letters. The documents fall within 13 major areas, or chapters, as spelled out in the table of contents, and then into more specific areas within each chapter. Each document has a descriptive title as well as a reference number, which identifies the chapter in which the letter can be found and, separated by a hyphen, its numerical placement within the chapter. In addition, there are two indexes from which to select the letter you need, one alphabetized by letter title and one by subject. After using the table of contents and indexes a few times you may find that, for your purposes, one of them proves more helpful to you than the others in locating the documents you want to use.

Customizing the letters. Once you've chosen the letter you wish to customize, you may want to make a copy of it on which you can do the editing. Keep the book open to that page, so you can refer to the original letter and the comments under it. The comments alert you to the important features of the letter—and assure that all essential information will be included.

In addition to the content of the model letters, pay particular attention to their tone and style. These factors determine the strength and effectiveness of your written communications.

Many of the letters and other documents in the book require very little customizing to make them appropriate for other situations, while some will need additional editing. The more complex letters provide excellent examples of how to handle particularly difficult situations.

When creating your own documents, consider combining paragraphs from several letters within the same category. This is particularly helpful when your needs fall somewhere between two model letters.

Review the letter when you finish to be sure you have changed all the information necessary to make the letter correct for your purposes. And, of course, proofread it to be sure there are no typographical errors or misspelled names.

Sales and Marketing 1

Sales and marketing are the lifeblood of most companies. Written communications cover many different kinds of activities in these areas. All of them are crucial to the success of a company, primarily because they are directly responsible for generating income or, in the case of communicating with the sales force, dealing with those who generate the income. The effectiveness of the written word is critical in all of these endeavors.

Sales letters. Although all business communications should be persuasive, persuasion is usually the *sole* reason for sales letters. While a face-to-face encounter provides a sales person with the ability to establish rapport with the customer, sales letters long have proven themselves powerful marketing tools as well. They are personal, command undistracted attention and can be precisely targeted to a market. Methods have been developed over the years which, when followed, yield highly productive results.

The alternative to the salesman's warm smile and sincere handshake is the "grabber." It captures the reader's attention and gives him a compelling reason to continue reading. The headline or opening sentence should involve him immediately. Among the time-proven grabbers are free offers, announcements of new or improved products, provocative statements and attention-demanding questions.

The body of the letter should demonstrate a need and then show how your product or service meets that need. Next, persuade the reader to make a purchase decision. The easier you make that decision for him, the more successful the letter will be. A reduction of the selling price or offering a money-back guarantee are strong inducements to purchase. Finally, ask for action: mail the order card, phone today. Keep the ordering instructions simple and clear.

Follow-ups. The cardinal rule is always to leave a "thread" that leads to the next contact, to a continuation of the relationship. Ending a letter with "Please call me if you have an interest in any of our products" will seldom elicit action. Much better is "I will call you in a week to hear your reaction to this proposal." Imagine that the steps preceding a sale are a dance and that you are leading.

Following up also means thanking people who give you leads or information about potential customers. Report your progress to date, if appropriate, and always let them know if you make the sale. It's simple courtesy.

Communicating with the sales force. Because most salespeople are on the road or unavailable, managers must communicate with them by memo or letter. The key is to be straightforward and to use a civil tone. Salespeople are no less sensitive to nuances than any other human beings. With their distance from the office, they may be prone to misunderstanding communications that aren't carefully worded.

Orders and shipping. Orders and shipping issues are part of the sales process in many organizations, since the salesperson will often also be responsible for fulfillment. The touchstone is to be pleasant and honest, particularly if there are difficulties in fulfilling the order.

Proposals, bids and quotations. Whether writing proposals, confirming terms, or changing terms and specifications, these letters have contractual ramifications. You may want to have them looked at by an attorney if significant amounts of money are involved. As with all customer correspondence, be clear, concise and polite.

Company Name
Address
City, State Zip

Date

Mr. and Mrs. Ned Hawkins
59 Winter Street
Easton, MD 21601

Dear Mr. and Mrs. Hawkins:

Congratulations on your new home and welcome to the Easton area! We wish you many happy years in this new location.

We at Chim, Chim, Cheree have been serving customers in Easton for over 50 years, and we would like to add your name to our list of satisfied customers. We are specialists in chimney cleaning, damper repair, masonry repair, and chimney cap installation. Please call me at 281-5333 to arrange an appointment for a **complimentary** fireplace inspection and consultation with one of the professionals from our staff. I've included our brochure, which tells you more about our company and services.

Again, welcome to Easton. I look forward to hearing from you.

Sincerely,

George Kendry

Enclosure

- Explain who you are and the services you provide.

- If possible, give an incentive for the customer to try your services (premium, discount, complimentary visit, etc.).

- Clearly indicate how you may be reached.

Company Name
Address
City, State Zip

Date

J & J Catering
103 Shady Lane
Nesconset, NY 11767

Dear Ms. Johnson:

Thank you for choosing AAAble Rents for your first catering job. I heard that it was a great success. The staff and I wish you and Mrs. Jones the best success with your new service.

At AAAble, we are ready when you need us. In addition to chairs, tables, china, silverware, table linens, and glasses, which you have already rented from us, we can also supply you with tents, candelabra, hollowware, party decorations, dance floors, and many other party supplies. Please call us soon!

Best regards,

John Miller
President

- Thank them for the business.

- Offer any additional services that you might have.

- Solicit more business.

Company Name
Address
City, State Zip

Date

Mr. John Siegler
Edge Tech
118 Collen's Ferry Road
Abbeyville, SC 29620

Dear Mr. Siegler:

Thank you for your order of last Tuesday; we appreciate new clients, as they are the lifeblood of our business. I am enclosing our latest company brochure, which describes our capabilities and terms of sale. I think you will find the section on small motors particularly interesting.

Our regional sales representative, Chuck James, will contact you next week to set up an appointment. At that time he can explain our products more fully and answer any questions you might have.

We look forward to serving you again.

Very truly yours,

Fred Spaninger
Vice-President, Sales

Enclosure

- Thank them for the business.

- Explain what you have enclosed and why.

- Establish the mechanism for doing more business with the customer, whether by mail, phone, or in person.

Company Name
Address
City, State Zip

Date

Mr. John Zimmerman
14 Sachem Village
West Lebanon, NH 03784

Dear Mr. Zimmerman:

Thank you for your order for carving chisels. You'll find that our tools will enhance your work and pleasure in woodworking. They are well-crafted, enduring, useful, and unique—the best that money can buy.

I'm enclosing a copy of our latest catalog. We have expanded into gardening tools in addition to our line of woodworking tools.

We look forward to hearing from you again soon.

Very truly yours,

Jason Sanderson
Vice-President, Customer Service

Enclosure

- Express appreciation for the business.

- Explain anything new or different in your catalog.

- Say that you're looking forward to doing more business.

Follow-up to Sales Call: First Follow-up to New Client/Customer (1-05)

Company Name
Address
City, State Zip

Date

Mr. and Mrs. John Farrell
3798 Canterbury Road
Cleveland Heights, OH 44118

Dear John and Fran:

It was a pleasure meeting you last week, and I thank you for the opportunity to introduce you to our insurance plans. I hope you have had the chance to look over the information on family protection, retirement income, and education plan that I left with you.

I will call you Thursday evening to see if you have any questions about our services. I hope to have the opportunity to work with you in planning your family's financial security and other insurance needs.

Sincerely yours,

Samuel T. Gold
Account Executive

- Thank them for the initial meeting.

- Establish a time when you will next contact them (at which time you can try to set up a meeting to close the sale).

Company Name
Address
City, State Zip

Date

Mr. Fred Johns
Kiddie Korner, Inc.
20 World Trade Center, Suite 3557
New York, NY 10048

Dear Mr. Johns:

It was a pleasure meeting with you last Friday. I'm glad we had the opportunity to discuss and, I hope, resolve some of the problems you had with our toy shipments three years ago. As I mentioned, we've upgraded our delivery system in the past year, which should prevent any reccurrence of late shipments and shipping errors.

I will call you in two weeks, after you've had the chance to look over our new catalog.

We look forward to doing business with you again.

Sincerely,

Adam Woodruff
Vice President, Sales

- Express appreciation for the client/customer's time.

- Follow up with what you discussed during the sales call (answer questions raised, send material requested, etc.). If the customer stopped doing business with you because he or she was dissatisfied, state how the problem has been, or can be, fixed.

- Always leave a thread—a link to your next contact.

Solicitation of Additional Business to Current Customer (1-07)

Company Name
Address
City, State Zip

Date

Mr. and Mrs. M. F. Dudley
42 Summit Drive
Whittier, CA 90605

Dear Toni and Marshall:

Because of the rapid appreciation of housing (and replacement costs) here in Southern California, we need to make sure your current homeowner's policy of $300,000 provides sufficient protection before we renew the policy on May 30. We are generally suggesting that our accounts increase their policies 10-15%.

If you've made significant improvements to your house in the last year, you'll need to think about an additional increase to the policy amount.

I'll call you next week to discuss your coverage.

Best wishes,

James Bowman

- If you're seeking additional business or an increase in an account, be sure to give a reason that makes sense to your reader.

- Leave the ball in your court—"I'll call you..." is much more appealing to a busy customer than "please call me."

Company Name
Address
City, State Zip

Date

Mrs. Betty Tovar
2030 Ocean Drive
Hallandale, FL 33009

Dear Mrs. Tovar:

We were sorry to see that your name has not been on our list for service contract renewals for the past two years. If you have had a problem with Friendly Air Conditioning, we would like to remedy it.

We have also expanded and improved our service fleet in the past year, and our prices have remained very competitive. We now have servicemen on call 24 hours a day and can guarantee that one will be at your place within an hour of your call.

I'll telephone you next week to see if I can answer any questions you might have about our new services. We would very much like to welcome you back as a Friendly Air Conditioning customer.

Sincerely,

David C. Hunter
Customer Service Representative

Enclosure

- Highlight any improvements in your products or services that have occurred since you last did business.

- Try to find out why they stopped doing business with you.

- Let them know that you would like their business back.

Response to Request for Information (1-09)

Company Name
Address
City, State Zip

Date

Mr. Donald Green
Green Ink Printers
2407 Halburton Road
Beachland, OH 44119

Dear Mr. Green:

Thank you for your request for more information on American
Adjustable Frequency AC Motor Speed Control products.

American has been producing quality AC motor controls since 1974,
and we have over 14,000 units in operation throughout the world. We
have an excellent reputation for quality, reliability, and service, and all
our products are designed, engineered, and manufactured in the U.S.A.

I've enclosed a catalog that describes our products.   Please contact me
for more sales information and application assistance. I would like to be
of further service to you.

Again, thank you for your interest in American Controls.

Sincerely yours,

Joseph G. Gest
Sales Manager

Enclosure

- Express thanks for their interest in your product or services.

- Let them know you're interested in providing more information and try to find out more
about what they're looking to buy.

Company Name
Address
City, State Zip

Date

Mr. Michael Handel
178 Pugsley Avenue
Brooklyn, NY 11201

Dear Mr. Handel:

May I use your name when prospective clients ask for a reference? You have been a valued client for over ten years, and you are well-known and respected as a piano teacher in our community—a perfect reference for a piano-tuning business!

I will call you in a few days for your answer. Thank you very much.

Sincerely,

Jason Russell

- Express how you appreciate their business.

- Make it sound like an honor and privilege to be "selected" as a reference. (Saying complimentary things usually helps.)

- Arrange to follow up.

Company Name
Address
City, State Zip

Date

Mr. and Mrs. Jonathan Walker
3500 Falmouth Road
Shaker Heights, OH 44122

Dear Mr. and Mrs. Walker:

Thank you very much for allowing us to use you as a reference for prospective clients interested in our window-washing service. We appreciate your time and value you as a client. As a token of our appreciation, I have enclosed a coupon good for 10% off our regular rates for our next visit.

Again, thank you.

Sincerely,

Orville Bruno

Enclosure

- Express your appreciation for the referral permission and for their business.

- When possible, include some token of appreciation for the use of their name.

Company Name
Address
City, State Zip

Date

Dear Homeowner:

Now that fall is here and you are getting things ready for the winter, it's time to think about your driveway. Does your driveway have cracks? Is it in need of sealing?

East Coast Seal Cote Co. specializes in asphalt driveway refurbishing. We seal cracks, large and small, and apply two coats of premium rubberized sealer to the entire surface. Our finish is guaranteed for two years.

If you would like a free, no-obligation estimate, please call 572-7800. You don't even have to be home for the estimate; we will leave it in your mailbox.

We look forward to helping your driveway look better and last longer.

Yours very truly,

Mark Bretton
Vice President, Sales

- Explain your services.

- Make it easy for them to respond.

- Ask for action—a response, an order.

> Company Name
> Address
> City, State Zip
>
> Date
>
> Dear Maintenance Manager:
>
> • Do you have concrete floors in your manufacturing area?
>
> • Do they require maintenance in heavy traffic areas due to cracking?
>
> • Would you like to end this maintenance headache?
>
> If your answer is yes to these three questions, we suggest that you try Glass-Coat brand sealer/resurfacer. Glass-Coat is a reinforced polycarbonate coating that goes on like paint and stands up even to heavy forklift traffic. It resists most chemicals and is nontoxic in the event of a fire.
>
> We feel so strongly that once you try Glass-Coat you'll want it in all your problem areas that we will send you a free sample to use as a test. If this sounds good, give me a call at 1-800-976-3871 for the name of our representative in your area.
>
> Sincerely,
>
>
> Tony Regalus
> Vice President, Sales

• Explain your product.

• Direct it to the most likely buying influence.

• Ask for a response.

Flyer (1-14)

SPRING CLEANUP

Dread cleaning up your yard this spring? We will do it for you at a price you can't afford to pass up!

Full cleanup: Rake out entire lawn; rake out dead grass, leaves, branches and debris from garden and flower beds; clean all lawn and driveway areas and pile debris neatly at the curb for city pickup.

Small-average lot	$60-75
Larger than average or small corner lot	$85-150
Large corner lot	$150-up
X-large lot	Call for estimate

Mini cleanup: Same work done as above except no beds are touched. Cost is 1/2 to 3/4 of above prices, depending on size of lot and lawn area.

For quick, reliable service, please call
Steve, Pete, or Joe Jetson
39 Provinceline Road
Princeton, NJ 08540
(609) 924-0111

All work done on first-come, first-served basis. References available upon request. Gift certificates available.

- Outline your services and quote typical rates.

- Make sure they know who to contact and where you can be reached.

- Distribute widely and frequently in targeted area.

Company Name
Address
City, State Zip

Name Our New Ice Cream Sundae Sensation!

Come in and taste our latest ice cream treat, a luscious concoction of mango, papaya, and coconut ice cream topped with chocolate and pineapple sauces, whipped cream, and candied grapefruit bits. Then dream up a name for this sundae sensation and fill out one of our entry forms.

If your entry is selected, you win a $25 gift certificate available for use at any one of our three Robert's Ice Cream Parlor locations: Landsdowne Square (downtown), West Road Mall, or South Landsdowne.

Hurry! The contest ends June 5. Be a winner, name a winner!

- Outline contest rules, deadlines, and awards.

- Contest should be geared to promote your business traffic (e.g., involve people coming to your store).

Company Name
Address
City, State Zip

Date

Mr. and Mrs. Ken Humphries
78 Fairview Road
North Branford, CT 06471

Dear Mr. and Mrs. Humphries:

This year we are again offering to our customers our prepayment option of a 5% cash discount on our seasonal mowing contract (April through November). Many of our customers prefer the seasonal mowing contract because of the convenience of writing one check and using one stamp.

If you decide to take advantage of this offer, please send us your check for $171.00 for the full year's mowing by April 30. If you decide to pay monthly, the seasonal charge will total $180.00.

If you have any questions concerning prepayment or your cost, please call me at 484-9333.

Sincerely,

Brian Victor

- State clearly the advantages and terms (including deadline of the offer) of the discount.

- Encourage your customers to call you directly. Giving a person's name is always better than saying "please call our office."

Company Name
Address
City, State Zip

Date

Mr. and Mrs. Frank Long
590 Farragut Hills Boulevard
Knoxville, TN 37920

Dear Mr. and Mrs. Long:

As a special offer to new customers, we will clean your living room, dining room, and hall carpets for a flat fee of $49.95. And that's not all—we will also clean any one of your bedroom carpets **at no added cost.** This offer is good through May 31.

We are extending this low, low price to you to demonstrate the fine quality of work we do, with the hope that you will join the list of the many satisfied customers we service.

I've enclosed a description of our company, our services, and our regular rates. You may be particularly interested in quotes from some of your Farragut Hills neighbors (p. 3 of the brochure). Please take a minute to call me at 773-4592 and schedule an appointment. I'm sure you'll be very satisfied.

Sincerely,

Jim Ballard

Enclosure

- Outline your offer clearly. People are very skeptical about offers like this and you must be very explicit.

- If you can get testimonials, use them in your promotional literature and refer to them in the letter.

Company Name
Address
City, State Zip

Ameritherm Temperature Controls invites you to the National Plastics Exposition and to the windy city of Chicago on November 2 and 3. You can view the full range of our temperature controllers for plastics manufacturing equipment at our company display in:

Booth number 164, 2nd floor of McCormick East

Our product specialists and sales representatives will be on hand to answer any questions you might have.

Our temperature controllers are also installed on the extruders in the following manufacturers' booths:

Davis Standard	Booth number 27
Wellex	Booth number 53
NRM	Booth number 71
Husky	Booth number 82
Glouster	Booth number 99
HPM	Booth number 125

We look forward to seeing you.

- Indicate what products you have on display.

- If your booth is in a difficult-to-find location, provide directions or a map.

- If your product is also part of other equipment at the show, indicate where it can be found (name of company and booth location).

Company Name
Address
City, State Zip

Date

Dear Beachwood Resident:

The Frameworks is opening a new store in the Beachwood Mall on June 1. To celebrate and to welcome you to our new store, bring in this letter and we'll take 25% off any ready-made frame or 15% off any custom frame you purchase before July 15.

We specialize in all kinds of metal, wood, and plastic frames and have over 300 different styles to choose from in our store.

Please stop in and see us soon.

Sincerely,

Susan Weston
Store Manager

- Make sure you can determine how the person heard of your offer (so you can determine the effectiveness of the campaign).

- Offer some enticement for responding quickly.

Company Name
Address
City, State Zip

Date

Ms. Theresa S. Rouse
Conference Coordinator
Southeast Venture Corporation
2000 21st Avenue South
Nashville, TN 37212

Dear Ms. Rouse:

If you are looking for a truly unique spouse activities program for your national sales conference in June, I believe my workshop, "The Beauty of Ikebana" (Japanese flower arranging), would provide a memorable experience.

The four-hour workshop offers insight into the meaning of particular ikebana arrangements, the history of the flowering arranging art in Japan, and an opportunity for participants to make and take home a small arrangement of fresh flowers. I bring to the workshop several arrangements to illustrate examples of different styles.

I've enclosed a brochure with color photographs, a description of my experience and education in ikebana, a client list, and a fee schedule to give you a better idea of what I can offer you. I will call you next week to discuss your program needs and answer any questions you may have.

Sincerely,

Silvia Platt

Enclosure

- Tie your seminar to a result the reader wants—i.e., an interesting and memorable program.

- Include supporting information (brochures, etc.) to give details and arrange to follow up.

Company Name
Address
City, State Zip

Date

To: Boston Area Foodwell Stores

For the Fourth of July this year, we will be running a special promotion on O'Grady's "Fire Breathing Barbeque Sauce." There will be a special point-of-sale display, coupons in the local papers, and radio advertising. This sauce has done well in test markets in New Hampshire and Virginia and should help sell chicken and pork in addition to beef.

The program will run from May 21 to July 9. We hope to move 40,000 bottles in this time period. Our sales representative, Dean Phillips, will contact you next week to give you further details of the program and to answer any questions you might have.

Sincerely,

Frank Hogan
Vice President, Marketing

- Explain the elements of the sales program.

- State the duration and objectives of the program.

- Indicate who the contact person is for the program.

Company Name
Address
City, State Zip

Date

To: Lumi-Co Distributors

Lumi-Co is pleased to announce the expansion of last year's growth program to include our new line of indoor and outdoor sodium lighting.

The program will run throughout this year and has a quarterly discount that gets better as the year progresses—provided you meet the agreed-upon sales levels. Our sales representative will be contacting you to review the details of this plan. Together we can make this year a "bright" year for everyone!

Yours very truly,

Vincent Cusano
Vice President, Sales

- Explain how the program works and what is included.

- State the duration of the program.

- Solicit participation.

Announcement of Advertising Campaign, Consumer Goods (1-23)

Company Name
Address
City, State Zip

To: All Chicago Area Managers of Billie Burger Restaurants

From: Ray Hanson, Promotion Manager

Date:

Subject: Spring/Summer Advertising Campaign

We are starting our Billie's Better Burger campaign in your area on April 21. This will coincide with national TV advertising during the Monday night baseball games.

The primary advertising in your area will be on WQOX and WNNB radio stations, as well as weekly ads and coupons in the Chicago Tribune.

We expect excellent response to this program, so plan your supplies accordingly. The program will run through June 30.

Let us know if there are any questions. Please have the weekly coupon totals ready to report with your weekly sales figure. Thank you and good luck!

- State when the campaign starts and ends.

- Describe how the advertising will be done; clearly state what actions you expect of the recipient of the letter.

- Have a feedback mechanism to record the success of your program.

Company Name
Address
City, State Zip

Date

Dear Distributor:

Frampton Gear Reducers is embarking on a large-scale advertising campaign for its new line of offset parallel gear reducers. We are targeting primarily the paper, stone and gravel, and chemical industries. We will be running full-page ads in *Chemical Age, Pulp and Paper Digest,* and *Gravel and Trap Rock News.* We will also be running similar advertising in *Power Design.* Ads will start in June and run through December.

We will make reprints available that are suitable for imprinting and mailing to your customers. We hope that this will stir up a lot of leads, and we are ready to help you close orders.

Good luck and good selling!

Yours very truly,

Bill Johnson
Vice President, Marketing

- Indicate who is targeted.

- State what advertising vehicle(s) will be used.

- Describe how long the program is to last.

Company Name
Address
City, State Zip

Date

Dear Customer:

We at North Shore Home Remodeling have been known for the past seven years for our excellent craftsmanship. Last year—the best in our history—more than 200 homeowners became North Shore customers. We look forward to continuing to serve the five towns on the North Shore.

This spring, we are expanding and will be starting our new division, North Shore Aluminum Siding, Refinishing, and Brick Cleaning. I'm enclosing a brochure that explains our new products and services. If you have been pleased with a remodeled kitchen or bath that we've built for you, you will love the way we can make the exterior of your home look brand new. Please call us at 790-6345 for a no-obligation consultation and quotation.

Sincerely,

Bruno Patella
President

Enclosure

- Establish the quality of your present product/service.

- Explain your new product/service.

- Make a tie between the old and the new product/service.

- Ask for action (quote, meeting, or order).

Company Name
Address
City, State Zip

To: Field Sales

From: Ken Daggs, Marketing Manager

Date:

Subject: Price Increase

On May 1, Powerflo will announce a 7 1/2% price increase on all plastic pumps and a 9 1/2% increase on the combination plastic/cast-iron pumps, effective June 1. Both prices are the result of increased PVC prices.

Orders entered before June 1 with shipment dates prior to July 1 will be priced at the old levels, and any orders entered after May 31 will be increased accordingly.

Please call me if you have any questions.

- Give as much advance notice as possible for a price increase, since the salespeople will want to prepare their customers.

- Give the amount of the price change, the date it will take effect, and a brief reason that salespeople can use with their customers.

Company Name
Address
City, State Zip

To: All Sales Reps

From: Ron Bryant, Marketing Manager

Date:

Subject: Power Mate Gear Reducers

Starting with shipments in June, all Power Mate gear reducers will have new and improved shaft seals. We have made the popular double lip seal standard across the line. This superior sealing system stands up to tough applications two and a half times better than the previous single lip seal systems.

We are offering this added feature at no additional cost. Please use the attached data sheet to explain the features and benefits of this new seal to your customers. We will be happy to help you work through any non-standard applications.

Thank you for your support. Please call me if you have any questions.

Attachment

- Tell how the product has changed and how to apply the change to get sales.

- Solicit feedback and offer further assistance.

Company Name
Address
City, State Zip

To: Field Sales

From: Ben Poole, National Sales Manager

Date:

Subject: Fred Porter Joins Our Team

It is with great pleasure that I introduce our newest sales engineer, Fred Porter. Fred has an extensive background in computer systems, particularly in positioning systems software.

Fred and his wife, Barbara, will be relocating to Richmond, where he will be joining our Southern office, handling accounts in Virginia, Kentucky, North Carolina, and South Carolina starting July 1.

Welcome aboard, Fred!

- Emphasize introduction in subject line.
- Give a short description of the person's background.
- Say when and where the person will locate.

Company Name
Address
City, State Zip

To: Tom Anderson

From: Bill Strejata, Regional Sales Manager

Date:

Subject: New Territory Assignment

As you know, Jim Fitzpatrick is leaving us next month, which will leave us one person short in the Boston office. I am asking you to assume responsibility for part of his territory, specifically southern New Hampshire, for the time being.

Please get together with Jim before he leaves. He and I have discussed the transition, and he plans to allow enough time so that he can introduce you to all his major accounts. I want you to make especially sure that we have a smooth transition of the Milekin Company account. We have spent a lot of time and effort developing this account, and we want to pass the baton with professional grace.

I will be in your office next Friday to see how things are going. We have every faith that you will handle this new territory in your usual highly professional manner. Good luck!

- Smooth transitions are vital to keeping customer goodwill. Give specific direction; ensure that the outgoing rep and the newly assigned rep talk to each other, and follow up.

Company Name
Address
City, State Zip

To: All Salesmen

From: Bob Potter, National Sales Manager

Date:

Subject: Fourth Quarter Bonus Bonanza

The last quarter of the year is traditionally our slowest quarter. To make things more exciting this year, we are offering an expanded bonus program. For orders placed in the fourth quarter, we will pay sales representatives an additional 1% commission on orders for immediate shipment. All product categories qualify, and bonus payments will be made on December 15th!

Get out there, stir up sales, and earn a nice Christmas bonus.

- Be specific about how the bonus works and to what products it applies. Also state time frames, limitations, and when the bonus will be paid.

Request for Meeting to Review Sales Performance (1-31)

Company Name
Address
City, State Zip

To: Jim Watson, Eastern Regional Sales Manager

From: Allen Beck, Marketing Manager

Date:

Subject: Second Quarter Performance

I've been reviewing your region's performance, and last quarter it was excellent! Certainly, 115% of plan is an outstanding result.

Your team posted over-plan sales in all product categories but two—chain and line. Is there a reason why these two groups were only 87% and 71% of plan respectively? I'll be in your area the first week of next month and would like to have dinner with you to discuss how we can help you get these two products on track.

My secretary will call yours to arrange a date.

- Be specific when you're talking about performance—generalized platitudes don't motivate anyone.

- Congratulate good performance first; suggest corrective actions for areas that need improvement later on.

- Take a problem-solving, rather than a punitive, approach.

Company Name
Address
City, State Zip

Date

Dear Executive:

We need the information requested in the enclosed questionnaire in order to prepare <u>The Marketer's Reference Guide</u>. Please take a minute and help us.

The Marketer's Reference Guide is a resource book highlighting the multitude of marketing and support services that businesses use in the greater Phoenix area. It's a valuable reference for your company because it indexes the local talent available to meet your marketing needs.

Whether your organization is in the market for direct-mail consulting, graphic-design help, a brochure writer, or an advertising/marketing agency, you can find what you need by looking through the 162 different categories of suppliers of services in this book.

We will send you future editions of The Marketer's Reference Guide free-of-charge if you return the questionnaire by September 30. Alerting us to your needs (by filling out and returning the questionnaire) will also enable us to invite you to specific trade shows geared to your interests.

Thanks for taking the time to complete and return the enclosed questionnaire. We promise that you will be the ultimate beneficiary.

Sincerely,

Marsha Becker
Editor-in-Chief

Enclosure

P.S. If you would like an additional copy of The Marketer's Reference Guide or need additional copies for other departments, you may order them for $19.95 ($10.00 off the cover price of $29.95) simply by enclosing with this questionnaire a check made payable to The Marketer's Reference Guide.

- It's very difficult to get people to return questionnaires. (Some people go so far as to enclose dollar bills with their requests.) Here the offer is a free reference book and invitation to trade shows.

- The P.S. will get read—and may get sales even if the questionnaire isn't filled out.

Company Name
Address
City, State Zip

Date

Mr. Robert Swan
2823 East Cudia
Phoenix, AZ 85018

Dear Mr. Swan:

Thank you for the information you provided for our 1988-1989 marketing campaigns questionnaire. As always, your cooperation has helped ensure the success of this project.

Your copy of the findings is enclosed. Please note that some of this information is extremely sensitive and should be treated as confidential.

We'll be back to request an update in September. In the meantime, we welcome any changes or corrections, which we will incorporate in our July newsletter.

Sincerely,

Brian Patenaude

Enclosure

- Questionnaires are marketing tools. Providing results to respondents rewards them for participation and gives you another chance to get their attention. People who have a long history of cooperation should be thanked and commended, even in a form letter.

Company Name
Address
City, State Zip

Dear Customer:

Thank you for visiting The Stork's Baby recently. I hope you found what you were looking for and that you were satisfied with the quality and the variety of baby products in our store.

Please help us by completing and returning this survey about our salespeople so that we can continue to improve the quality of our service. It is very short and will only take a few minutes of your time. Thank you very much for your help.

Sincerely yours,

Joanne Wright
Manager

Did a salesperson wait on you within a reasonable amount of time?
  [ ] Yes   [ ] No

Was the salesperson knowledgeable about the merchandise?
  [ ] Very   [ ] Somewhat   [ ] Not at all

Were you treated with courtesy?
  [ ] Yes   [ ] No

Did the salesperson mention:
      Our Free Special Order Service?   [ ] Yes   [ ] No
      Our Shower Planning Service?   [ ] Yes   [ ] No

Overall, how would you rate your salesperson at The Stork's Baby?
    [ ] Excellent   [ ] Good   [ ] Average   [ ] Poor

Any suggestions or comments regarding our salespeople?
_____
_____

If anyone was particularly helpful, please let us know.
_____
_____

- Explain how the feedback you receive will help you improve the quality of the salesforce.

- Mention any special services which may have been overlooked.

- Thank the customer for his or her time and assistance.

Company Name
Address
City, State Zip

Date

Mr. Hiram Kerlinsky
Kerlinsky Auto Parts
73 Noble Avenue
Longmeadow, MA 01006

Dear Mr. Kerlinsky:

In reviewing our accounts we noticed that we have not received any orders from your store for our Maxi-Pipes Chrome Exhaust kit during the last six months. In the preceding year, you had ordered an average of 10 kits per month. Naturally, we hate to lose a steady customer.

It's important to us that we keep informed of our customers' degree of satisfaction with our products and service so we can continue to serve them well. It's particularly important that we learn why old customers no longer order from us.

Won't you please help us by completing the following questionnaire and returning it to us in the enclosed stamped envelope? It will only take a minute and your answers will help us provide better services in the future.

Thank you for your time, and we hope you'll be placing an order with us soon.

Sincerely,

August Henry
Sales Manager

Why did you stop ordering Maxi-Pipes Chrome Exhausts? (Check all that apply.)
   [ ] Dissatisfied with quality of product
   [ ] Dissatisfied with promptness of delivery
   [ ] Dissatisfied with payment terms
   [ ] Experienced customer service problems
   [ ] Other (Please explain.)

_____

_____

What will it take to get your business back?

_____

_____

- Ask direct questions—you'd be surprised at what people will tell you. Besides, you have nothing to lose.

- Express interest in getting the business back.

Company Name
Address
City, State Zip

Thank you for stopping by our booth at the Cleveland Outdoor Expo. Would you please help us by completing the following survey? As you'll see, it's a brief one and will only take a minute or two to complete. Then, either hand it to one of our sales representatives in our booth or place it in the attached return envelope and drop it in the mail. No postage is required.

Your answers are important because we analyze the information to help us learn more about our customers and their desires and to provide better products in the future.

Again, thank you for your time and your interest.

SPIFFY CYCLES CUSTOMER SURVEY

1.   Name:_____
       Address: _____

2.   Date:

3.   Why did you stop by our booth?
       [ ] Looking to buy a bicycle [ ] Attracted by display
       [ ] Spiffy's reputation   [ ] Other (please specify)

4.   Have you ever heard of Spiffy before? [ ] Yes   [ ] No

5.   If so, where?
       [ ] Owned one before   [ ] Friend/relative
       [ ] TV/magazine ad   [ ] Saw in store
       [ ] Other (please specify)

6.   Based on what you have seen and heard, would you buy a Spiffy cycle?
       [ ] Yes [ ] No

7. Are you interested in a bicycle for yourself or for someone else?
    [ ] Self   [ ] Other adult   [ ] Child

8. Have you ever owned a bicycle?
    [ ] Yes   [ ] No

9. Birthdate: _____

10. Marital status: [ ] Married   [ ] Single

11. Occupation: _____

12. Age of each child living at home: _____, _____, _____, _____

13. Which group describes your family income?
    [ ] Under $15,000   [ ] $35,001-$45,000
    [ ] $15,000-$25,000   [ ] $45,001-$55,000
    [ ] $25,001-$35,000   [ ] Over $55,000

14. Which of the following credit cards do you use regularly?
    [ ] Bank (Visa, MC)   [ ] American Express, Diners Club
    [ ] Gas, department store [ ] None of these

• Express appreciation for filling out the questionnaire and let them know why the information is valuable.

• Indicate how easy it is to complete the questionnaire and to return it.

• Make sure the questionnaire *is* easy to fill out.

Company Name
Address
City, State Zip

Date

Mr. Conrad Sullivan
Sullivan Consulting Company
213 Riverway
Boston, MA 02215

Dear Mr. Sullivan:

Thank you for your recent order (PO #437-B) of stationery from The Inky Printing Company. We are currently processing your order for 2,000 letterheads, 1,000 second sheets, and 1,000 envelopes. I expect your order to be ready within the next two weeks; we will notify you when it is ready for pick-up.

Again, thank you for doing business with us.

Sincerely,

Joseph T. Fries

- Express your appreciation for the order.

- State each item of the order and, if possible, the expected date when it will be ready.

- Make sure you follow up as promised.

Company Name
Address
City, State Zip

Date

Mr. Roger G. Jackson
Sugar & Spice & Something Nice Co.
Beachwood Mall
Beachland, OH 44119

Dear Mr. Jackson:

Thank you for ordering 10 cases of Cajun Cooking Magic spices. Your order (PO #S-43CC) is being shipped via the Package Express Company (Bill of Lading #IG46P00L) and should arrive in 7-10 days (their estimate). I've enclosed an invoice for the spices. I hope I can be of further service to you.

Sincerely,

Frank T. Beck
Sales Representative

Enclosure

- Express appreciation for the order.

- Detail what was ordered, who is shipping it, and when it is expected to arrive (if possible). Include all relevant purchase order and shipping numbers in case there are problems later.

Company Name
Address
City, State Zip

Date

Mrs. Amy Rowland
54 Lincoln Street
Glen Ridge, NJ 07028

Dear Mrs. Rowland:

Thank you for your recent order of a "Christine" doll from Dreamgirls.
As you know, our dolls are handmade in West Germany.
Unfortunately, orders for "Christine" dolls this Christmas season have
surpassed our expectations, and the doll is out of stock at the moment.
We expect another shipment of dolls in two weeks, and as soon as it
arrives, we will ship the doll to you via express mail, at our expense, so
that your little girl will not be disappointed on Christmas morning.

I'm sorry for the inconvenience, and I thank you for your understanding.

Sincerely yours,

Henry D. Krieger

- Apologize, give the reason for the delay and, if possible, let the customer know when to expect delivery.

- Show the customer you care about the order by going out of your way—in this case, Express Mail—to expedite delivery.

Company Name
Address
City, State Zip

Date

Mr. Robert Somes
900 West Rahn Road
Dayton, OH 45449

Dear Mr. Somes:

I am returning your check for $153.00 because we no longer make the foul-weather gear (item G357) you ordered. I'm sorry to disappoint you, but that item has not been available for over six months now. We do make several other styles of foul-weather gear, and I hope you'll find one of these new styles, pictured in our new catalog that I've enclosed, to your liking.

I hope we can be of further service to you.

Very truly yours,

Jeff Downing

Enclosure

- Express empathy that the merchandise ordered is not available.

- If payment has been made, explain how you've dealt with it (returning their check, crediting their account, etc.).

- Offer comparable alternative merchandise if available.

Company Name
Address
City, State Zip

Date

Mr. William Skillins
29 New Street
Port Monmouth, NJ 07758

Dear Mr. Skillins:

Thank you for ordering the ski mask (item no. 69M) from our catalog. However, we are unable to process your order because you didn't indicate your color choice. The ski mask comes in red, navy blue, and black.

Please call me at (800) 495-5000 with your preference, so I can send you your ski mask as soon as possible.

Sincerely yours,

Lance Handel

- Explain why you're unable to process the order.

- If a corrective measure needs to be taken before the order can be processed, detail what needs to be done and who is to do it.

Company Name
Address
City, State Zip

Date

Mr. Anthony Santos
Ace Dance Troupe
80 Broadway
Massapequa Park, NY 11758

Dear Mr. Santos:

The 15 beige grass skirts, silver tops, and headdresses that you asked us to make for you are finished, and I've shipped them to you by UPS, insured. You should be receiving them around July 28.

I'm enclosing our invoice #4219 for the order, which totals $672.50, including shipping costs. Thank you again for your order; I look forward to providing you with other costumes in the future.

Best wishes,

Leilani Lahaina
Manager

Enclosure

- Indicate what is being shipped and when delivery is expected.

- Include the invoice number and amount, plus any other relevant information.

- Solicit future business.

Company Name
Address
City, State Zip

Date

Dr. Charles Friedman
Ring Medical Center
67 Main Street
Belchertown, MA 01007

Dear Dr. Friedman:

We've received the 25 boxes of No. 2 rubber gloves (Purchase Order #12-8945J) that were backordered, and I am sending them to you by Jetline Air Freight (shipment #22-B-6732). They should arrive within a week.

I'm sorry for the problems this delay may have caused you. We look forward to serving you again soon.

Sincerely,

Paul T. White
Customer Service

- Indicate what is being shipped and when and how the shipment should arrive.

- Express regret for the delay.

- Put in a plug for future business.

Company Name
Address
City, State Zip

Date

Mr. Russell Downing
207 Montana Avenue
Englewood, FL 33533

Dear Mr. Downing:

The BMW 325e you purchased through our European Delivery Program has arrived and is ready for pick-up. Please give me a call at 397-6622 so we can arrange a convenient time for you to come in; we are open from 9 a.m. to 6 p.m. Monday through Saturday. When you come, please bring with you a photo i.d. (driver's license) and the packet that you received from the BMW factory in Munich when you purchased the car.

I look forward to hearing from you.

Sincerely,

George H. Canfield
Customer Service

- Let the customer know what your business hours are and what he or she needs to do in order to pick up the merchandise.

Company Name
Address
City, State Zip

Date

To: Thomas B. Slocum
      42 West Oak Road
      Sherman, TX 75090

Statement for Services

March 1 - March 15

    March 1
    General Housecleaning   4 hrs. @ $15.00 per hr. $60.00

    March 8
    General Housecleaning   4 hrs. @ $15.00 per hr. $60.00

    March 15
    General Housecleaning   2 hrs. @ $15.00 per hr. $30.00
    Yard Maintenance   2 hrs. @ $20.00 per hr. $40.00

                        Total: $190.00

Payment is due upon receipt

- Give exact dates and hours of service.

- Specify hourly rates and total charges.

- Mention when bill is to be paid.

Company Name
Address
City, State Zip

Date

Mr. Stanley Jarvis
519 Sutton Place NW
Washington, D.C. 20027

<u>Statement for goods delivered</u>   April 12, 1988

Qty. 4   "Jiminy Cricket" dwarf shrubs @ $150.00 ea.

subtotal	$ 600.00
delivery charge	$ 35.00
total	$ 635.00
less deposit	$ 100.00
amount due	$ 535.00

Payment is due upon receipt.

- Note date of delivery.

- Specify, exactly, goods and quantities delivered.

- Account for all charges exactly, crediting deposits.

- Note when bill is to be paid.

Company Name
Address
City, State Zip

Date

Mr. Henry Rossbach
Skating Program Director
Perkasie Recreation Board
379 Old Hill Road
Perkasie, PA 18944

Dear Mr. Rossbach:

I would like to request the opportunity to quote for this year's ice skating show costumes. The Creative Costume Company has been making costumes for ice skating, ballet, dance, and theater productions for over fifteen years. We are known for our fast, reliable, high-quality work and reasonable prices. Our list of satisfied customers in your area includes the Cherry Hill Recreation Board Ice Show, the Doylestown Dance Troupe, and the Quakertown Thespians Company. I have enclosed pictures of some of the costumes we have made.

I would very much like to meet with you to get more information on your ice show costume requirements (approximate quantities, material, styles, etc.) so that we may submit a quote. May I see you next Thursday morning? I will call on Monday to check if this is convenient for you.

I look forward to meeting you and having the opportunity of doing business with you. Thank you.

Sincerely,

John Hathaway
Sales Manager

Enclosures

- State what you would like to quote on and why you think the customer would be interested in a quote from your company (include information about your company if the customer does not know you: brochures, samples, a client list, and testimonials are all helpful).

- Ask for the information you need to submit the quote if you don't already have it.

Company Name
Address
City, State Zip

Date

Mr. Rudyard Hamilton
3402 East 214th Street
Cleveland, OH 44117

Dear Mr. Hamilton:

It was a pleasure meeting with you last week. Thank you for your time and for giving us the opportunity to quote on our home, automobile, yacht, life, and disability insurance rates.

By analyzing your personal needs and financial goals, I believe we have come up with a coverage plan that will provide you with more than adequate protection for yourself and your family but will save you money over your present coverage policy. I have enclosed copies of the various proposed plans and rates.

I will call at the end of next week to see if you have any questions.

Sincerely,

Don Aggers
Account Executive

Enclosures

- Express appreciation for their time and the opportunity to present your quote.

- State what you have enclosed and highlight special features.

- Establish a time to follow up.

Company Name
Address
City, State Zip

Date

Mr. Aaron Plunkett
Odyssey Athletics
1402 Blackford Turnpike
Augusta, GA 30907

Dear Mr. Plunkett:

In response to your recent inquiry, we are pleased to submit the attached quotation for Stargazer baseball shirts, as outlined in the attached specifications. We can ship these within six weeks after we receive your order.

We sincerely appreciate your inquiry. If you need additional information, please feel free to call me at 555-3343.

Very truly yours,

Geoffrey Dungood
Sales Manager

Enclosure

- Remind the reader of his interest in your product.

- Highlight any information you may want the customer to take special notice of—for example, the delivery schedule.

- Offer to provide additional information if the customer requires it.

Proposal (1-50)

Company Name
Address
City, State Zip

Date

Mr. Martin Beech
32 Cricklewood Road
Milford, CT 06460

Dear Mr. Beech:

Thank you for giving Foliage Factory this opportunity to inspect your landscape plants and recommend a comprehensive treatment program. During my March 3 inspection of your property, I found black vine weevils infesting your rhododendrons. These insects are the cause of the notches on the leaves. They are a serious problem and need to be controlled as soon as possible. In addition, your maple trees have leaf spot and powdery mildew diseases, and the arborvitae have tipblight.

I recommend five treatments for your trees and shrubs annually— an application of dormant oil in the late winter in order to destroy insect eggs, followed by three treatments (one each in early spring, late spring, and summer) for continuing insect and disease control; and a late fall application of fertilizer to encourage root growth and keep the plants strong through the winter. Foliage Factory uses only the finest materials and state certified horticulturists.

Each treatment costs $33.00. There is a 10% discount if you pay for the year's five visits in advance. For your convenience, we will return each spring to continue the service unless we hear from you. You may discontinue the service at any time. If you are not pleased with the results of any treatment, let me know and I will re-treat your trees and shrubs at no extra cost. You have nothing to lose and a better landscape to gain.

If you have any questions, please call me; otherwise I will call you on Monday to set up a schedule for the treatments.

Sincerely,

Kevin MacKay

- Express appreciation for the opportunity to present your proposal.

- Say exactly what you will provide and what the customer will gain from your proposal (benefits).

- Set up a time when you will call to discuss the proposal. Don't wait for the prospect to get back to you.

Company Name
Address
City, State Zip

Date

Mr. John Bruckel
Bruckel and Associates
Fairlane Town Center
Dearborn, MI 48125

Dear John:

I'm writing to make sure that you received our proposal for your office computer system and that everything was as we had discussed over the telephone.

Do you have any questions? We have two of the units in which you were interested in stock; shall we hold them for you? I will call Monday to discuss how we might proceed.

Sincerely yours,

Sarah Wickersham
Account Manager

- Request confirmation of the proposal's receipt and offer to clarify any questions.

- Ask for a decision on the order.

- State any additional actions you have taken or intend to take.

Revised Proposal Cover Letter (1-52)

Company Name
Address
City, State Zip

Date

Ms. Jill Bessemer
St. Mary's Hospital
1187 Wall Street
Austin, TX 78754

Dear Ms. Bessemer:

I'm enclosing our revised proposal for the printing of your admission forms (RFQ 18-9910). By changing from a four-part form to a three-part form, we can reduce the cost by $1,230.00. I have also included the second color on the first form at no additional charge.

I hope this new proposal meets your needs and your budget. We look forward to receiving your business.

Sincerely,

James Buckner
Sales Department

Enclosure

- Highlight what was changed and why.

- Solicit more feedback (if necessary).

- Ask for the order.

Company Name
Address
City, State Zip

Date

Mr. Dale Snyder
The Pine Tree Inn
45 Commodore Street
Middlebury, VT 05753

Dear Mr. Snyder:

Thank you for requesting a quote on the landscaping for the inn's renovation. We are most interested in submitting a proposal for your consideration.

Before we submit our proposal, we have a few questions that we would like you to clarify:

1. Will all the landscaping work need to be done in July, or can it be spread out over July and August?

2. Will you be supplying topsoil from elsewhere on the property, or will the contractor have to supply it?

3. Will you require all refuse trucked away, or is there a location on site that can be used as a landfill?

I will call you next Tuesday to discuss these details if I have not heard from you before then.

Sincerely,

Adam Taylor

- Express your interest.

- Make your questions as specific as possible; certainty on the details will help you make an intelligent bid.

- Set a time to follow up for the answers.

Request to Extend Decision Deadline (1-54)

Company Name
Address
City, State Zip

Date

Mr. Keith Cockerham
Appleton Airport
1011 N. Lindale Drive
Appleton, WI 54914

Dear Mr. Cockerham:

As I told your assistant, we just received your request for quotation RFQ 1991 for the new runway lights. It must have been delayed in the mail. May we have an additional week to work on this specification? I have already faxed the specifications to the factory and am preparing a bid package for the contractors. We should be ready to review our bid with you by next Friday.

Unless I hear differently from you tomorrow, I will assume that the extension is acceptable. I will call you if the factory has any questions. Thank you for your patience and consideration.

Sincerely,

Gene Harrison
Vice President

- In an urgent matter like this, you will have phoned, but you will want the facts in writing. Send the letter by overnight service, fax, or messenger.

- Ask for a specific amount of extra time, give the reason for requesting it, and request an immediate response if your request is to be refused.

- Thank them for their understanding.

Company Name
Address
City, State Zip

Date

Mr. Trevor Fleming
Fleming Paving Co.
3029 Michigan Avenue
Indianapolis, IN 46202

Dear Mr. Fleming:

I'm confirming that we have extended the deadline for submitting bids in response to our RFQ 1993 (Parking lot paving) until 5 p.m., May 15, as we discussed on the phone this morning.

Thank you for your interest; we shall notify you of the results of the bid selection by June 10.

Sincerely,

Howard Loomis
Vice President

- State the project to which you are referring, as well as the new deadline.

- It is helpful to provide the date by which you'll be notifying them of your decision—you can cut down on the calls you'll be receiving to inquire about the decision.

Confirmation Letter, Terms Accepted (1-56)

Company Name
Address
City, State Zip

Date

Mr. Gary Longobucco
Concept Marketing Tools
36 Briarwood Road
Greenbrook, NJ 08812

Dear Mr. Longobucco:

Thank you for your order (PO# 10-87-C). Greentree Printers agrees to accept the special terms of net 45 days on this order, rather than our usual net 30 days, because your company will display samples of the catalog at the trade show with an appropriate credit to Greentree Printers.

We look forward to working with you on your catalog.

Sincerely,

Fran Schultz

- Identify the order and the terms that have been accepted, as well as any special conditions.

- Thank them for the business.

Company Name
Address
City, State Zip

Date

Mr. Jim Bunnell
Center Heights Shell Station
Ferry Center Road
Morgantown, WV 26505

Dear Mr. Bunnell:

I would like to confirm the price and terms of the paving of the lot for your Shell Station.

- Net price: $3,270.00

- Payment terms: 10% with order
                          40% after completion of grading
                          50% after completion of paving

I'm enclosing the invoice for the first 10%. Thank you for selecting AJ Paving. I'm sure you will be pleased with the results.

Sincerely,

Andy Jackson
President

Enclosure

- State the terms clearly.

- Indicate what you've enclosed.

- Express appreciation for the business.

Company Name
Address
City, State Zip

Date

Mr. Greg Ring
Brewer Paper Company
41 Acme Road
Brewer, ME 04412

Dear Greg:

Thank you for your order (PO #12-81-77C, #2 Boiler rebuild). We have already begun the foundation design work and expect to have prints ready for approval to you in three weeks, as promised.

There is one item open on this order: the final payment. We would like the last 25% to be paid within 30 days of completion, rather than the 45 days your financial people suggested. If this is agreeable to you, we will proceed with the acknowledgment in this fashion.

Thank you again for your order. We are looking forward to a smooth start up.

Very truly yours,

Kevin Bauer
Vice President, Sales

- Express thanks for the order.

- State what the exception is.

- State what impact the resolution of the open item has on the progress of the order.

Company Name
Address
City, State Zip

Date

Mr. James Lopez
Essex Engineering Company
75 Hickory Avenue
Forest, VA 24551

Subject: PO #18-7711-B 100HP Motor

Dear James:

Thank you for your order. Before we start engineering on this order, I just want to clarify one point. Your specification states "Class B insulation." Our standard is "Class F," which is the next higher temperature rating. It is superior to B in every way and provides you with more thermal "life" in your motor.

Unless you tell us otherwise within 10 days, we will design and build the motor with "Class F" insulation.

We very much appreciate your business.

Sincerely yours,

Roger Cook
Vice President, Sales

- Explain the changes in specification and their consequences.

- Thank the customer for his business.

Company Name
Address
City, State Zip

Date

Mr. Gary Burdette
3620 Atlanta Highway
Athens, GA 30306

Dear Mr. Burdette:

We would like to confirm the changes to the contract on Order
#GMT-001762.

1. You will require the heavy-duty suspension.

2. You request the 306 V-8 engine.

3. You will pay cash and will not use our financing program.

The above changes should not affect the delivery schedule of your
pickup truck. However, they will add $402.86 to the price. Your truck
should be delivered in 10-12 weeks.

Thank you for choosing Athens Motors.

Sincerely,

Ed Schmidt
Sales Manager

- Detail the changes.

- Explain the consequences of the changes.

- Thank the customer for his business.

Company Name
Address
City, State Zip

Date

Mr. Ron Gratovich
Hardi Extruder Company
106 Quarry Road
Charleston, WV 25301

Dear Ron:

We would like to confirm the terms of the consignment stock of motors that we have agreed to place in your building.

1. When you draw on the consigned stock, your purchase order will trigger us to replenish the stock and invoice for the motors taken.

2. At the end of the year, a physical inventory will be taken and any adjustments will be made.

3. Either party can discontinue this agreement on two month's notice.

This program has worked very well at other companies like yours. We are looking forward to working more closely with you.

Very truly yours,

Bill MacDougall
Vice President, Sales

- Describe the ordering and billing mechanism.

- State the length of the deal.

- Thank them for their business and express optimism in the program.

Company Name
Address
City, State Zip

Date

Mr. and Mrs. Roger Lawrence
4509 Southwest 22nd Circle
Delray Beach, FL 33444

Dear Roger and Kitty:

It was so nice to see you again. I'm glad you liked the plans I proposed for the library. The soft rose color you chose for the carpet will look wonderful with the chestnut paneling and will tie in very nicely with the rest of the downstairs.

As usual, I've enclosed two copies of the contract detailing the cost of the materials (carpeting, window treatments, wallpaper, paint, and furnishings) and projected costs for the labor involved. Please sign and return one copy to me along with a check for the indicated deposit so that I may start ordering the materials as soon as possible. The other copy is for your records.

Thanks again for your business. I enjoy working with both of you very much.

Very truly yours,

Jonathan J. Monroe

Enclosures

- Indicate what is to be signed, why, and what else the client should do (e.g., return contract, send deposit).

- Express appreciation for the business.

Company Name
Address
City, State Zip

Date

Mr. Edward Ecklemeyer
Universal Electric Company
720 Stewart Avenue
Ithaca, NY 14850

Dear Ed:

Our Sales Order #GA-39482 for Universal Electric Co. (purchase order #PEC-409) requests that we transmit revised drawings for approval. The prints are enclosed with this letter; please return them by February 21. Should the prints not be returned by that date, we will have to extend the Sales Order Ship Date according to our published cycle times after the prints are returned to Athens.

Please let us know your best estimate as to when we should be receiving the approved drawings.

Thank you.

Sincerely,

Robert R. Reed
Manager, Customer Service

- Specify when the deadline is for returning the approved drawings.

- Make certain to outline the consequences of not returning the drawings on time.

Company Name
Address
City, State Zip

Date

Mr. Robert Wickersham
Wickersham Plumbers
78 Pine Street
Hayward, CA 94544

Dear Mr. Wickersham:

Because Kingsley Building Company is a prime contractor for the State
of California, we are required to verify that all our subcontractors comply
with the EEOC standards. Please send me a letter by April 20 stating
your compliance with these standards so that we may proceed with our
pending order for your supplies.

If you do not have the statement of EEOC criteria at hand, the state's
regional EEOC office can send it to you.

Thank you for your cooperation.

Sincerely,

Mark Vianni
Vice President, Personnel

- State why you need to have verification of compliance and by what date you need the letter.

- If you are dealing with a business that may not have experience in this area, be helpful and guide it in the necessary direction.

Advertising and Public Relations 2

Advertising and public relations, though related in their objective of increasing acceptance of a product, service or idea, use very different approaches to reach those objectives. While public relations is frequently described as free advertising, its primary goal is to make potential buyers and clients aware of the company and products—to keep its name before the public. The primary objective of advertising is to move the buyer from awareness to purchase. In both cases, the idea is to create positive images that will attract potential customers. Both advertising and public relations must be consistent with the objectives of the business and its approach to the market in order to succeed.

Advertising. When requesting rates from print and broadcast media, be specific as to what you want and why you want it. After receiving rate information, it's always a good idea to meet with the sales person to discuss the advertising schedule and negotiate the best rates. Working with an advertising agency can sometimes be a rocky road. The letters in this section help in dealing with some of the more difficult situations.

Announcements of new businesses, branch offices, employees and such should, as a rule, be short and to the point. The challenge is to get the reader's attention, and then give him the single message you want to communicate. Brevity and focus are the keys here.

Public relations. To understand how to put together a press release, it's helpful to see what route the press release takes when it leaves your office. First, it finds its way to an editor's desk at a newspaper, magazine or broadcasting station.

The editor weeds through a pile of press releases and finds a few that look as if they would be of interest to his audience. A staff writer uses the press release as background material or rewrites the release into a story, sometimes barely changing it for the final version.

To have the best chance for publication, a press release must, therefore, be in a form that makes sense to a journalist. *Who*, *what*, *when*, *where*, *why* and *how* are the basic questions a journalist asks. Incorporate the answers to these questions in your press releases. What makes the event you are describing "newsworthy" must be clear and prominent. Be concise and accurate. And don't try to oversell your release. Journalists have a built-in baloney detector.

Hiring Advertising Agency (2-01)

Company Name
Address
City, State Zip

Date

Ms. Regina Welles
The Welles Group
47 Madigan Avenue
Lisbon, OH 44432

Dear Regina:

The display ads are great. The print campaign you outlined is the best thing we've ever seen proposed. I guess we have no choice but to give you the account!

We were so excited about our meeting that we want to get this show on the road immediately. Let's get together and discuss a printer.

Next week we'll sign contracts over lunch. Call us soon to arrange the details.

So, congratulations! And thanks.

Sincerely,

Paul Blanton
Vice President, Marketing

- Simple is best. Say congratulations and tell them what happens next, and that's about it. Be upbeat and get things off on the right foot.

Company Name
Address
City, State Zip

Date

Mr. Steve Waring
The Ad Hoc Company
89 Deer Park Road
Milford, PA 18337

Dear Mr. Waring:

The Wheelhouse Discount Auto Dealership is planning a big promotion to announce the new model year, and we are interested in your agency. Please contact our Advertising Manager, Fred Tracy, to set up a meeting to discuss your fees and how you would propose to handle our account.

We want to produce two 30-second television spots and five radio spots to be aired on local stations and cable systems. We have seen some of your locally-produced commercials and were impressed with their quality and directness.

Please contact Fred as soon as possible. We want to get going with this immediately.

Sincerely,

Evan Mitchum
Advertising Director

- Tell the prospective agency what you plan to do (in general terms) and what you expect the agency to do. Your clarity will speed the process.

- Be specific about who should be contacted and when.

Company Name
Address
City, State Zip

Date

Ms. Janet Wein
The Alpha Agency
1412 Sunrise Highway
Sandusky, OH 44870

Dear Janet:

At our annual review last Friday, the Board of Directors was quite
disappointed at the soft sales growth for the last year. We have decided
to review our entire promotional effort, including our advertising
relationship with The Alpha Agency.

I'm sure you will want to be part of this review. This letter is meant to
give you an opportunity to gather some information to present your side
of the story. Please contact my office to set up a meeting.

I expect to hear from you soon.

Sincerely,

Michael Deere
Marketing Director

- This is not a pleasant task, so don't try to be too chummy. Just get to the point.

- Give them an opportunity to respond, at their initiative—but be sure they know it should be done ASAP.

Company Name
Address
City, State Zip

Date

Mr. Arthur Bonner
The Creative Partnership
23 Eaves Street
St. Louis, MO 63111

Dear Arthur:

As you know, MicroData was recently acquired by General Systems, Inc. We have found it necessary to streamline many of our operations, and all of our promotions will now be handled by the Marketing Department of the parent company in New York. We regret to inform you that MicroData will no longer be needing the services of The Creative Partnership.

We are sorry that we must end what has been a mutually beneficial relationship. Thank you again for all the work you have done for us.

Very truly yours,

R. Stanley Steele
Vice President, Marketing

- Although not all terminations will be as friendly as this, it is preferable to avoid being too negative. Try to be upbeat without being false—no need to kick them when they're down.

- If possible, conclude on a cordial note; priorities may change again in the future.

Company Name
Address
City, State Zip

Date

Ms. Julia Cavanaugh
Advertising Director
The Valhalla Register
Valhalla, NY 10595

Dear Ms. Cavanaugh:

The Quilt Barn is planning a Spring Sale, and we would like to advertise in The Register. Please send us your rate sheet, along with information about the amount of lead time The Register requires for advertisements.

If you have any special requirements for the artwork and copy to be printed, please enclose these specifications with the rate sheet.

Sincerely,

Wilma Greves

- Short and sweet. All you want is their rates and lead time (how soon before publication the ad needs to be submitted), and that's all you need to ask for.

- Cover your bases by asking if they need anything special. The chances are they don't, but you don't want to find that out too late.

Request for Magazine Advertising Rates (2-06)

Company Name
Address
City, State Zip

Date

Mr. John Bloska
Advertising Sales Manager
Business Ventures Magazine
12 Vulcan Road
Allentown, PA 18100

Dear Mr. Bloska:

We are interested in placing several advertisements in your magazine and would like to know what your rates are. Please call me or send us a rate card as soon as possible.

Our plans are to place a two-page ad in your June issue and subsequently to place a full-page ad in the next five issues. We are having the artwork done right now. If you have any special requirements for the printing of artwork, please forward those with your rate card.

We also need to know what the lead time is for the submission of ads.

If you have any questions, call me immediately.

Sincerely,

Mark Holloway
599-4328, Ext. 3

- Perhaps even more important than rates is the lead time. Magazines have a huge lead time, six months or more in some cases, so plan ahead.

- Don't forget to cover yourself by asking for their printing requirements.

Company Name
Address
City, State Zip

Date

Ms. Evelyn Wise
KING-TV
2 Battle Avenue
Seattle, WA 98101

Dear Ms. Wise:

Our company will be buying television time in August for a back-to-school shoe promotion, and we are making inquiries now to lay the groundwork. Please have a sales representative call me at 645-2300 to discuss advertising on your station.

Our preliminary plan is to run 30-second spots during the last two weeks of August. We want airtime every day during the late afternoon movie for those two weeks, and possibly during the late night movie as well, depending on how far our budget will take us.

I realize that you book these spots well in advance, and I would appreciate your immediate attention in this matter.

Sincerely,

Steve Young
Vice President, Marketing

- Broadcast advertising rates (despite rate sheets) are extremely variable, and you will probably want to negotiate them face-to-face.

- Most spots are booked months in advance, so the first thing you should do is inquire about availability and set up a meeting.

Work Agreement with Freelancer (2-08)

Company Name
Address
City, State Zip

To: Date:

Guilford Associates, Inc. (Guilford) hereby requests you to prepare for and on behalf of
Guilford, the following:

_____

Description of Work   Date Due

Guilford agrees to pay you $ on receipt and acceptance of the work. You
understand that the labor performed is a "work made for hire" and that Guilford shall own
all the rights to the work in the name of Guilford or otherwise. You hereby warrant that the
work will be an original work that has not been in the public domain or previously created,
and that the work will be free of any unauthorized extractions from other sources. You
further understand that Guilford shall have the privilege of referring to you in promotional
and advertising material.

Please signify your acceptance of this agreement by completing the form below and return
one copy to us at your earliest convenience.

_____
For Guilford Associates, Inc.

To: Guilford Associates, Inc.

I agree to perform the work listed above, and I accept the terms of this agreement as
stated above.

_____
Signature

_____
Social Security Number
(Required by Internal Revenue Regulations)

- Your agreement should be crystal-clear as to ownership of materials produced, such as
  articles, artwork, or anything else created by the freelancer, and that these materials shall be
  original.

- Insist that freelancers sign agreements (thereby protecting you) and provide social security
  numbers (saving you time later).

Company Name
Address
City, State Zip

Date

Mr. Sol Linman
Linman Printing
14 Press Way
Harrison, NY 10528

Dear Sol:

Well, it finally happened. Nuevo Promos just got too big for its britches, and we had to move to a bigger office. So from now on, if you're looking for the best advertising agency since the dawn of mankind, you'll just have to go to:

Nuevo Promos
112 Atlantic Street
Stamford, CT 06906
(203) 555-4141

Call us, and we'll have Jim Prior, the account executive for your area, stop by your office to discuss your promotional needs. We will continue to offer maximum creativity at very reasonable rates.

Hope to hear from you soon.

Sincerely,

Linda Hernandez

- This letter is a fairly routine one, but do what you can to keep it from being too boring. Have fun with it and give them a reason for following up.

- Be sure the new address stands out clearly, and always include the phone number, even if it *hasn't* changed.

Company Name
Address
City, State Zip

Date

Ms. Sandra Deale
Editor
New England Video Production News
310 Charles Bank Road
Boston, MA 02113

Dear Ms. Deale:

Video Eyes—a new division of Prince Marketing—combines the creative expertise that is Prince's hallmark with a new, state-of-the-art video production facility.

The core of Video Eyes is a creative service team of independent professionals who work on projects as needed. Production managers, directors, screenwriters, computer-graphics artists and post-production specialists are all on call at the new facility.

The heart of the new subsidiary—the apple of Video Eyes—is the new post production facility. Built around a CMX edit controller, it offers full featured edit capability with list management, frame accuracy, and digital effects from a FOR A 440 TBC. Add to this full-frame graphics capability and eight-track audio mixing, and it all spells sophistication.

Sophistication is great, but more important to the video producer is configuration. All of Video Eyes capabilities are available for one remarkably reasonable rate. No add-ons, and no surprises when the bill comes. It's all right there, to be used as the production requires.

Video Eyes is located at 15 East Street, Cambridge, MA 02138. Rate sheets are available upon request.

Sincerely,

Dick Navarro
Director, Creative Group

- Treat the new subsidiary as a separate company and make sure the reader knows where to find you. Don't belabor the fact that it has been spun off from the parent. Your reader is more likely to be interested in what the subsidiary does.

- A simple mention of the parent company suggests its expertise is available to the subsidiary.

- Do some selling. Tell the reader what makes you better than everybody else.

HARVEY H. PITNEY, STEVEN P. SUPER

AND

PAUL W. GORDON

TAKE PLEASURE IN ANNOUNCING

THE FORMATION OF

PITNEY, SUPER AND GORDON

A PROFESSIONAL CORPORATION

ENGAGED IN THE GENERAL PRACTICE OF LAW

3042 CENTURY PARK
LOS ANGELES, CA 90041

(213) 554-3211

- This is a formal announcement—appropriate to professional service firms. It would not be appropriate to such businesses as a plumbing contractor or a beauty parlor.

Regional Health Care, Inc.

is pleased to announce that

Barbara Chappell, M.S.W., C.I.S.W.

has joined the firm's Santa Fe Office

as a Psychiatric Social Worker

14 Elmont Ave.
Santa Fe
638-4218

- An announcement of a new employee gets the company's name before the public and implies that your company is growing and prosperous.

From Here to Maternity

is pleased to announce

that we now offer

A COMPLETE LINE OF CHILDREN'S WEAR

INCLUDING INFANTS' SIZE 0 TO CHILDREN'S 6X

SERENDIPITY SQUARE PLAZA

6 HIGH SCHOOL AVENUE

PROVIDENCE RI

(401) 654-0234

HOURS:

MONDAY - SATURDAY 10-9
SUNDAY 12-5

Ask for Joan or Thomasina!

- Focus on your unique capabilities (here, combining two related product lines in one store).

- Give the state name and area code if you operate in an area close to the state line.

Tina's Florists

has changd its name to

BUDS, BANGLES, AND BEADS

to reflect the addition of crafts supplies...

We'll continue to serve you with all kinds of floral designs,

and, as always, we're happy to sell a single orchid

or the full arrangements for a formal wedding.

Come see us.

We're at the same address:

340 Alderman Way (Across from the Shopper's Market)
Westfield

Or give us a call at 623-0999

- Although many people suggest ads with lots of long copy, a relatively concise one like this will be less likely to dilute your points.

- If you're not sure about the design the ad should take, consult with your local paper.

Company Name
Address
City, State Zip

WILD STEVE HAS OPENED A NEW STORE IN SCOTTSDALE!

Dear Neighbor:

Central Arizona has gotten Wilder since Wild Steve opened an all new store at the Apache Mall in Scottsdale! And this store is the Wildest one yet, with 25,000 square feet of the hottest fashions at the coolest prices!

To celebrate the Grand Opening, Wild Steve is giving away free tote bags to the first 1,000 customers. So come on down and check out Wild Steve's incredible selection of women's fashion jeans for under $30, our full range of colorful tops, and Arizona's biggest collection of exercise wear!

And when you're in Phoenix or Tempe, check out our other fantastic stores.

Wild Steve's will really drive you Wild!

- Give people an incentive to use your new branch—convenience, service, selection, pricing, etc.

- Assume nothing. Pretend they've never heard of you before and remind them of what your business is all about.

- Mention your other established locations.

Company Name
Address
City, State Zip

Date

Mr. Robert McClatchey
McClatchey and Varnum
340 Windmere Road
Winnetka, IL 60093

Dear Bob:

After long consideration, Vulcan Products has decided that our public relations needs will be handled by McClatchey and Varnum. Congratulations!

We based our decision on your firm's excellent track record of dealing with mid-sized manufacturing companies. Your extensive client list, as well as the satisfaction expressed by those companies, made you the obvious choice.

As we have discussed in our preliminary meetings, Vulcan Products requires a full-service public relations approach. All inquiries not of a sales nature will be referred to McClatchey and Varnum, all of our press releases will be handled by your firm, and we will meet soon to discuss the updating and revamping of our other printed materials.

We would like to get a one-year contract signed and financial arrangements finalized as soon as possible. Please contact our legal department to work out the details and set up an appointment.

McClatchey and Varnum is an excellent firm, and we are excited about working with you. Let's hope this is the beginning of a long and profitable relationship for everyone involved.

Sincerely,

Thomas Whitehead
President

- This is a formal communication in what is probably already a dynamic relationship. Give them the good news, be sure everyone knows what's expected of them, what the next step is, and sign off.

Company Name
Address
City, State Zip

Date

Mr. Frederick Gelso
Warwick Public Relations, Inc.
109 Conch Avenue
Tampa, FL 33609

Dear Mr. Gelso:

Cableview has decided to hire a firm to handle the public relations for our Tampa system. We are interested in your firm and would to discuss your services and fees.

Specifically, we need a firm to handle our brochures, releases, the annual report, and other written communications. Telephone inquiries and letters will be handled by our Public Affairs department, which will also coordinate our relationship with the outside public relations firm.

Please call to set up an appointment to discuss your services.

I look forward to hearing from you.

Sincerely,

Mark Obern
Executive Vice President
987-3321 Ext. 43

• Simple is best—tell them what you want and ask for the price. That's it.

Company Name
Address
City, State Zip

Date

Mr. Timothy Applebaum
News Director
WDSR-TV
1111 Main Street
Nicollet, MN 56074

Dear Mr. Applebaum:

Thank you for your invitation to be a guest on your program "Movers and Shakers." I will be at your studios at 11:00 a.m. on Tuesday, August 3 for the taping of the show.

My understanding is that the topic to be discussed is the recent acquisition of Affiliated Systems, Inc. by the Honeyman Corporation. I will represent Affiliated, Mr. James Knox will be there to give Honeyman's side of the acquisition process, and we will both be asked questions by members of the local business press who have not yet been chosen.

I have been informed that it is best not to wear a white shirt on television. If there are any other "tricks of the trade" I should know about, please contact my office. Also, if you could let me know who the interviewers will be when they are selected, I would appreciate it.

I look forward to it. See you then.

Sincerely,

Bart Willoughby

- State your acceptance, then give the time, date, and place for the interview in the first paragraph. Put any other details to be sorted out in the first paragraph.

- Be certain the topic is mutually agreed upon in writing. There is no such thing as an open-ended interview. The last thing you want is any surprises when the tape rolls.

Company Name
Address
City, State Zip

Date

FOR IMMEDIATE RELEASE

Faust FX Expansion Card Adds 80386 Power to 80286 PCs

The Faust EX Expansion Card is the latest addition to the Cinque Computer Products line. Built around the sophisticated 80386 microprocessor, the Faust EX combines power and speed to put any 80286 IBM-compatible computer on the cutting edge of the latest technology.

The Faust EX requires only a single expansion slot and 20 watts additional power. It can be easily installed using ordinary tools. The 80386 microprocessor can handle twice the load of a conventional 80286 microprocessor in one-quarter the time. The Faust EX comes complete with an external communications port that makes networking convenient and easy.

For more information, contact Cinque Computer Products, 207 Tarry Way, San Luis Obispo, CA 93401 (1-800-555-4567).

- *What* and *why* goes in the first paragraph as succinctly as possible. You are announcing a new product, not trying to sell it—your goal is to get the reader to remember the product name.

- *How* gets detailed in the second paragraph, along with significant features. The source of the information goes at the end.

Company Name
Address
City, State Zip

Date

FOR IMMEDIATE RELEASE

Basta Pasta Incorporated is opening its new pasta factory in Brooklyn on June 15. Soon all America will be able to savor the fresh buttery noodles and other pasta varieties from Basta Pasta.

Twenty years ago, Sal and Doris DeCiccio opened a family-style Italian restaurant in Bayside, Queens. They served the same delicious pasta that they had served to their family. It was so tasty that soon people were coming from all over the New York and New Jersey area to sample the authentic Italian taste. The DeCiccios thought "Why not make the pasta available to everyone, not just the customers at our restaurant?"

And so Basta Pasta Incorporated was born. Local residents can still get authentic Italian spaghetti, tortellini, and stuffed shells at the restaurant in Bayside. And now shoppers across the country will be able to get the pastas at their supermarkets, too!

Basta Pastas are made from only the finest ingredients—pure, golden semolina and country fresh eggs. Aside from the traditional family favorites, like manicotti and linguine, Basta Pasta also makes specialty pasta—red pepper pasta, cheese and basil pasta, even pumpkin pasta! And every box of Basta Pasta comes with a recipe for one of Doris DeCiccio's favorite pasta sauces. Now consumers can learn the secrets behind the spicy red clam sauce, or the sophisticated lemon and chicken linguine sauce.

Once your customers have tried these pastas, they'll keep coming back for more.

For wholesale orders, call our toll-free Pasta Hotline: 1-800-YO-BASTA

- Because people remember stories, it's useful to construct a narrative. Talk about why and how the business was created, and why your product or service is really necessary and/or unique.

- Be complete in discussing your product line or service. Target your audience and give them an easy way to reach you.

Company Name
Address
City, State Zip

Date

Mr. Andrew McGaffigan
Host, "Business In The News"
WNJR-AM
1210 Union Turnpike
Rahway, NJ 07065

Dear Mr. McGaffigan:

Acoustic Engineering is pleased to announce that John W. Hill will be joining the company as Special Assistant to the President. Mr. Hill will oversee new product development, as well as report directly to the President on staffing and corporate development.

Mr. Hill comes to Acoustic Engineering from the Douge Corporation, where he was Chief Engineer as well as Operations Manager of the loudspeaker division. Previously, he designed public address systems for Theatre Sounds, Inc.

Mr. Hill is a graduate of Princeton University. He lives in Manhattan with his wife, Frances, and daughter, Melanie.

Sincerely,

John Almas
President

- Begin with new position and responsibilities.

- Professional history, in the second paragraph, should include relevant items in reverse (most recent to earliest) order.

- Keep listing of personal items to a minimum.

Company Name
Address
City, State Zip

Date

FOR IMMEDIATE RELEASE

Dixie Advertising is pleased to announce that Laura Kiner has been named Vice-President, Account Supervisor. Ms. Kiner has been an Account Executive with Dixie for over five years. Her new responsibilities will include overseeing eight Account Executives as well as guiding the continued growth of Dixie Advertising. Ms. Kiner has generated accounts worth over $2.5 million in business for Dixie and has been the prime mover in the firm's recent successful campaigns for Southern Air Transport and Frontierland Amusement Park. She lives in Atlanta with her husband, Tad, and son, Tim.

- Talk about new job responsibilities first, then the previous position.

- Don't get bogged down in the specifics of the new position.

- Keep personal details to a minimum.

Company Name
Address
City, State Zip

Date

FOR IMMEDIATE RELEASE

The First Hartford Bank is proud to announce that Chief Executive
Warren Hardman has been named to the Board of Directors of the
United Way.

Mr. Hardman recently celebrated his twenty-third year as an employee
of First Hartford. Long active in community affairs, he also sits on the
board of Saint Stanislaw's Hospital and is past President of the Rotary
Club of Middlesex County. Mr. Hardman feels it is a privilege to
represent the Bank in such an important capacity. "I can't think of an
organization that makes more of an actual difference in the community.
I hope I can help them maintain that tradition."

The United Way raises money for a number of well-established
charities, including the American Red Cross and The Cancer Society,
through a partnership with business and community leaders.

- Keep biographical details brief and relevant to the award/achievement.

- Blow your horn, but softly.

- Include a brief explanation of the award/achievement at the end.

Company Name
Address
City, State Zip

Date

FOR IMMEDIATE RELEASE

Robert McDonald, President of McDonald Financial, Inc., and Christopher T. Martin, President of Plan-Financial, Inc., announce that their two firms will merge on November 30.

The new firm, which will be called Lifetime Financial Planning, Inc., will be located at 54 State Street, New Haven, Connecticut 06511. The telephone number is (203) 787-2982. Mr. McDonald and Mr. Martin are well-versed in financial planning, each having more than ten years of experience in the field. Mr. McDonald is a lifetime resident of the New Haven area; Mr. Martin has lived in the area since attending Yale University.

Lifetime Financial Planning is prepared to help individuals develop a financial plan at any stage in their career. The firm will specialize in aiding small-business owners and providing services to executives in local corporations.

The two firms have worked extensively with numerous local organizations and individuals. Current clients include Seth Warner, Inc., Financial Management, Inc., and Managed Plans.

- This is a typical news release—relatively low key in view of the usual overblown approach.

- Be sure to ask your clients' permission to use their names in any publicity.

Company Name
Address
City, State Zip

Date

FOR IMMEDIATE RELEASE

Edward McVay Belding has been named a partner in the law firm of
Anderson & Lakewood, 150 South Ninth Street, Minneapolis, Minnesota
55428. Mr. Belding was formerly a partner of Tilson, Johns, Zapata,
and Thorpe of Minneapolis. Lewis Lakewood is the senior partner of
Anderson & Lakewood.

Mr. Belding is a graduate of Carleton College and the University of
Michigan Law School. He served in the Marine Corps in Lebanon.

- You can go into more detail—about academic honors and job history, for example—but it's well to keep it simple. Always review copy with the person concerned, and respect his or her wishes as to what's included or left out.

Company Name
Address
City, State Zip

Date

FOR IMMEDIATE RELEASE

Martin Firearms Celebrates 70th Anniversary

Martin Firearms, a world leader in manufacturing quality pistols and
rifles since 1918, is celebrating its 70th anniversary. With its
headquarters located in the original factory building in Schenectady,
New York, Martin Firearms employs 161 people in both corporate and
manufacturing capacities. Martin Firearms is an industry leader in
sportsman's rifles and supplies handguns to many police departments in
the United States and Canada. Last year, over 15,000 pieces were
shipped around the world. No serious gun collection is complete
without a custom-made Martin Firearms hunting rifle.

- Just the facts. Try to keep it under 100 words. Tell them what you do, where you do it, how many people it takes, and what your sales are.

- Include one or two salient features if you have the room. In this case, the reader is told that this is a company whose stock in trade is quality, not volume. Although this kind of piece is primarily informational, give readers something to remember you by.

Company Name
Address
City, State Zip

Date

FOR IMMEDIATE RELEASE

Martin Firearms Celebrates 70th Anniversary

Martin Firearms, a world leader in manufacturing quality pistols and rifles, is celebrating its 70th anniversary. As part of its anniversary program, the company will conduct tours of the plant at 40 DeLong Drive in Schenectady, demonstrating all aspects of gun manufacturing, on Friday, July 11, from 10 am to 4 pm.

With its headquarters located in the original factory building in Schenectady, New York, Martin Firearms employs 161 people in both corporate and manufacturing capacities. President Preston Martin, a grandson of founder Joseph Martin, started his firearms career working summers in the tool and die shop, entered sales following his graduation from Union College in 1962, and became president in 1983.

Martin Firearms is an industry leader in sportsman's rifles and supplies handguns to many police departments in the United States and Canada. The .38 Patrol Officer's Special was adapted by the Dallas and Boulder, Colorado, police departments this year and is in use in more than 300 police departments nationwide. Last year, over 15,000 pieces were shipped around the world. No serious gun collection is complete without a custom-made Martin Firearms hunting rifle.

The company won the prestigious "Sam Houston" award six years in succession, 1981-1986, for its contribution to the sport of riflery. The award is presented each year to the rifle manufacturer who does the most to promote safety on the range.

Martin Firearms' most famous handgun was the one specially crafted and manufactured for General George Patton. The World War II officer's famed pearl-handled revolver was built to U.S. military specifications by Martin Firearms, by special order of the general. It now resides in the Smithsonian Institution in Washington.

- A longer version of a company press release is particularly well suited to local media, but can easily be edited by any publication. In it, the company can expand on the virtues of its products or services and its personnel.

- Stress recent accomplishments, sales achieved, honors won, etc.

Company Name
Address
City, State Zip

Date

Mr. George Mackie
Editor
Finance News
282 Palm Avenue
Altamonte Springs, FL 32701

Dear Mr. Mackie:

I was embarrassed to find the January copy of Finance News on my
desk—since I haven't even thanked you for the great way you featured
my article "CFO's Guide to the Newest Spread Sheets" in the December
issue.

At least, being late gives me a chance to pass on the fact that I've had a
lot of positive comments on the article.

I have two more ideas for articles, which I'll run by you as soon as they
"jell."

Best wishes,

Paul Ahlstrand

- Any time you get press exposure, be sure to thank those responsible.

- Prompt thank-you's are always better, but being late is no excuse for not expressing your
appreciation.

Customer Relations 3

Customer relations letters are frequently referred to as "goodwill" letters since many of them are designed to engender positive feelings on the part of the reader. But there are also letters in this category which notify customers of changes to your business, deal with meetings, appointments and payments, and one of the most sensitive issues of all, handling customers whose checks have bounced. Because it is critical to maintain the best of relations with customers, the letters in this chapter are among some of the most important a business person will ever send.

Changes in business. When announcing changes in your business—from a price increase to a new salesperson in the territory—you should present those changes in the most positive way possible. Even seemingly negative situations can provide an opportunity to stress the professionalism of your company, both in the way you handle the news and in the sensitivity shown for the customer.

Complimentary letters. While these may be among the easiest to write, beware of complimenting someone on a trivial matter. It only serves to undermine your credibility. When complimenting an individual, choose a situation that truly warrants the attention.

The fact that you've taken the time to write a personal note indicates that you're interested in the customer and puts you and your company in a good light. Do not use this type of letter to make a direct solicitation for business.

Meetings and appointments. In addition to the obvious need for covering the specific arrangements, these letters should sell you and your company. After all, the purpose of a meeting is to generate business.

Payments and returns. Letters concerning payments range from the easy "Thank you for the prompt payment" to the more difficult clarifications regarding incorrect payments, and credit/exchange policies, to no-nonsense communications regarding payment problems such as returned checks. Clarity and a rational tone are essential, for these qualities will help you to resolve problems while keeping your existing customers. After all, they are the best source for future business and for referrals to potential new customers.

Company Name
Address
City, State Zip

Date

Mr. William Trexler
Frameworks
200 Station Road
Great Neck, NY 11022

Dear Bill:

I was delighted to hear how popular our "English Manor" line of picture frames has been with your customers. We have just added a new line of Art Deco frames that appeal to customers with a similar eye for current trends. I have enclosed a brochure with color photographs of each of the ten sizes in the line, as well as measurement and component information and prices. I'm sure this line will be as big a winner for you as the "English Manor" line has been.

I'd like to be able to ship an introductory assortment of 100 frames as soon as I get a purchase order from you. Once you've looked at the photographs, you might find you prefer particular sizes. We'll be glad to put together a shipment that includes exactly the mix you want.

I'll call you early next week to discuss how you'd like to proceed.

Best regards,

Sally Potter
Sales Representative

Enclosure

- To get a current client interested in a new product, mention how much success they've been having with a product of yours they already carry.

- Be sure to include as much specific information on the new product as you can.

- Let the customer know exactly what you need to know to proceed with a first shipment and arrange to follow up on the order.

Company Name
Address
City, State Zip

Date

Mr. Chester Walker
Walker's Hardware
415 Main Street
Little Rock, AR 72203

Dear Chet:

Effective April 1, we're forced to increase the dealer's price of our "Handyman's Tool Kit" to $13.65 per unit (based on lots of 24).

For the past year we have had to pay increasingly higher prices for top-grade steel and are no longer able to absorb all of this increase ourselves. Since our goal is to continue to provide high quality tools for the avid do-it-yourselfer, we believe that the best course is to continue using this supplier. We hope you'll agree that even with the new price, the "Handyman's Tool Kit" remains an excellent value.

Best regards,

Michael Kowalski
Sales Representative

- Express regret that you have to increase prices.

- State specifically:
    — what the product now costs
    — when the increase is effective
    — why it's necessary

Company Name
Address
City, State Zip

Date

Mr. Chester Walker
Walker's Hardware
415 Main Street
Little Rock, AR 72203

Dear Chet:

I'm pleased to report that effective April 1, we'll be decreasing the dealer's price of our "Handyman's Tool Kit" to $11.75 per unit (based on lots of 24). We have signed a more favorable price contract with our high quality steel supplier and are happy to be able to pass this savings on to you.

We hope this price decrease will contribute to your continued success with the "Handyman's Tool Kit" line.

Sincerely,

Michael Kowalski
Sales Representative

- Since everyone loves to save money, be sure to bring it to the customer's attention whenever you can pass on a cost savings.

- Let them know that quality hasn't suffered even though the price is lower.

Company Name
Address
City, State Zip

Date

Ms. Patricia Loomis
PSM Office Systems
79 Wildwood Turnpike
Millburn, NJ 07041

Dear Ms. Loomis:

We have extended the hours for our copying and printing service in order to accommodate our customers' needs. We are now open from 8:00 a.m. to 9:00 p.m. Monday to Friday, 9:00 a.m. to 6:00 p.m. on Saturday, and 9:00 a.m. to 1:00 p.m. on Sunday.

We hope that you will take advantage of our longer hours soon.

Sincerely,

William Ring
Millburn Branch Manager

- Tell them what is new or different and why you've done it—to help them.

- Ask for their business.

Company Name
Address
City, State Zip

Date

RMG & Associates
185 South Broad Street
South Euclid, OH 44121

Dear RMG & Associates:

We regret we will no longer be able to accept returns for cash at Lesher Supplies. However, we will be happy to exchange your returned goods, with receipt attached, for credit towards any other purchase in our store.

Thank you for your understanding and for your business.

Sincerely,

Jane Noel
Manager

- Clearly outline your new policy; explain how it differs from the old policy.

- Express appreciation for their understanding/cooperation.

Company Name
Address
City, State Zip

Date

Mr. Samuel Hanson
Universal Machine Tool Co.
389 Oak Street
Paso Robles, CA 93446

Dear Mr. Hanson:

As you know, Jim Tynan has left our sales office to become an applications engineer at our head office in Chicago. Kevin Smith will be your new account manager. Kevin has worked for us for five years in our order administration department. We are pleased to have him in our office, and I'm sure he'll do an excellent job in servicing your account. To assure that the transition is smooth, I will be working with Kevin for the next two months.

I will introduce him to you on our next sales call on Thursday.

Sincerely,

Tom Trent
Sales Manager

- Give the qualifications of the new salesperson and sell him or her to your customer.

- Confirm the next meeting and assure the customer that you will help make the transition from one salesperson to another as painless as possible.

Company Name
Address
City, State Zip

Date

Dear Client:

We are pleased to advise you that we have entered into an agreement with the clearing house of Little, Ursine & Co., Inc., a long established and prestigious member of the New York Stock Exchange, to clear our customer accounts. The direct effect of this action will be that on or about May 2, your account will be carried by Little, Ursine & Co., Inc. rather than our present clearing firm, Nugent, Golden & Co.

As our clearing firm, Little, Ursine & Co., Inc. will be responsible for holding securities and cash, settling transactions, collecting dividends, issuing confirmations, and looking after the various details incidental to the clearing of accounts. In conjunction with the foregoing, the securities in your account will be insured for $2,500,000. The first $500,000 of protection, which includes up to $100,000 of protection for cash, is provided by SIPC, and the balance is provided by an insurance policy purchased by Little, Ursine & Co., Inc. from the Lolander Casualty Company.

Unless we hear from you to the contrary, your account will be delivered to Little, Ursine & Co., Inc. on or about May 2. Please call us with any questions you may have.

Very truly yours,

Michele May
Vice President, Operations

Enclosures

- Customers need to be informed of any change in administrative arrangements. Give them enough information so that they feel comfortable that everything is under control.

- Offer to answer any queries they may have—this increases the comfort level.

Company Name
Address
City, State Zip

Date

Mr. Stuart Chapman
Director, National Accounts
Loomis/Jones
200 Park Avenue
New York, NY 10010

Dear Stuart:

Congratulations on becoming Director, National Accounts. It came as
no surprise to any of us here—Loomis/Jones has a widely recognized
eye for sharp talent. I am sure you'll meet with the same success in
New York as you did in Houston and hope that you take with you
pleasant memories of your two years here in Texas.

Best regards,

Lois Simmons
Realtor

- Everyone appreciates recognition when they move up the corporate ladder. Brief, sincere congratulatory notes when customers enjoy success are important to maintaining a good client relationship.

- To avoid sounding insincere, avoid excessive detail in wishing the person success.

Company Name
Address
City, State Zip

Date

Mr. Charles Borden
Omni International Trading, Inc.
800 South Wacker Drive
Chicago, IL 60606

Dear Charlie:

Congratulations on your new position at Omni International. I was delighted to hear you'd moved into management and know Omni International will be glad they found you. I'm sure this is just the first in a long series of moves up the professional ladder.

Best of luck to you—I hope we continue to see one another at the monthly DCG luncheon.

Sincerely,

William Simpson
Manager, Customer Relations

- Take every opportunity to keep in contact with current clients. Congratulating someone on a promotion provides an ideal opportunity—it's a happy occasion, and your taking note of it shows you're alert.

- Don't be unnecessarily effusive. It's easy to step over the line between applause and flattery. For example, saying "I know you'll be President someday" exceeds the bounds of reality.

Company Name
Address
City, State Zip

Date

Dr. Kenneth Pond
Department of Nutrition and Food Science
Cornell University
Ithaca, NY 14850

Dear Ken:

I've just finished reading the article in today's issue of *The Washington Post* in which you were quoted regarding calcium deficiency in teenage girls. I've always considered you to be one of the world's experts on calcium deficiency, and I'm glad that a respected newspaper such as *The Washington Post* agrees with me.

I hope you are well. I expect to be going to Ithaca later this spring; if so, I'll be sure to call you so we can get together. I'm currently working on marketing orange juice with added calcium for my company, and I'd like to discuss a couple of ideas with you.

Congratulations again on being quoted in such a prestigious source.

Best wishes,

Harlan D. Jones

- Indicate where you read or heard the quote.

- Tie the event or issue in with your own business affairs if feasible—don't force it.

Company Name
Address
City, State Zip

Date

Mr. Horace M. Long
H. M. Long and Company
54 Pine Street
West Lebanon, NH 03784

Dear Horace:

Thank you for inviting me to your open house. It was a wonderful party, and I enjoyed meeting your associates very much.

Congratulations on your beautiful new office. The view you have of the river is spectacular, and I like the way you've redesigned the interior, especially how you've opened up the roof to let in more light. It's hard to believe that place was once a hat factory!

I wish you all the best in your new location.

Sincerely,

Jim Fuller

- Include your wish for their business success in the new office.

- Be as specific as possible, especially with customized designs that the tenant will be particularly proud of.

Company Name
Address
City, State Zip

Date

Mr. Larry Lobeck
Manager
Tamale Towers
1489 Federal Road
Houston, TX 77005

Dear Larry:

On my sales call to your restaurant last week, I noticed that you were breaking ground for an addition. Congratulations on the expansion of your business.

Please let me know if I can be of any help in meeting your increasing needs for Tres Equis Beer. I look forward to working with you in serving your additional customers.

Sincerely,

Paul Logan

- Compliment the owner or manager on the obvious success of the business.

- Express an interest in serving the additional business, if appropriate.

Company Name
Address
City, State Zip

Date

Dr. Peter Rowe
Cleveland Clinic
3908 Euclid Avenue
Cleveland, OH 44110

Dear Dr. Rowe:

I very much enjoyed your article about the value of "orphan drugs" in the Sunday, March 15 edition of *The Plain Dealer.* I completely agree with you that our society will be in trouble unless something is done to stimulate the continued production of these drugs.

I am a distributor of one of these drugs, TRX-94, and I would like very much to speak with you about some of the points you discussed. I'll call you next week to see if we can arrange a convenient time to meet.

Sincerely,

Warren K. Hamlish

- State where you read the article and what you enjoyed about it.

- Make clear your connection with the topic, especially if you anticipate further contact. You want the letter's recipient to think about your interests before such contact.

Company Name
Address
City, State Zip

Date

Mr. George Unger
35 Peter Street
Newton, MA 02158

Dear Mr. Unger:

Thank you for your letter suggesting that we have a pick-up and delivery service for our dry cleaning stores. I think it's a good idea, and my partners and I will be looking into the feasibility of having such a service.

We at Hawley Dry Cleaning are always looking for ways to improve our services to our customers.

We appreciate your taking the time to write us. Thank you for your continued patronage of our stores.

Sincerely,

Robert J. Hawley
Manager

- Express appreciation for any suggestion that a customer thinks will improve your business.

- If you have taken action due to the suggestion, state what you've done.

- Express thanks for their being a customer.

Acknowledgment of Compliment to Company/Employee (3-15)

Company Name
Address
City, State Zip

Date

Mr. John G. Farmer
15 Bermuda Street Wharf
New Orleans, LA 70117

Dear Mr. Farmer:

Thank you for writing and letting us know how much you enjoyed staying at Cypress House during your recent visit to Charleston. My wife, Betty, and I both take great pride in the restorations we have made to Cypress House; we are happy that our guests enjoy what we have done.

I'm enclosing the recipe for She-Crab Soup that you requested. Jim Tate, our chef, was delighted when I relayed to him how much you enjoyed the soup.

It was a pleasure having you here with us, and all of us at Cypress House hope that you'll visit us again in the near future.

Best wishes,

Sam deWinter

Enclosure

- Express appreciation for the business, as well as the compliment, and ask for continued patronage.

- Make the reply as personal as possible and show that you have valued the compliment enough to relay it to those responsible in your business.

Company Name
Address
City, State Zip

Date

Mr. George Poole
Director of Human Resources
Robomatix, Inc.
100 Renaissance Plaza
Detroit, MI 48226

Dear George:

It was a pleasure catching up with you on Thursday and hearing that Robomatix wants to proceed with training for mid-level managers. I'm sure we can put together a program that is every bit as successful as the one we did for your support staff last year.

I believe we could proceed most quickly and productively if you, Marty, Gene, and I got together for a few hours one day next week to discuss program development, scheduling, and costs. By then I'll have developed a few possible program formats that can serve as the basis for our discussion about just what type of program best meets the company's objectives.

Either Tuesday, Wednesday, or Thursday of next week is fine for me— I'll leave it up to you, Gene, and Marty to choose a date and time that is most convenient for you. I'll call you on Friday after you've had a chance to check your schedules.

I look forward to seeing you again soon.

Best regards,

Howard Stamp
President

- Be sure to mention what you hope to accomplish at the meeting (informal agenda) as well as who should be there.

- Show willingness and flexibility to work within others' schedules.

- Set a time to confirm plans.

Company Name
Address
City, State Zip

Date

Mr. George Poole
Director of Human Resources
Robomatix, Inc.
800 South Wacker Drive
Chicago, IL 60606

Dear George:

I'm glad you, Gene, and Marty all have time available next Tuesday
morning, May 8, to discuss the program for mid-level managers. I'll be
at your office at 10 so we'll have a few minutes to review the formats
I've developed before we all meet at 10:30.

I'm planning to bring a few overheads with me to give you all an idea of
the teaching materials I've found particularly effective with groups like
yours. Can we arrange for a small conference room with an overhead
projector?

I look forward to seeing you again and to moving ahead with plans when
we meet next week. Thanks for making it all happen.

Best regards,

Howard Stamp
President

- State the date, time, and location of your meeting.

- Mention any equipment you need and why you need it.

- Express appreciation to the person who set up the meeting.

Request for Associate to Attend Meeting (3-18)

Company Name
Address
City, State Zip

Date

Mr. John Gates
HiTech Office Systems
500 Saratoga Road
Gastonia, NC 28052

Dear Mr. Gates:

Thank you for choosing NC Advertising for your expansion campaign. We look forward to working with you in making the next year the best in HiTech's history.

May I bring along my associate, Pauline Green, when we meet on Wednesday, April 25? Pauline is our expert on promoting service businesses, and she'll be able to highlight the areas your company should emphasize in your promotions.

Sincerely,

Martin Michaels
Account Supervisor

- Give a reason why your associate will be an asset at the meeting.

- Touting an associate's or subordinate's expertise enhances the image you project, demonstrating your security and self-confidence in your own position.

Company Name
Address
City, State Zip

Date

Miss Robin Waite
The Stork's Store
7754 West 97th Place
Overland Park, KS 66204

Dear Miss Waite:

It was a pleasure speaking with you on the phone last week. Thank you for your interest in Daisy Diaper Covers. It's always cheering to find people who care about the ecology and want to avoid disposable diapers. We are the revolutionary alternative to diaper pins and rubber pants. As our enclosed brochure explains, our patented design allows air to circulate but won't let wetness pass through, so clothes are kept dry while heat does not build up in the diapers, reducing the chance of diaper rash. Our velcro fasteners make changes easy and eliminate sharp pins.

I will be in your area the week of April 15. May I stop by at 2:30 p.m. on Wednesday, April 17, to show you some of our samples and answer any questions you may have about our diaper covers? I will call next week to confirm with you that this time is convenient for you. I look forward to meeting you.

Sincerely,

Mike Parris
Sales Representative

Enclosure

- Be specific as to the time, date, place, and purpose of the appointment.

- Set up a time to confirm the appointment.

Company Name
Address
City, State Zip

Date

Mr. and Mrs. John Spangler
2740 Duhallow Way
South San Francisco, CA 94080

Dear Cynthia and John:

Thank you for calling and letting me know that you're interested in putting your condominium on the market. I would be very pleased to represent you in this sale. I look forward to coming over to appraise your place and to providing you with a comparative market analysis. I'll also discuss with you how I can help you get the best possible exposure and the best possible price for your property.

As we agreed over the phone, I'll be at your condominium next Thursday at 2:00 p.m.

Very truly yours,

Helen R. Hoffman

• State the date, time, and place of the appointment, as well as what you hope to achieve.

Company Name
Address
City, State Zip

Date

Mr. Michael Preston
North Communications
670 White Way
St. Paul, MN 55404

Dear Mike:

It was a pleasure meeting with you last Friday. Thank you for letting me show you how Coleman Productions can handle all your program needs and improve your video productions.

I'm enclosing the literature that you requested on our computer graphics and animation services along with a copy of our demo tape, which I thought you'd find interesting. I will call you next week to see whether you have any questions. I look forward to exploring the possibilities of our working together.

Sincerely yours,

Wilfred I. Binstock

Enclosures

- Follow up on what occurred during the meeting (e.g., request for more information) in order to get more contact if your aim is to solicit business.

- Be assertive but don't act, particularly early in a relationship, as if doing business is a certainty.

Company Name
Address
City, State Zip

Date

Mr. Conrad Stephens
CS Electronics
4892 Vista Way
Phoenix, AZ 85016

Dear Mr. Stephens:

Thanks for all your help setting up my appearance at the regional
business development meeting today. I feel that it went very well and
that you deserve a great deal of the credit.

I have one favor to ask. Is it possible for someone to send me a list of
the people who attended the meeting? I generally create a seating
chart so I can link names and faces, but unfortunately I had no time to
do that. If it's easier, just jot the names at the bottom of this letter and
return it to me. Again, thank you very much.

Best wishes,

Barry O'Connor

- Get the thank-you up front and reinforce it at the end.

- Since names are all important in sales (in life?), asking for a list of attendees is perfectly
  appropriate (and essential for follow-ups).

- Asking the reader to reply by writing on the letter itself makes a prompt response likely.

Apology to Customer for Missing Meeting (3-23)

Company Name
Address
City, State Zip

Date

Mr. Kyle Taylor
The Warren Group
708 Worth Avenue
Palm Beach, FL 33480

Dear Kyle:

I'm sorry I missed our meeting last Tuesday. As I explained to your secretary over the phone, all flights out of Boston on Monday and Tuesday were canceled due to the snow storm we had. I'm glad my colleagues from Atlanta were there to present our proposal to you. I have already spoken with them, and they have briefed me on the concerns you expressed during the meeting about the scheduled delivery dates. I'm researching that right now, and I'll call you on Monday with some answers.

I would also like to schedule another meeting with you before the end of March. Is the morning of March 26 convenient for you?

Sincerely,

Tim Bournehoft
Sales Engineer

- Explain why you missed the meeting.

- If the meeting went on as scheduled without you, get information as to what went on and what your responsiblities, if any, are.

- Schedule another meeting if necessary.

Company Name
Address
City, State Zip

Date

Mr. Dwayne Newall
City Life Insurance, Room 1550
43 Madison Avenue
New York, NY 10010

Dear Dwayne:

Please forgive me for missing our lunch Tuesday. My problem was an overturned tractor trailor on I-95. You may have heard about it on the news. Had I been near an exit, I might have had a shot at it, but as it was, I sat in my car for close to two hours.

Then, when I finally got to New York, I heard you had already left for your cruise. I hope that you'll forgive me and that we can try to meet again when you return.

Best wishes,

Barbara Jackson

- Apologies are best delivered on the phone or in person. In this case, that obviously wasn't possible. Next best is a hand-written note on personal stationery. For a business associate, company letterhead is also an alternative.

Company Name
Address
City, State Zip

Date

Ms. Linda Jackson
32 Seymour Road
Atlanta, GA 30344

Dear Ms. Jackson:

I've enclosed your check for #325 for $532.23, which was returned by your bank because of "insufficient funds." Because I'm sure this problem is the result of an oversight or some mistake on the bank's part, please call me at 655-3241 and tell me how to proceed.

Sincerely,

Carlos Erickson
Vice President

Enclosure

- People are funny about having their honesty called into question. If you have a long-standing relationship with the customer and there is no history of previous problems, a polite letter like this one will get the results you want.

Company Name
Address
City, State Zip

Date

Ms. Linda Jackson
32 Seymour Road
Atlanta, GA 30344

Dear Ms. Jackson:

On April 4, we redeposited your check #325 for $532.23, as you requested in our April 3 phone conversation, and it has again been returned to us marked "insufficient funds." We are sure this is as embarrassing for you as it is frustrating for us, but we must insist that you call us immediately and make arrangements to pay your bill by money order or cashier's check so that we may keep your account current.

Sincerely,

Carlos Erickson
Vice President

- Switching from "I" to "We" (meaning the firm) makes this letter sound sterner.

- A check that has been returned a second time is a signal that your once-solid customer may be having financial difficulties. But if he or she pays up at this point you may want to forget the matter.

Company Name
Address
City, State Zip

Date

Ms. Linda Jackson
32 Seymour Road
Atlanta, GA 30344

Dear Ms. Jackson:

We have not heard from you since your check (#325) for $532.23 was returned by your bank a second time. If we do not receive payment within seven days, we will have to place your account with a collection agency, with all the unpleasantness (and damage to your credit rating) that this implies.

Sincerely,

Carlos Erickson
Vice President

• Transferring an account to a collection agency will assure that you've lost your customer, so you should provide the customer with one more chance to pay before doing so.

Thank You for Prompt Payment (3-28)

Company Name
Address
City, State Zip

Date

Ms. Lynn Pearl
320 Pipers Lane
Columbus, OH 43228

Dear Ms. Pearl:

On May 10, we received your payment of $95.00 for April lawnmowing and weeding services. We have noticed that in the year you've been our customer, you have paid well in advance of the 15th every single month. We'd like to reward your promptness—this kind of payment schedule is an immeasurable help in running our business.

Starting with this month, we'll deduct 2% from your monthly bill each time you pay by the 15th.

Thank you again for your patronage.

Best wishes,

Glen Hansen
President

- Reliable, loyal customers should be rewarded. A simple "thank you" might have been enough in this case, but issuing a small discount packs more of a wallop.

- In small firms, the president should sign the letter.

Company Name
Address
City, State Zip

Date

Ms. Maddie Ford
543 Abner Doubleday Way
Gaithersburg, MD 20760

Dear Ms. Ford:

Thank you for your payment of $73.95 for your recent order of swimming pool supplies. You might like to know more about our swimming pool maintenance contract, which spares you the task of carrying heavy containers of chlorine and algacide and ensures that your pool is at all times clean and safe. In your area, a pool maintenance contract usually includes a twice-monthly visit by one of our professional service people as well as all necessary supplies. The actual cost varies depending on the size and location of your pool, but it is usually about the same expense as performing the work yourself.

Mr. John Hardy, the professional responsible for your area, will be maintaining the pool of one of your neighbors next week, and he will call you to see if you would like a free estimate.

Sincerely,

Kyle Lapham
President

- Try to interest the customer by filling a need—in this case, one implied by the need to carry heavy containers of pool cleaning supplies.

- If you promise someone will call, set up some system to ensure that they actually do so.

Company Name
Address
City, State Zip

Date

Ms. Cassie Tate
Tables by Tate
18D Beach Road
Melbourne, FL 32951

Dear Ms. Tate:

Enclosed are the table linens you ordered on April 10 and our invoice #MFL-4X09 for $898.37. Please note that if we receive payment within 10 days, you may discount the invoice by 4%. This discount is double our usual 2% discount and is available only during this quarter, so I urge you to take advantage of it.

We hope you enjoy the linens and that you will call us with another order soon.

Yours very truly,

Sandra Lockwood

Enclosure

- Offer a special discount for early payment when cash flow is a concern.

- Let the customer know right away what he/she did to qualify for the discount—stating your time requirement exactly.

- Urge the customer to take advantage of the opportunity.

Payment Received, Pre-payment Required in the Future (3-31)

Company Name
Address
City, State Zip

Date

Mr. Harold Bloom
Asheville Park Towers, Apt. 7
700 Biltmore Avenue
Asheville, NC 28803

Dear Mr. Bloom:

Today we received your payment of $550.00 for catering services we performed at your Christmas party. Unfortunately, this is the third time you have paid for our catering services more than 60 days after the date of the invoice, despite our stated policy of payment within 10 days. As you can understand, a small business like ours must pay close attention to cash flow. Our suppliers demand cash up front, and we must have sufficient cash on hand to pay them.

In the future, we'll have to require that you pay for our catering services in advance. After a year, we'll be glad to reconsider our position since you have been a good customer in the past.

Sincerely,

Kerry Wolfe
President

- All the reasons given in the letter are valid—small businesses live and die on cash flow. You may lose this customer—but you probably can't afford to keep him on this basis.

- You'll notice there's no—"please call me if you have any questions" in this letter. You want to sound (and be) firm.

Company Name
Address
City, State Zip

Date

Mr. J. B. Boone
Cape May Pools
236 Justine Avenue
Houma, LA 70360

Dear Mr. Boone:

We have received your check #9749 for $1,610.24 in payment of our
May statement. Although our statement showed shipping charges,
Cape May was entitled to deduct this cost ($77.24) because the
statement was paid within seven days. We have credited your account
for these charges, and the credit will be reflected on your June
statement.

If you have any questions, or if we can be of further service, please call
us at the telephone number below.

Sincerely,

Bernard Holt
555-2900, ext. 37

- Customers delight in being told that they're due money, and it reflects well on the supplier if you notice the error and credit the customer promptly.

- Avoid making the customer feel that he or she made a stupid mistake.

Company Name
Address
City, State Zip

Date

Ms. Margot Robertson
150 North Pine Street
Branford, CT 06405

Dear Ms. Robertson:

We received your check #540 for $48.00 for our driveway plowing last month. I think you must have overlooked the usual surcharge of $12 for plowing after the second storm, when the snowfall exceeded 8 inches.

There's no need to pay us separately for the surcharge; we will add it to SnowBusters' next monthly statement.

Thank you for your patronage.

Sincerely,

Bryce R. Goodhue

Attachment

- Even if an unpaid item was clearly stated on an invoice, assume an inadvertent oversight if dealing with a regular customer. (People sometimes don't read statements carefully.)

- Reminding a customer of your reasonable attitude reflects well on your company and will build good will.

Company Name
Address
City, State Zip

Date

Mercury Video Deliveries
200 North Michigan Avenue
Chicago, IL 60611

Dear Accounts Payable Supervisor:

We have received your payment of $198.54 (check #2361) for our invoice #002189. Unfortunately, you have a balance due of $12.30 because you have overlooked the relevant tax and freight charges.

Please send your check as soon as possible so that we can stop the computer's collection letter sequence, which most people find extremely annoying.

Very truly yours,

Robin Johnson
Collection Supervisor

- It's better to have a person's name, even for form letters, but this salutation is better than "Gentlemen."

- Be sure to include all relevant information: amount paid, check number, and invoice number.

- The ending sentence humanizes the "form" letter.

Company Name
Address
City, State Zip

Date

Mr. Dorman F. Hillhouse, CPA, P.C.
600 Skiff Street
Baltimore, MD 21213

Dear Mr. Hillhouse:

Enclosed is our check #2032 for $212.50. You apparently paid your
June bill for computer services twice, resulting in an overpayment of that
amount. Ordinarily, we would give you a credit, but since you have
plans to close the office for the months of July and August, we believe
you would prefer to have a check.

Have a good vacation.

Best wishes,

Chris J. Risch

Enclosure

- Most customers do not object to receiving a credit. You must provide a check if the customer requests one, however.

- In this case, the writer knows the customer personally, so wishing him a good holiday is totally appropriate.

Company Name
Address
City, State Zip

Date

Mrs. Helen Stargis
14 Oak Terrace
Rutland, VT 05701

Dear Mrs. Stargis:

As requested, here is a copy of our invoice #2160543 for the merchandise we shipped to you on March 17. I've also enclosed a copy of our newest catalog; we welcome your next order and hope that you will call us whenever we can help you.

Yours very truly,

Warren Palmer
Billing Department

Enclosure

- Refer to the invoice enclosed by number and note the date of shipment.

- Take advantage of every opportunity to interest your customer in another sale. You might consider adding a handwritten "P.S." referring to a specific product. Research shows that the "P.S." gets read first.

Company Name
Address
City, State Zip

Date

Mr. Tony Walters
420 Lakeland Boulevard
Kokomo, IN 46901

Dear Mr. Walters:

We received your return of the model 42Z11 Zip-o-mat power saw
(invoice #120211) and are happy to exchange it for model 51X12, which
we hope is more suitable to your needs. Since model 51X12 is priced
lower than model 42Z11 (at $89.95), we have credited your account
$20.00.

I've enclosed a copy of our new spring catalog in which we feature a
new line of small handheld power tools that appeals to home woodworking enthusiasts like yourself. Please call at 1-800-246-6660 or use
the form in the catalog whenever you would like to place another order.

Sincerely,

Donald VanHoff

Enclosure

- Show you're truly interested in seeing that the customer gets what he or she needs.

- Refer specifically to the model ordered, shipping invoice, and amounts billed. State how
  under or overpayment will be handled (i.e., we credited your account).

Company Name
Address
City, State Zip

Date

Mr. Eugene Jarvis
10 Polk Place
Lorton, VA 22416

Dear Mr. Jarvis:

We are sorry to hear the model 1240G Deluxe Router we shipped you on March 4 (invoice #22610) did not fulfill your expectations and are happy to credit your account $129.98 for its return.

I've enclosed a copy of our new spring catalog. We feature a complete line of power tools designed specifically for the home woodworker. Please use this catalog's order form or call us at 1-800-246-6660 whenever we can help you with another order.

Sincerely,

Donald VanHoff

Enclosure

- Express regret that your product didn't satisfy the customer.

- Take every opportunity to get the customer interested in other products.

Company Name
Address
City, State Zip

Date

Mr. Clint LaPointe
154 Bormann Road
Cazenovia, NY 13035

Dear Mr. LaPointe:

We're sorry the model 182CZ handdrill you ordered (invoice #26675) did not arrive safely and are happy to refund your $62.95 (enclosed check #8669). Unfortunately, we have no more model 182CZ drills in stock, since we discontinued the line this spring.

Here is a copy of our new summer catalog, which features a complete line of tools for the home woodworker. Model 184CZ (p. 22) is closest in price and speed to the 182CZ. We hope you will consider ordering the 184CZ, which has two more drill bits than the older model.

We apologize for any inconvenience you suffered and hope we will have another opportunity to ship you one of our fine products.

Sincerely,

Donald VanHoff

Enclosure

- Express sincere apologies for any customer dissatisfaction.

- Refer specifically to order, invoice, and check numbers and amounts.

- Show interest in continuing the customer relationship by suggesting other suitable products.

Company Name
Address
City, State Zip

Date

Ms. Deborah Bovan
Designer Depot Company
25 Green Road
Shaker Heights, OH 44122

Dear Ms. Bovan:

I'm glad you called to check on the status of the 25 sweaters you sent back to us two weeks ago. After checking our records carefully, I find that we have not received your returned sweaters. Please contact your shipper to start tracing the shipment. I'm sorry, but we cannot be responsible for returned goods that are lost in transit. However, if you send me the details in writing (sales order number, shipping company name, shipment number, date it was shipped, etc.), I will gladly help you trace it from this end.

Please keep me posted. We value your business and look forward to assisting you whenever possible.

Sincerely,

Sean McIntyre

- Be clear as to who will be responsible if the returned goods are not located.

- Express interest in resolving the matter and in helping when possible.

Handling
Customer Complaints 4

There are no complaint-free businesses. In fact, dissatisfied customers who silently take business elsewhere are a far worse problem than those who complain. A customer who complains can usually be salvaged. Businesses should take the time to solicit feedback from their customers, especially unhappy ones.

Ideally, complaints should be handled on the phone. A customer's complaint can best be understood in a conversation. If the customer cannot be reached, or a discussion doesn't resolve the situation, a letter is required. In any case, a letter confirming the details of the conversation should be sent.

Whether the customer's complaint has any basis or not, the letter writer needs to acknowledge in some way that the company welcomes hearing from the customer for any reason. Even seemingly frivolous complaints can reveal significant needs for improvement in customer relations. The tone of the letter should reflect the fact that company people are approachable and ready to help if possible.

Justified complaints. If the complaint is justified, the company should respond immediately, offering to "make things right" if possible, or offering alternative solutions if that's not possible. The tone should not be defensive or cringing. After all, mistakes happen, even in the best run company. If the company has made an error, admit it promptly and make amends as best you can. Because customers are so accustomed to shabby treatment, promptness in satisfying them may even make them into public relations people for your firm. They may comment to others on the company's unusual responsiveness.

Partially justified complaints. The key here is in the approach you take. Focus on the fact that the customer is partially right. Ignore the fact that this also makes him or her partially wrong. It's far harder to get a new customer than to keep the good will of an old customer. If there's any element of truth in what the customer is saying, it is better to agree (and make things right, even if it costs money) than it is to get into a no-win argument. Similarly, in cases of misunderstanding, the thrust is for the company to take at least part of the responsibility (a miscommunication has two possible causes—a garbled message or an inattentive receiver.)

Unjustified complaints. If you believe the customer is unjustified, ask for clarification—it may be that he has not expressed himself well and the complaint is the result of a simple misunderstanding that can be easily cleared up. If you are unable to respond positively, an honest, straightforward "no," along with the reasons for the refusal, is best. If the company is not responsible, suggest the action the customer can take to get satisfaction elsewhere, without actually blaming someone else. It's unlikely the customer is trying to cheat the company, and accusing him of that will ensure undying enmity. This type of ill will can spread to other customers of your company.

To sum up, respond positively and promptly to all complaints—and consider even the most vituperative attack as providing valuable information about customer relations.

Company Name
Address
City, State Zip

Date

Mr. Frank Delaplaine
830 N. Carrollton Avenue
Baltimore, MD 21217

Dear Mr. Delaplaine:

Here's the breakdown that you requested of the billing on your sound
system (PO #88177-B, Factory Order 96N-00182):

Suborder	Description	Amount
1GA	amplifier	$ 106.24
2GA	turntable	$ 261.89
3GA	speakers	$ 649.41
	Subtotal:	$ 1,017.54
	State tax (5%):	$ 50.88
	Freight:	$ 17.50
	Total:	$ 1,085.92

I hope this will allow you to pay the invoice. If you have any further
questions, please call me at 889-6249.

Respectfully yours,

James Conklin

- Be clear—show all discounts, taxes, freight, etc.

- State your expectations—that the customer will either pay the invoice or call.

Company Name
Address
City, State Zip

Date

Mr. Bruce Feinstein
35 Main Street
South Hadley, MA 01075

Dear Mr. Feinstein:

I would like to apologize for the error we made on our invoice DCI-92J, dated June 15. I'm canceling that invoice and reinvoicing you as follows:

12 tables @ $11.48 each		$137.76
48 chairs @ $2.05 each		98.40
12 tablecloths @ $1.88 each		22.56
24 5-piece place settings @ $3.24 each		77.76
	Subtotal	$336.48
	Tax (4.5%)	15.14
	Total	$351.62

I hope this resolves the issue to your satisfaction. I look forward to doing more business with you in the future.

Sincerely,

Bill Simmons

- Explain what action you will take (reinvoice, credit, accept deduction, etc.)

- Solicit more business.

Company Name
Address
City, State Zip

Date

Mr. Robert J. Hudak
45 Yankee Peddler Path
Madison, CT 06443

Dear Mr. Hudak:

Thank you for calling last week regarding our error in your billing last month. Your check (#489) was credited to the wrong account due to an error in our computer records. I have corrected the situation, and I'm very sorry for the inconvenience that our error has caused.

Please take a moment to review our records and confirm that we now have your information correctly in our computer:

Cardholder:	Robert J. Hudak
Address:	45 Yankee Peddler Path
	Madison, CT 06443
Home phone:	(203) 245-4872
Work phone:	(203) 266-6079
Account number:	128-9771-553

Thank you for your understanding. We look forward to serving you in the future.

Sincerely,

Bill Salvatore
Credit Manager

- Apologize for the error.

- State the action you took or to be taken by another party (e.g., submit corrected information).

- Confirm the correctness of your present records.

Company Name
Address
City, State Zip

Date

Mr. Hasan Kebebian
Kebebian Rugs, Inc.
578 Broad Street
Lorton, VA 22079

Dear Mr. Kebebian:

I'm sorry that we have not been able to deliver as scheduled your shipment of rugs from India. Unfortunately, the dock workers' strike in New York has prevented the unloading of the ship. I expect that the strike will be over soon and that we can deliver your shipment within the next month.

I apologize for the delay and inconvenience this has caused you. I will notify you as soon the strike is over.

Very truly yours,

Jim Castalucci
Customer Service Representative

- Explain the reason for the delay.

- Give your best estimate of reschedule.

- Express empathy, whether the delay is caused by you or by others.

Apology for Shipment Error (4-05)

Company Name
Address
City, State Zip

Date

Mr. Stan Walton
15 Federal Road
Hemlock, NY 14466

Dear Mr. Walton:

I'm sorry we sent you the Mahogany Queen Anne Footstool Kit (No. 347A) instead of the Cherry Queen Anne Footstool Kit (No. 347B) that you ordered. I am sending you the correct kit today. Please return the mahogany kit to us by UPS with insurance; we will reimburse you for all shipping costs.

Again, I apologize for the inconvenience this has caused you. Thank you for your help and understanding. We truly appreciate your business and look forward to serving you again in the near future.

Sincerely,

Jason Fine
Customer Service

- Acknowledge the error and express your apology.

- Say what you have done and/or what the customer should do to corrrect the error.

Company Name
Address
City, State Zip

Date

Mr. David Young
38 Petrified Tree Pass
Billings, MT 59101

Dear Mr. Young:

I'm sorry to learn about the damage to the sofa that you purchased from us last month. Our driver has determined that the damage occurred in shipment (most likely from the manufacturer's warehouse to our store).

I've ordered an exact replacement from the factory, and I've been told that it will take four to six weeks to get here. I'll call you as soon as it arrives, and we will arrange a convenient time for delivery.

I am very sorry for the inconvenience this has caused you. I'll be in touch very soon.

Sincerely,

Bob Chamberlain
Manager

- Acknowledge the party responsible for the damage.

- Outline corrective action taken or to be taken.

- Make sure that you follow up as promised.

Company Name
Address
City, State Zip

Date

Mrs. Lucille Jackson
1150 Oriole Street
Baltimore, MD 21217

Dear Mrs. Jackson:

Please accept my sincerest apologies for the rudeness you experienced at our restaurant last night. There was no excuse for the way you were treated, and the person involved is no longer employed at PJ Willy's. PJ Willy's prides itself on being a family restaurant where good food and good service are always "on the menu."

I hope that you will try us again. Please call me at 459-3398, and I will be very happy to take your reservations for a dinner for two on the house. Thank you for your understanding and for bringing this matter to my attention.

Very truly yours,

Bill Robinson
General Manager

- Acknowledge and apologize for the rudeness.

- Outline the corrective action to be taken.

- Ask the customer to try you again and offer an incentive (a free dinner) for doing so.

Company Name
Address
City, State Zip

Date

Mr. Patrick Blakely
964 Monroe Avenue
Malden, MA 02148

Dear Mr. Blakely:

I am sorry that the instruction manual for operating your new Frostee-Lite ice cream maker was missing. I am sending you a new manual along with a booklet of recipes for some wonderful ice cream and sherbet delights that you might like to try.

Thank you for your understanding and for selecting Frostee-Lite. I'm sure you will be very pleased with your new ice cream maker.

Sincerely,

Jana Rossman
Customer Service

Enclosure

- Apologize for the missing documentation.

- Enclose the missing documentation.

- Express appreciation for the business.

Company Name
Address
City, State Zip

Date

Mr. Sal Marino
Fast Start Automotive Products
30 Broad Street
Milford, CT 06460

Dear Mr. Marino:

We're sorry to learn of the damage to our latest solenoid shipment (PO# 77J-4P). You should file a damage claim with the trucking firm, as our standard terms and conditions of sale state "FOB factory." Our responsibility therefore ends when the trucker signs for the shipment. I have enclosed a copy of the trucker's pick-up slip, showing that the shipment was in good condition, in case this will help you in filing a claim.

We have enough stock on hand to reship your order. If you would like us to do so, please call us with a purchase order.

Sincerely,

John Bloom
Customer Service Manager

Enclosure

- State clearly who is and who is not responsible.

- Be as helpful as possible to the customer.

- Express empathy.

Company Name
Address
City, State Zip

Date

Mr. George G. Mallion
The Computer Science Corporation
66 Geese Lake Drive
Oberlin, OH 44074

Dear Mr. Mallion:

Thank you for writing us about your irritation concerning the delay in CSC's receipt of four (4) MacDonald Customized Video Display Terminals (CSC PO# 3214; our invoice #80-1219-G).

The delay, however, was not caused at our end. As specified in your Purchase Order, we shipped via Transcontinental Truckers before July 14. The terminals were actually picked up on July 12, as you can see from the enclosed copy of the bill of lading (Transcontinental #55-MC-9906).

Unless I have misunderstood something, it appears that Transcontinental is responsible for the delay. Please let me know if I may help further in this matter.

Sincerely,

James B. MacDonald
Enclosure

- Acknowledge the customer's complaint. Reference all purchase orders, invoices, etc.

- Be direct about where the fault (if any) lies.

- Appear flexible; there may be additional issues the customer will raise subsequently.

Company Name
Address
City, State Zip

Date

Miss Estelle deWinter
380 Orion Circle
Palm Beach, FL 33480

Dear Miss deWinter:

I'm sorry to hear about the rudeness you experienced while shopping at our store. I wish there was something we could do to prevent such unpleasant events from occurring but, unfortunately, we cannot always observe peculiar behavior in people who come through our store, or intercept them as an incident develops.

I hope this incident will not give you a bad impression of Fashion Fair stores. We value you as a customer, and I look forward to seeing you again.

Sincerely,

Kathy Goodman
Manager

- Express understanding for the customer's feelings.

- Establish that there was nothing you could have done to prevent the rudeness from occurring.

- Express hope that the incident will not affect your customer's patronage and that he or she will try you again.

Company Name
Address
City, State Zip

Date

Mr. Francis D'Attalo
905 Wingate Road
Rochester, NY 14692

Dear Mr. D'Attalo:

Thank you for calling to check on the status of the shirts you ordered from us (Item 53J, Order #29746) three weeks ago (July 28). I have looked into your order, and everything is on schedule. Perhaps you did not notice that on the bottom of the order form we have noted that any items that are monogrammed, such as your shirts, will require a delivery time of four to five weeks instead of the usual two to three weeks.

Your shirts should be arriving next week. I believe that you will be very satisfied with your Wellington Bay shirts. Please let me know if I can be of any further assistance.

Sincerely,

Glenn Hanks
Customer Service

- Clarify what the delivery time is for the order.

- Refer to the item as specifically as possible (Sales# or PO#, etc.).

- Express goodwill and willingness to help out further.

Company Name
Address
City, State Zip

Date

Mr. Jonas Rew
30 Golden Hill Drive
Philadelphia, PA 19140

Dear Mr. Rew:

I've tried to reach you by phone because I feel problems should be dealt with in person. However, I have been unable to catch you at home this last week, and I don't want our disagreement to go on much longer.

I understand from J. C. Gilbert, our stylist, that you were very unhappy with Radar's grooming last Monday. She said you felt we had "dandified" and "emasculated" Radar by putting him in a "business suit." As we discussed when you brought Radar in, Airedales cost $20 more to groom because their clip is very difficult. For example, they must retain "eyebrows," always difficult to achieve with such energetic dogs. During our conversation, I felt you were familiar with the way Airedales looked after they had been clipped. I'm very sorry for the misunderstanding.

Nevertheless, I must insist you pay your account in full. We spent considerable time removing burrs and snarls and gave Radar a flea bath as well as clipping him. I'm afraid the aesthetics of the cut have no bearing on the necessity to pay for work performed.

I look forward to receiving your check for $40.00 as soon as possible.

Sincerely,

Lyman Gordon

- Acknowledge that the customer may have misunderstood, and detail clearly the work performed, but firmly insist on your right to payment.

Company Name
Address
City, State Zip

Date

Miss Karen Steinkraus
289 Holden Avenue
Lansdowne, PA 19050

Dear Miss Steinkraus:

Along with this letter, I'm sending back the sheets (Sales #4503) that you returned to us. I'm sorry to hear that they were not the color you expected, especially since there were color swatches as well as color photographs of the sheets in the catalog. Unfortunately, as we have indicated in large type on the bottom of our order form, we cannot accept any items for return or exchange that have been monogrammed, unless there is a defect in either the material or workmanship.

I apologize for the inconvenience our policy has caused you. Thank you for your understanding.

Sincerely,

Paul Hatfield
Sales Manager

Enclosure

- Outline the terms of sale specifically and indicate where that information is located in the sales literature that the customer already has (e.g., the order form, the catalog).

- Clarify the misunderstanding.

- Express goodwill.

Company Name
Address
City, State Zip

Date

Mr. George Stang
2500 Chardon Rd.
Willoughby, OH 44094

Dear Mr. Stang:

I am sorry to hear you are dissatisfied with the capacity of your Patsy Ice Cream Maker, Model IC-BIG, which makes one quart. I cannot understand why you thought it would make a half-gallon since our ad, the box and the owner's manual clearly state the quantity that each operating cycle will produce is one quart.

I think that your using the Patsy Model IC-BIG you will find that the one quart capacity is quite convenient. Also, since the operating cycle is only 30 minutes, another batch can be prepared quickly.

Sincerely,

Carmen Linn
Customer Service

- Clarify the misunderstanding by stating the product specifications and where the information can be found in the sales literature.

- If possible, explain why the product specifications are positive features.

Company Name
Address
City, State Zip

Date

Mrs. Aileen Yamamoto
372 Center Street
Granada Hills, CA 91344

Dear Mrs. Yamamoto:

I have received your letter concerning the A-Pro 1900 hairdryer that you recently purchased. I'm sorry that you misunderstood the product specifications. As indicated in the sales literature, the hairdryer is designed to be used only on 115 volts, 60 hertz electrical current; it cannot be used on 220 volts, 50 hertz current.

Our policy is to accept authorized returns within 30 days of purchase if the product is returned in the original box. I have enclosed a shipping label for your convenience.

If you wish, we will send you a refund check for $28.95 upon receipt of the hairdryer. However, if you are interested in a hairdryer that runs on 220 volts, 50 hertz electrical current, I suggest the A-Pro 2400 model. It is very similar to the A-Pro 1900 and lists for the same price, $28.95. We also carry a model that can be used on both 115 volts and 220 volts, the A-Pro 3500. It is extremely popular and lists for $36.95. Please write me or call our toll-free, 24-hour number, (800) 991-6000, if you wish to make arrangements about either of these models. We can ship the 2400 model at no cost to you or the 3500 model upon receipt of an additional $8.00 (in both cases, upon receipt of the 1900 model you now have).

Sincerely,

Tim Comcheck
Customer Service

Enclosure

- Acknowledge the customer's specific complaint and state the courses of action available.

- If you have other products that fit the customer's needs, steer the customer toward them. The customer will be more satisfied, and you'll have kept the sale.

Company Name
Address
City, State Zip

Date

Miss Krista Hemeyer
206 Peachtree Lane
Athens, GA 30613

Dear Miss Hemeyer:

I'm sorry to hear of the damage to your A-Pro 1900 hairdryer during your trip to Italy. Unfortunately, we cannot be held responsible for this damage, which occurred because the hairdryer was plugged into a 220 volt, 50 hertz electrical outlet. As specifically indicated on the box, on the documentation inside the box, and on the actual product, the A-Pro 1900 is designed to be used only on 115 volt, 60 hertz electrical current. No return is therefore possible.

Sincerely yours,

Tom Comcheck
Customer Service

- Clarify the product specifications and indicate where they can be found in the sales literature.

- Explain why no return is possible.

Company Name
Address
City, State Zip

Date

Mr. Robert Metz
Euclid Orthopedic Group
358 Euclid Avenue
Euclid, OH 44117

Dear Mr. Metz:

I'm glad to hear that you are pleased with the quality of sharpening that EdgeTech has provided. I hope that you will give us the opportunity to serve you again.

I'd like to clarify a misunderstanding we may have had regarding delivery terms and turn-around time. The rates that we quoted you for the sharpening of your surgical instruments is based on the normal Wednesday afternoon pickup from your office and delivery to your office on the following Monday morning by our representative. If you require a pickup other than on Wednesday afternoon, there is a special charge of $10.00 per order, but the sharpening price is still the same as quoted per surgical instrument. If you require an overnight turnaround, there is again a special pickup charge of $10.00 and, in addition, the sharpening rates are 15% above the regular quoted rates.

Please let me know if you have any questions. I look forward to your business.

Sincerely,

Jason Green
Account Manager

- Specifically state the delivery terms in question and clarify the misunderstanding.

- Express appreciation for the business.

Company Name
Address
City, State Zip

Date

Ms. Eileen Johnson
42 Ferry Lane
Concord, NH 03301

Dear Ms. Johnson:

Larry Crosby, our Credit and Collections Manager, has told me of your intense dissatisfaction with the way your father's recent auto repair was handled here in our shop.

I am terribly sorry that you and your family have had these difficulties. Please be sure that I will give the entire matter a very thorough review. Mr. Johnson's repairs were extremely complicated. It will take me some time to review this with the mechanics involved and the Shop Manager, but after I have completed my investigation, I would very much like to meet with you and your father to discuss the problem he experienced. Is there a possibility that you will be visiting your parents over the holidays? If so, perhaps we can arrange a mutually convenient time to meet.

I asked Mr. Crosby to hold up any further collection proceedings until I have discussed the matter with you and your father in person. I will be in touch as soon as I have completed my review. I would appreciate your speaking to your attorney as soon as possible to delay the legal action he contemplates—that would serve no one's best interests.

Sincerely yours,

Pierce Franklin Thomas
General Manager

- No one really wants legal action. Try to forestall it by offering to establish the facts and have a face-to-face discussion.

- The tone should be reasonable but not apologetic. You do not know if your company is at fault or what action you wish to take if it is. Do not make specific reference to the "facts." If they disagree with the customer's version, you'll engender hostility.

Credit and Collections 5

Strangely enough, when matters of credit and collection come up, businesspeople often forget that they are writing to other human beings. More than that, they forget that they are writing to *customers*, people whose business they value. It is absolutely essential that you treat everyone with courtesy and understanding, and that includes customers who have not paid their bills or customers to whom you cannot yet extend credit for one reason or another.

In fact, the collection process begins with the sale. Overselling—selling to someone who truly cannot afford an item or a service or to someone who doesn't need the item or service—often creates massive problems later on. Credit and collections are actually part of the selling process, since the sale is not really complete until the seller receives payment.

Credit letters. Many people have been offended or hurt by the way creditors have dealt with them in the past. As a result, refusing credit is a very ticklish issue, and the tone of any letter should be extremely sensitive. Offering to provide credit after the customer has established a track record is a good way to present the bad news positively. Remember, though, that you do no one a favor if you extend credit to someone who is truly not creditworthy.

Collection letters. To avoid having to write collection letters in the first place, make it as easy as possible for the customer to pay on time by offering discounts for timely payment, by providing self-addressed envelopes, or by making it an option to charge the payment to a major credit card. The easier you make it, the more likely you are to get what you want—first, attention to your bill among the plethora of pieces anyone receives in the course of the day and second, actual and prompt payment.

If your customer is late in paying, however, you need to establish an automatic sequence of collection letters. It has been documented that the longer the customer goes without paying, the less likely you are to see any payment, even if you turn the account over to a collection agency. Collection sequences follow a standard pattern—notification or reminder, inquiry, appeal, demand, ultimatum. It's correct to start any collection sequence with a notification that payment has not been received (a statement of fact) and an inquiry as to whether a problem exists.

Despite all the "the check is in the mail" jokes, someone may not have paid because of events beyond his or her control. The U. S. Postal Service may be at fault or the business or person may have moved or be on vacation. If a personal tragedy has occurred (a death in the family perhaps), sending a hostile letter will not only lose you a customer, but may blacken your reputation with other potential customers.

Of course, if you ask people whether there's a problem, they may actually respond by calling and telling you what it is. Although this is precisely what you want (you want to keep the communication going at almost any cost), you'll need to have someone available to talk with them and possibly to negotiate an extended payment schedule.

If your reminder and/or inquiry doesn't work (the two letters are frequently combined), then you'll need to have a letter that appeals to the customer's sense of fair play. You have provided a service or a product; the customer owes you something in return. You then proceed to demanding payment and to an ultimate threat to turn the account over to a collection agency. At each stage, though, whether you adopt the moderate tone of the first sequence of letters or the stern tone of the second sequence, keep your determination to treat the customer with sensitivity and honesty. Treating a slow payer with politeness is difficult, but the ability to do so may preserve that customer's goodwill in the future.

Request to Customer to Complete Credit Application (5-01)

Company Name
Address
City, State Zip

Date

Mr. George Maxham
265 Coast Boulevard
Jenner, CA 95450

Dear Mr. Maxham:

We're pleased to hear you'd like to establish a credit account with
H. R. Stoneham Corporation and look forward to the opportunity to
serve you on an ongoing basis.

We do require that credit applicants complete the enclosed application
form before receiving formal credit approval. Once we've received your
completed form we'll notify you within three weeks regarding its
acceptance.

If you have any questions about the form or our approval requirements,
please call me at 1-800-268-4269. I will be pleased to help you provide
the information we need.

Yours truly,

Marion Stanley
Credit Manager

Enclosure

- Use a cordial tone to maintain a good relationship with an existing or potential customer and let the customer know you appreciate the patronage.

- Specify when the applicant can expect a decision.

- Let the applicant know how to request assistance.

Company Name
Address
City, State Zip

Date

Mr. Richard Miller
MZM Incorporated
116 Brookpark Road
Houston, TX 77055

Dear Mr. Miller:

Thank you for your purchase order ST-1950. So that we may extend
our normal terms of net 30 days, please furnish us with the following
information:

1. your annual report
2. name of your bank, account number, and contact
3. names of two suppliers with whom you are presently
   doing business.

We look forward to serving you, and we feel that extending 30-day
payment terms is part of that service. Thank you for your cooperation,
and for your order.

Sincerely,

Bill Small
Credit Manager

- Ask for the information (be specific) you need to make a good decision. Remember, it's your money that they are asking to use!

- Express appreciation for their cooperation and for their business.

Company Name
Address
City, State Zip

Date

Ms. Martha Johanneson
Manager, Credit Department
Northrop Department Stores
Nashua, NH 03060

Dear Ms. Johanneson:

Thomas Slate (Acct. #2276052) has named your company as a credit reference in his application for an account with our store. We are now reviewing Mr. Slate's application and would appreciate your providing the following information regarding your experience as one of Mr. Slate's creditors:

- length of credit relationship
- amounts billed monthly and annually
- promptness in payment/delinquency

As soon as we receive this information, we can complete processing Mr. Slate's account. We would appreciate your prompt reply.

Thank you.

Sincerely,

Harold Lowe
Credit Department

- Give the name and account number of applicant.

- Specify information you need.

- Ask for prompt action, noting the importance of the report in your decision.

Company Name
Address
City, State Zip

Date

Mr. Calvin McCormick
Credit Manager
Webster Products, Inc.
4442 Withey Highway
Flint, MI 48503

Dear Mr. McCormick:

One of our credit applicants, Perkins/Neville Associates of Grand Rapids, MI, has named your company as a credit reference. Before extending credit to an applicant, we require information on that applicant's experience with other creditors. Would you please furnish a credit report on Perkins/Neville, including length of relationship, amounts billed annually, and promptness of payment?

We would appreciate your response soon so that we can complete our review of Perkins/Neville's application within a month.

Thank you for your cooperation.

Sincerely,

Stanley Johnson
Credit Department

- Identify the credit applicant about whom you seek information.

- Specify information you need.

- Note the time span in which you need a response.

Approval of Credit, Retail (5-05)

Company Name
Address
City, State Zip

Date

Ms. Nancy Vosburgh
13 Fairfax Court
Richmond, VA 23225

Dear Ms. Vosburgh:

We at Temple Department Stores are pleased to welcome you as a
Temple Card holder. We think you'll find the Temple Card opens the
door to enjoying many valuable services, including easy credit terms
and advance notice of special sales.

Please validate the enclosed Temple Card by signing your name in ink
in the space indicated on the back. You can then use it when you shop
in any one of our four stores in the greater Richmond area. We have
also enclosed a copy of our credit terms specifying how your account
will be billed each month.

Again, welcome to our family of Temple Card Holders!

Sincerely,

Merrill Cottle
Billing Department

Enclosure

- Cordially welcome the new credit customer.

- State what the customer needs to know/do before using the account.

- Include written notice of credit terms.

Company Name
Address
City, State Zip

Date

Mr. Jack Martin
Yankee Modular Homes
72 Quincy Road
Boston, MA 02127

Dear Mr. Martin:

Thank you for your recent order. We have a long history of serving new businesses. Your initiative in providing low-cost homes in an urban setting is bound to draw a large clientele.

Because a steady cash flow is important to us, however, we approve very few credit accounts. Although the credit reference you provided is favorable, you will need to establish two more credit references to charge orders exceeding $1,000.

We do, though, offer a 5% discount on cash orders. Please indicate on the enclosed copy of your order form whether you want to place a cash order now.

We will review your application in three months. If at that time you have established additional references, we will accept a credit order.

We wish you the best of luck in your new endeavor.

Sincerely,

John Snyder
Vice President, Accounting

- Credit is refused for a variety of reasons. A regular customer may have fallen behind in payment. A young credit candidate or new business may have no credit history. A customer may have a history of being delinquent on credit payments.

- Exercise good judgment in refusing a candidate for credit to avoid legal action.

Company Name
Address
City, State Zip

Date

Ms. Katherine Woodley
14 Elmhurst Street
Marietta, GA 30086

Dear Ms. Woodley:

Thank you for showing your interest in becoming a Thomas Furniture Mart credit account holder. We're happy to know you appreciate the fine quality of our merchandise as well as our wide selection of contemporary and traditional home furnishings.

We've received your application and are sorry that we cannot extend you credit at this time. One of our requirements for credit is that applicants have lived in the area for at least one year. As a newcomer to Marietta, you do not meet that requirement.

We hope, though, that you will continue to shop at Thomas's and that you will resubmit your application after you have met our residency requirement.

Sincerely,

Perron F. Towers
Credit Manager

- Thank the customer for the application.

- Refuse the request graciously and regretfully.

- Specify *why* the application was refused.

- Invite the applicant to try again should circumstances change.

Company Name
Address
City, State Zip

Date

Mr. W. G. Randall
Purchasing Agent
P&W Leasing Company
200 Fairwood Lane
Detroit, MI 48215

Dear Mr. Randall:

As of March 31, we have not received your February payment. Have you forgotten? Please check your records.

If you have already sent your payment, please disregard this notice and accept our thanks for your payment.

Sincerely,

W. P. Johnson
Collection Manager

- A first reminder for payment reflects your understanding that some minor problem may have delayed payment. You assume that the customer has every intention of paying and needs only to be reminded.

Company Name
Address
City, State Zip

Date

Mr. W. G. Randall
Purchasing Agent
P&W Leasing Company
200 Fairwood Lane
Detroit, MI 48215

Dear Mr. Randall:

You have been a valued customer for many years, and you have always been conscientious about paying your bills within the 30-day payment period.

Your good credit rating has enabled you to purchase from us on convenient payment terms at a substantial discount. Because of your prompt payment record, we have been glad to serve as a reference when you have applied for credit with other suppliers.

To keep your good credit rating and to continue receiving a substantial discount, payment of your account is necessary. Are you having some problem that we can help you with?

By sending your check for $350.00 in the enclosed stamped envelope, you will bring your account up-to-date and protect your credit rating. If this is not feasible, please call or write me today.

Sincerely,

W. P. Johnson
Collection Manager

Enclosure

- As frustrating as it is to send out a reminder and still get no response, assume that the customer has overlooked your payment request, or that other circumstances are preventing payment.

- Be specific as to the payment required and make it easy for the customer to pay you (the return envelope).

Company Name
Address
City, State Zip

Date

Mr. W. G. Randall
Purchasing Agent
P&W Leasing Company
200 Fairwood Lane
Detroit, MI 48215

Dear Mr. Randall:

This morning I received your file with a big OVERDUE stamped on it. I receive customer files only when some serious problem has occurred.

Your order was shipped over four months ago, and we still have not received a payment from you. As you are in business, Mr. Randall, you must realize that we cannot afford to carry this debt on our books any longer.

To preserve your credit privileges, please do one of the following:

- Remit the full amount of $350.00 today.
- Send us $150.00 as partial payment, with the balance payable by June 30.
- Explain your situation, and let us know what you can do to meet your obligation.

Your immediate response is necessary.

Sincerely,

Mark Bowman
President

- Avoid overt threats, but convey your desire to collect the overdue payment immediately. Having a senior company official sign the letter will signal urgency.

- Allow the customer to make a payment without losing face.

Company Name
Address
City, State Zip

Date

Mr. W. G. Randall
Purchasing Agent
P&W Leasing Company
200 Fairwood Lane
Detroit, MI 48215

Dear Mr. Randall:

We are sending this letter to you with regret that previous efforts to obtain payment of your account have been unsuccessful.

We sent a bill for $350.00 for payment by March 1. Over the past four months, we have tried to get you to fulfill your obligations to us. We assumed, since you had an excellent credit rating and have always been responsible in paying your bills before, that some small oversight was to blame.

Please send us your payment for the overdue bill within five days so that we do not have to turn your account over to a collection agency.

Sincerely,

Mark Bowman
President

• Do not send an ultimatum unless you are able to back it up. By sending this letter, you can encourage customers to reevaluate their priorities. If their finances are in disorder, you will not get results until this stage.

• You are no longer interested in excuses, but only want your payment.

Company Name
Address
City, State Zip

Date

Mr. and Mrs. Lawrence Sternin
1246 South Branch Parkway
Westwood, NJ 07675

Dear Mr. and Mrs. Sternin:

We're delighted you're enjoying your new living room furniture, including our popular Relax-a-lounger. However, it has been two months now since we delivered your furniture, and we have yet to receive your payment for $2,375.60 (Invoice #46237, copy enclosed). Have you already put a check in the mail to us?

If not, please give this matter your attention today, since we want to be able to extend you credit the next time you shop for quality home furnishings.

Sincerely,

Claire McManus
Billing Department
555-3222, ext. 102

Enclosure

- A polite, cordial reminder encourages the customer to settle the matter immediately. You want to be paid *and* keep the customer.

Collection Letter, Stern Tone, Letter #2 (5-13)

Company Name
Address
City, State Zip

Date

Mr. and Mrs. Lawrence Sternin
1246 South Branch Parkway
Westwood, NJ 07675

Dear Mrs. and Mrs. Sternin:

Unfortunately, we still haven't received your $2,375.60 payment
for merchandise you purchased January 5 (Invoice #46237, dated
January 12). Because your account is three months past due, we are
now forced to add a late charge of $23.75 in accordance with our credit
policy. The new balance is $2,399.35.

Please be sure to settle your account with us today. If you have
difficulty paying the full amount now, please call me today to discuss
arranging a payment schedule.

Yours truly,

Claire McManus
Billing Department
555-3222, ext. 102

- Note *how* and *why* late charges were assessed.

- Offer to adjust the payment schedule. It's better to get the money slowly than not at all.

Company Name
Address
City, State Zip

Date

Mr. and Mrs. Lawrence Sternin
1246 South Branch Parkway
Westwood, NJ 07675

Dear Mr. and Mrs. Sternin:

Your letter has been referred to me by Claire McManus of our Billing
Department. Because you have failed to make any payment on Invoice
#46237 for $2,399.35 (including late charges) or to contact us to
arrange a payment schedule, we have been forced to initiate
procedures to repossess the furniture you bought at our store.

We will be contacting you to arrange a date for repossession if we do
not receive full payment from you within two weeks. Please make every
effort to ensure that we are not forced to take this drastic action.

Sincerely,

R. Lane Peterson
Executive Vice President

- Have the collection letter written by someone high in the company and threaten action only after repeated attempts to secure payment have failed and the customer has shown no intention of cooperating.

- Note that you regret the severity of your action, which leaves the door open for the customer to settle.

Collection Letter, Stern Tone, Letter #4 (5-15)

Company Name
Address
City, State Zip

Date

Mr. and Mrs. Lawrence Sternin
1246 South Branch Parkway
Westwood, NJ 07675

Dear Mr. and Mrs. Sternin:

Regrettably, we are forced to repossess the five items of furniture we delivered to you on January 5, due to your failure to pay the $2,399.35 you owe for them.

On May 5, representatives of our company will arrive at your home at 10 a.m. to collect:

(1) queen-size sleep sofa (model 206G)
(1) "Corona" coffee table
(2) "Corona" end tables
(1) "Relax-a-lounger" (model 460L)

We had hoped to avoid this extreme action by offering you flexible credit options to lessen the difficulty you face making payments. However, your unwillingness to cooperate with our billing department has left us no choice.

Sincerely,

R. Lane Peterson
Executive Vice President

- When notifying a customer of intent to repossess, list the items involved and set a date for repossession.

- Send the letter via certified mail, return receipt, so you will have evidence that the customer was aware of your intentions.

Company Name
Address
City, State Zip

Date

Mr. and Mrs. Lawrence Sternin
1246 South Branch Parkway
Westwood, NJ 07675

Dear Mr. and Mrs. Sternin:

We were unhappy to find that we could not gain admittance (to take delivery of our merchandise) when our representatives arrived at your home on May 5. R. Lane Peterson, our chief financial officer, has turned over your file to me, and, as president of the company, I have decided that legal action is necessary.

Our decision to repossess our merchandise came only after several months of our repeated attempts to come to payment terms with you. Your continuing lack of cooperation leaves us no choice but to turn this matter over to the County Sheriff's office for resolution. All our future efforts to contact you will be through that office.

Sincerely,

William Travis
President

- As a last resort, refer the matter to law enforcement authorities.

- Having the company president write the final letter underlines the gravity of the situation and demonstrates that everyone in authority has considered the matter carefully.

Response to Credit Report, Misleading Report (5-17)

Company Name
Address
City, State Zip

Date

Mr. Edward Bonnard
Equitable Credit Check
6789 Loyola Drive
San Jose, CA 95125

Dear Mr. Bonnard:

Kindly include this letter in our company's credit file. Although in the main the material you summarized is correct, your summary does not provide a clear picture of the history of our business and therefore may be misinterpreted by lenders.

Our company, Simple Tools, has actually been in business since December 31, 1976. However, for the first five years, it was known as Thomas Canner, DBA Simple Tools. We incorporated as Simple Tools, Inc., on December 31, 1981, and that is the date you give for the inception of the business.

I look forward to receiving a revised summary including this additional information.

Sincerely,

Thomas Canner
President

- Credit bureaus must include pertinent information in their files if that information is verifiably correct. It's worthwhile to check occasionally to make sure that their files are complete and accurate.

- Always request written verification that a change has been made.

Company Name
Address
City, State Zip

Date

Ms. Leila Foxx
Equitable Credit Check
6789 Loyola Drive
San Jose, CA 95125

Dear Ms. Foxx:

As I stated on the phone, the information in your files relating to our mortgage payment history is erroneous. As you can see from the attached statements provided by Howland Savings Bank, the holder of our mortgage, we have never been notified of foreclosure proceedings, as stipulated in your file. In fact, our company's payment record is exemplary, as you can clearly see.

I will look forward to seeing a new synopsis of our company, indicating that this grossly false statement has been corrected, and to seeing, as you promised on the phone, copies of letters detailing the correct information to all those who have made inquiries about our credit standing.

Sincerely,

Georgia T. Kroner
Vice President, Finance

Attachments

- A good credit rating is vital in business. If you learn of a false statement, ensure that the credit bureau corrects it as soon as possible and that they send correction statements to anyone they have misinformed.

Dealing with Suppliers 6

The most important thing you can remember when writing letters to suppliers is to be clear. Tell your reader exactly what you need and when you expect it, or what you are going to provide and when. When making requests for information, as in inquiring about credit terms, you will help yourself by making the request as specific as possible. If you take the time to think through your needs and communicate them clearly to the supplier, you have a better chance of receiving a precise answer and, therefore, a better opportunity of making a sound business decision. Compliments and suggestions should be direct and unambiguous; don't get bogged down in flowery platitudes or general observations.

Are we speaking the same language? These days, people in business are constantly confronted with terminology and jargon. Refer to merchandise in the supplier's terms, use dates and numbers from invoices and bills of lading in your correspondence and, if necessary, look up the name of the part in the manual so that it is correctly identified in your communications. Be sure everyone knows what is going on.

Referring to invoice numbers, recalling dates and stating exact amounts is particularly important when your letter is expressing dissatisfaction. Command of these routine items demonstrates that you have looked into the matter carefully, have weighed the possibilities, and still find something unsatisfactory. A supplier who wants to keep your business will be more likely to see your side of a problem if you are precise, while remaining reasonable in tone.

I'm sorry, you're sorry. When you are inconvenienced by a supplier, remember that *your* company may inconvenience someone somewhere along the line. The best thing you can do is to assume that everyone wants to do a good job. Respect the professionalism of every supplier and insist that they respect your professionalism, too. This will create the best working environment for everyone.

Company Name
Address
City, State Zip

Date

Ms. Samantha Willis
Sales Representative
Fabrics First Incorporated
12 Calico Plaza
Darien, CT 06820

Dear Samantha:

Both the "Garden Chintz" pillow line and your new specialty quilts are selling almost faster than we can keep them in stock. Since your products seem so popular with our customers, we are interested in carrying other items of a style and quality similar to that of the pillows and quilts—perhaps table accessories or throw rugs. Please send brochures and price information on any of these types of products you now have, and I will then call you to discuss an order.

Sincerely,

Ramona Thomas
Purchasing Manager

- If you're particularly happy with a certain product, let the supplier know.

- Be as specific as you can about the kinds of products about which you want more information.

Company Name
Address
City, State Zip

Date

Mr. Ed Kelton
Kelton's House and Window Cleaning Service
345 Percheron Drive
Melbourne, FL 32935

Dear Mr. Kelton:

As we discussed on the phone, we look forward to your providing office-cleaning services every Tuesday and Friday evening (beginning May 17). To ensure you're paid regularly and promptly, we'd like to be billed on the last day of each month for the services you have provided that month. We will then pay each bill within 30 days of the date we receive it.

We hope this credit arrangement is satisfactory to you. If not, please call me to discuss alternatives.

Yours truly,

Roger Palmer
964-3321

- State the circumstances of your agreement with the supplier.

- Specify the credit terms you would like to establish.

- Leave the door open for discussion if your suggestion does not satisfy the supplier.

Inquiry about Credit Terms (6-03)

Company Name
Address
City, State Zip

Date

Mr. Gordon Harvey
Harvey Power Equipment
1220 Brookhaven Blvd.
Augusta, GA 30906

Dear Mr. Harvey:

Good Earth and Lawn is expanding its services this year to include the northern half of the city. We have serviced residential and commercial accounts in the southern neighborhoods for the past nine years. I have enclosed a list of our larger accounts.

For our expansion, and to upgrade existing equipment, we will need three (3) 12 h.p. riding mowers (36" rotary), four (4) self-propelled mowers (20" rotary) and two (2) weed and brush cutters.

As I'm sure you can understand, there will be a time lag between our initial use of the equipment and our receipt of fees for work performed. I would, therefore, appreciate receiving information regarding your firm's billing and credit terms.

Thank you.

Sincerely,

Miles Templeton

- Mention (for the supplier's benefit) your company's background; put yourself in as good a light as possible.

- Specify what type of goods or services you're considering buying. Explain why you want credit.

Company Name
Address
City, State Zip

Date

Ms. Yvonne Frost
Peerless Dry Cleaners
2507 Durango Dr.
Billings, MT 59101

Dear Ms. Frost:

Several of our waiters at the Lucky Seven Restaurant, on Main Street in Billings, have told us of the superior drycleaning service you offer. We have now agreed to provide weekly uniform drycleaning to all of our staff members and are interested in contracting for these services. We would like to deliver approximately 25 uniforms (shirts and trousers) for cleaning each Tuesday morning and have them returned to us by noon the following day.

Before we decide on a particular service, we need to know what discount you are prepared to offer for this type of order and what the weekly charge per uniform would be. Would you please call me by Wednesday with this information?

Sincerely,

Bart Tolland
443-7627

- Suppliers like to know where their business comes from—do mention any referrals from satisfied customers.

- Estimate as closely as possible the volume and regularity of the service or goods you require. This information is essential in figuring discounts.

Company Name
Address
City, State Zip

Date

Sales Manager
Croft Office Systems
75 Main Street
West Orange, NJ 07052

Dear Sales Manager:

Our secretarial service company will be upgrading our word processors.
We would like you to quote the following for immediate delivery:

Quantity	Description
(2)	Macintosh SE computers
(2)	2400 Baud modems
(1)	Laserwriter
(1)	300 dpi scanner

Your bid, including payment terms and/or credit options, should be
submitted to me no later than Friday, July 28.

Sincerely,

David Pierce
Manager

- Be specific about what you want them to bid on (including quantities and the projected delivery date), when they are to respond, and to whom they are to send the bid.

- Ask about payment terms, as these may influence your purchasing decision.

Company Name
Address
City, State Zip

Date

Mr. David Lewis
XYCOMA Telecommunications
59-304 Hapaki Street
Aiea, HI 96701

Dear Mr. Lewis:

We're sorry to inform you that we did not choose your products for the PBX expansion for our Honolulu office. Your preferred delivery cycle of 18 weeks is too long, given our specified requirement of 12 weeks. Your quote for the 12-week delivery cycle was about 10% higher than the successful bidder.

Thank you, however, for the detailed bid you provided. We will be sure to call you when we have telecommunications needs in the future.

Sincerely,

Kathy Gandalf
Office Manager

- Writing this type of letter is not pleasant, but should not be put off.

- Tell a company why it was not selected, if it is constructive.

- Be cordial and thank them for their effort (you want them to quote again).

Company Name
Address
City, State Zip

Date

Mr. Fred Costello
Costello Castings Corp.
57 North Drive
Akron, OH 44301

Dear Mr. Costello:

Thank you for your letter and for your interest in supplying castings for our brake assemblies. Since yours is a new company and because our tolerances are so exact, we would have to see more of a track record before we consider you as a supplier. In addition, our turn-around times are quite demanding, so we would need more references than you can provide at this time.

We are, however, always looking for reliable new suppliers, and I would be interested in hearing from you again in about six months, when you've gotten through the start-up phase.

Sincerely,

Jeff Craven
Manager

- Be specific about why you are refusing to do business.

- If there's a possibility that you might do business with them in the future, let them know when to contact you again.

Company Name
Address
City, State Zip

Date

Mr. Wilson Cutting
Cutting and Simat Associates
405 39th Street NW
Washington, DC 20015

Dear Mr. Cutting:

Thank you for coming to St. Louis to deliver your proposal for your
"Time Management in the 1990's" seminar to our policy committee.

After reviewing all proposals with Mike Meyers, Marvin Quigley, and
Hank Kramer, we have decided to use Jones & Vandendorpel, a local
St. Louis firm.

We do appreciate your time and wish you continued success with your
programs. Please keep us on your mailing list so we can stay current
with your offerings.

Sincerely,

Louis T. Silverman
Vice President, Personnel

- Writing rejection letters is difficult, but essential. Proposals are time-consuming to write, and vendors deserve the courtesy of a response.

- To avoid "why didn't we get the contract?" phone calls, state the reason in the letter (second paragraph—*presumably local firms are less costly*).

Company Name
Address
City, State Zip

Date

Mr. George Marra
Fasteners Unlimited
2608 Industrial Highway
Cleveland, OH 44129

Dear Mr. Marra:

Under separate label, via United Parcel Service, we are returning the remaining 36 commercial grade staplers from our trial order of 50 (invoice #2306) for credit. Please apply the credit to our account.

Although this type of stapler is effective and does interest some of our customers, it has not been as successful for us as your other two grades—general office and industrial. I think that the commercial grade has too limited an application for our customer base, which is divided between professional offices and industrial manufacturers.

I'm sorry this new item didn't work out because we've had good results with your other products.

Sincerely,

Robert Gordon

- State what you are returning and how it is being shipped.

- Let the supplier know *why* you were dissatisfied (as objectively as possible), providing pertinent but not excessive details of the situation.

Sender's Name
Address
City, State Zip

Date

Mr. Thomas Wasserman
General Products Repair Center
5600 Raines Road
Odessa, TX 79760

Dear Mr. Wasserman:

I am returning for repair the enclosed "Splash Mate" AM/FM bath/
shower radio, Model 560Z, which is covered under warranty #2094798
(copy enclosed). Since I bought it three weeks ago, the radio has
inexplicably failed to work whenever I turn on the shower. If the radio
cannot be repaired, I hope you will send me a replacement that is in
good working order.

Thank you.

Sincerely,

Rebecca Purvis

Enclosure

- Be sure to note the model number and warranty number.

- Give as much information *as you can* about the problem you're having and the circumstances under which the product does not work.

Company Name
Address
City, State Zip

Date

Mr. William Carabetta
Bath Bazaar
3678 Cumberland Pike
Nashville, TN 37228

Dear Mr. Carabetta:

On March 25, you installed a Jet Splash 20 hot tub in our hotel. For two weeks, the tub functioned perfectly, giving our guests many hours of relaxing bathing. In the past week, however, we've had problems with the tub's water-heating mechanism. We have been unable to raise the tub's water temperature higher than 75 degrees Fahrenheit.

We would like our guests to be able to enjoy the tub as they did when it was functioning properly. I believe service and repair calls come under the terms of the tub's warranty and would like to have a service technician come to the hotel as soon as can be arranged. I will call on Friday to determine the first available date.

Thank you.

Yours very truly,

Gordon Cameron
Assistant Manager

- Give all the important details—what you bought, when you bought it.

- Be as specific as possible about the type of problem you're having. Even if you don't know what caused it, describe the symptoms.

- Be clear about how you would like the matter resolved.

Company Name
Address
City, State Zip

Date

Mr. William Carabetta
Bath Bazaar
3678 Cumberland Pike
Nashville, TN 37228

Dear Mr. Carabetta:

Thank you for offering to send your repairman, Ted Evans, to service
our hotel's hot tub. I will look forward to seeing him on Tuesday
between 7 and 10 am.

If, as you suspect, the problem is with the temperature control
mechanism, it is my understanding that both parts and labor are
covered under the warranty. If the problem is with the hotel's hot water
heater, we are responsible for repairs.

Thank you again for your prompt attention and courteous service.

Yours very truly,

Gordon Cameron
Assistant Manager

- Express appreciation for the service to be provided.

- Outline any and all conditions that have been agreed upon. This will help ward off future
  misunderstandings.

Company Name
Address
City, State Zip

Date

Mr. Robert Evans
Concord Office Supplies, Inc.
Bicentennial Drive
Nashua, NH 03060

Dear Mr. Evans:

I am returning with this letter a recent shipment of 2,000 personalized ballpoint pens (order #21392943). Upon examination of the pens, we discovered that our company name had been misspelled. As your records will confirm, the order specified that each pen should read:

Lombardo Limousines
Coach of Kings

Please make the necessary correction and send another shipment of 2,000 pens as soon as possible.

Yours truly,

Carl Lombardo

- Be sure to refer to your order by number.

- State exactly why you were dissatisfied with the quality of the product.

- State how you would like the matter remedied.

Company Name
Address
City, State Zip

Date

Mr. Joseph I. Zale
Zale's Contracting
6624 West High Street
Richmond, VA 23230

Dear Mr. Zale:

We've received your invoice (#2562) for carpentry work in our office. We'd very much like to pay you, but as we discussed on the phone on May 14, there are still several items that must be attended to before the job is finished. These include the countertop formica and the additional shelves in the supply closet. We cannot efficiently run the production side of our business until these tasks are done.

We will be delighted to send you a check when the work is completed.

Sincerely,

Thomas Lotus
Senior Vice President

- The name of this game is "leverage," and you have every right to withhold payment. Putting it in writing will forestall or delay legal action.

Company Name
Address
City, State Zip

Date

Mr. Peter Hyman
Accounts Receivable
South California Medical
4035 Ripley Boulevard
Venice, CA 90291

Dear Mr. Hyman:

We are unable to process your invoice #8092 for disposable linens.
This invoice represents only a portion of our purchase order #42658,
and we cannot pay until the entire purchase order has been filled.

You are correct in thinking that we had a different policy in the past.
Unfortunately, we have had problems with vendors who submitted
invoices for part of a purchase order and later submitted invoices for the
entire purchase order. The resulting confusion forced us to institute a
new policy. Please submit a new invoice as soon as the entire order
has been filled.

Sincerely,

James P. Darrow
Accounts Payable

- Always state the main point first.

- Although clearly you've changed the policy (because of dishonest vendors or ineptness on
  the part of your people), assigning blame is counterproductive. Referring to "confusion" is
  more politic.

Company Name
Address
City, State Zip

Date

Mr. Leonard Mercer
Revere Office Equipment
42 Mercer Road
Natick, MA 01760

Dear Len:

As you can see from the enclosed envelope and your invoice (#3429) for $1,395, your invoice of April 19 was delayed in reaching us because it was addressed to the wrong town. We did not receive it until today.

When I talked with you on the phone about a FAX, you said that the list price for the FAX 103 was $1,795, that Revere's usual price was $1,395, and that you would be able to sell one to us at $1,295. When I visited the store, no one was able to give me an exact price, but I was told that you'd call me when you returned. Since I did not hear from you, I assumed that the $1,295 price would be charged.

I would appreciate it if you would check your records and let me know whether there would be any problem in reissuing the invoice at $1,295. Please note that the invoice should be made out to Totoket Associates and that the mailing address is Box 298, Reading, MA 01867.

Sincerely,

Jamieson Perkins

Enclosure

- In something of this magnitude, "putting it in writing" is essential. Following up with a phone call is also a good idea.

- Decide before sending the letter how rigid or flexible your position is so you'll be prepared to react to the supplier's response.

Company Name
Address
City, State Zip

Date

Mr. John Stuart
Customer Service
Roundo Computer Supply Co.
1122 State St.
Camden, NJ 08109

Dear Mr. Stuart:

Please send us the documentation for Micromouse Write 1.2 that we purchased from you on May 11. As you requested in our phone conversation earlier today, I am enclosing a copy of our receipt.

Yours truly,

John H. Sullivan

Enclosure

- When possible, call the service department before writing in order to include in your letter whatever information the seller requires and to be certain you are writing to the appropriate person. If a call is not possible, include the full name of the product and enclose proof of purchase.

Cancellation of Order (6-18)

> Company Name
> Address
> City, State Zip
>
> Date
>
> Miss Rosemary Randolf
> Acme Toys for Tots Co.
> 22 Rider Street
> Evanston, IL 60202
>
> Dear Miss Randolf:
>
> Please cancel our order (#1707-56) for 200 "Wooden Animal Puzzles for 2-4 Year Olds." We have just found a large number of these puzzles in our storeroom and do not have need for more at this time. We will place a new order when our present supply runs out.
>
> Yours truly,
>
>
> Jonathan Evens
> Vice President

- Be certain to include the order number and full name of the product.

- If you believe there will be a question about why you are canceling the order, give the reason, particularly if the supplier is a regular one. Courtesy never hurts.

Company Name
Address
City, State Zip

Date

Ms. Marianne Murphy
Murphy Employment Agency
2208 Irvine Street
Lowell, MA 01850

Dear Ms. Murphy:

We appreciate your efforts in sending us Tammy Renhouse on Monday in response to our request for a temporary secretary who could use Microsoft Word on a PC. Unfortunately, we have had to let Ms. Renhouse go after the first half-day. She had never worked with a PC. As a result, she was of no value to us, and she took up my valuable time asking questions.

You have provided us with good temporary help in the past, and I assume that Ms. Renhouse was less than forthright with you about her abilities. We look forward to using your agency again.

Yours truly,

Maria Scanlon
Office Manager

- Be sure that you make clear what services you required, how the individual failed, when the temporary began work, and when you let the temporary go.

- Let the agency know whether this event alters your relationship.

Company Name
Address
City, State Zip

Date

Mr. Ennis Thompson
Customer Service Dept.
Forest Cable Co.
37 Garibaldi Street
St. Louis, MO 63134

Dear Mr. Thompson:

During the past week, Forest Cable technicians have twice failed to keep appointments to install a surge protection system for our computer equipment. On both Tuesday, May 17, and Friday, May 20, I arranged for our data communications supervisor to be on site from 9:00 am to noon to accommodate the schedule of your service crew. On neither day did the installation technician arrive, nor did he call to explain why the appointment had not been kept. This lack of concern has caused us both serious inconvenience and valuable time.

I would like to believe that Forest Cable values our company as a customer, but quite honestly, the events of last week do not support that view. Can I depend on you to arrange dependable installation at our mutual convenience sometime next week? We have enjoyed the services your company has provided in the past and look forward to reestablishing our relationship on a more pleasant footing. I will call you on Friday to arrange the appointment.

Yours truly,

Beth Dowling
Vice President, Operations

- State specifically why you are dissatisfied. Mention the dates and times when service was unsatisfactory (or non-existent).

- Make it clear how you would like to resolve your issues with the supplier and arrange to discuss the matter further.

Company Name
Address
City, State Zip

Date

Mr. Manfred G. Weiss
The Office Furniture Mart
273 Bliss Road
East Longmeadow, MA 01028

Dear Mr. Weiss:

I am sorry to hear that you are unable to provide the six Junior
Executive Desks (model EX-102) that we ordered. I'm surprised that
such a popular model was discontinued. The alternative desk you
suggested (Secretarial Desk, model EX-101) would not fit our needs as
it is smaller than what we require.

We will have to search elsewhere for these desks but will look forward
to dealing with you again in the future.

Sincerely,

Randall Pierce
Purchasing Manager

- Reiterate your request and the remedy offered.

- State why you cannot accept.

- Even in refusals, be cordial and leave the door open for future dealings.

Company Name
Address
City, State Zip

Mr. Ted Oldey
Parkway Printers
1406 Topstone Parkway
Gaithersburg, MD 20879

Dear Ted:

Enclosed is a check for $4,508.52, covering the balance due on Purchase Order 788-10 for the recent printing of our catalog.

While I think we both developed a few gray hairs over the printing difficulties, I have to praise you and your company for being sensitive to my needs and responding quickly and professionally.

The catalogs look great and we will be needing a new printing in about two months.

Again, thanks for your cooperation during this difficult situation.

Kindest regards,

Harold Cousins
President

- When things go awry during a project, and the supplier gives his all, it makes sense to tell him you appreciated the help.

- If additional work will be coming his way shortly, tell him so.

Company Name
Address
City, State Zip

Date

Ms. Marianne Murphy
Murphy Employment Agency
2208 Irvine Street
Lowell, MA 01850

Dear Ms. Murphy:

I believe I have a suggestion that will help you and us. If you could test typists before sending them out on a job, we could both be assured that they can do the work they say they can do.

I know you cannot test every individual on every machine, but you could test, and therefore validate their ability, on the several machines you have in your office. You might also ask for references if typists say they had experience on certain machines at certain places.

I hope this idea will be useful to you.

Yours truly,

Marjorie Williams
Office Manager

- Open the letter with a statement that is sufficiently compelling for the recipient to continue to read. People get free advice all the time; they continue reading only when they perceive some personal value.

- If you are writing to someone you deal with personally, show understanding of that person's problem.

Company Name
Address
City, State Zip

Date

Mr. Harry Sarnoff
Food for Thought Caterers
20 Carson Drive
Omaha, NE 68114

Dear Mr. Sarnoff:

Thank you for the wonderful help your entire staff provided in feeding
the participants at our annual meeting on April 20. The room looked
lovely, the flowers were beautiful, the service was excellent and, most
important, Chef Michael's food was exceptional. You more than kept
your promise of being "the best in all ways."

You will hear from us again soon.

Yours truly,

Harry Singh
Director of Communications

• Keep it short and sweet but be sure to include, whenever possible, who should be
complimented, what that person or people did, and when it happened.

Company Name
Address
City, State Zip

Date

Mr. Carl Sanderson
Sanderson Electrics
2288 Seventh St.
Cambridge, MA 02138

Dear Mr. Sanderson:

You are indeed fortunate to have as dedicated an engineer as William Southwick. Bill worked with me for hours to ensure that our lighting design will now meet our needs. He was concerned that each area of the shop have lighting appropriate to the work that will be done in that area and that, should we alter the production flow, we will be able to alter the lighting as well.

I have told Bill how much I appreciate his attention to detail, but I wanted to tell you as well. If you feel it is appropriate, feel free to include this letter in his personnel file.

Yours truly,

Harold Wolfson
Construction Coordinator

- Be sure to include the name of the employee and a brief description of what the employee did that you found especially helpful.

- If you are writing to a large organization, you might ask that your letter be added to the individual's personnel file or send a copy to the person you are complimenting.

Company Name
Address
City, State Zip

Date

Mr. Douglas Vreelander
Manum Custom Parts, Inc.
Central Manufacturing Park
Camden, NJ 08122

Dear Mr. Vreelander:

Enclosed is our check #3098 for $3,097.62, which covers the balance
due on invoice #28602. I believe this will bring our account up to date
until we receive the shipment of parts due next month.

Sincerely,

Christopher Worth
Accounting Department

Enclosure

- Be sure to note your check number, the amount of the check, and the invoice your payment covers.

- Confirm that this payment brings your account up-to-date.

Company Name
Address
City, State Zip

Date

Ms. Andrea Rollins
City Bank
222 State Street
Topeka, KS 66604

Dear Ms. Rollins:

Please transfer, immediately, two thousand dollars ($2,000.00) from Handerson Service Co.'s savings account #23456789 to Handerson Service Co.'s checking account #785624983.

Yours truly,

George Handerson
President

- Be sure to include the account number and the name in which the account is listed.

- The person who signs the letter should have the authority to make transactions in the account from which funds are being withdrawn.

Company Name
Address
City, State Zip

Date

Ms. Constance Whitley
Accounts Receivable
Fabrics First Incorporated
12 Calico Plaza
Darien, CT 06820

Dear Ms. Whitley:

Enclosed is our check #694 for $247.82. We regret that we
inadvertently underpaid the balance due on invoice #27706 last month
and hope that you will accept our apology for the error.

Sincerely,

Lane Peters
Accounts Payable

Enclosure

- When you're wrong, admit it promptly.

- Don't go into excessive detail. This letter skips any mention of the people involved and thus avoids assigning blame.

Sender's Name
Address
City, State Zip

Date

Mr. Paul Carlson
Carlson and Maxwell Travel Consultants, Ltd.
185 4th Avenue
New Rochelle, NY 10802

Dear Mr. Carlson:

Enclosed is our check #6714 for $789.55, covering the extra charges for the off-site planning meeting that Apex held at the Long Pond Conference Center last month. We apologize for the lateness of this check, but we had to wait for Long Pond to send us the paperwork on our two extra attendees before we could process your invoice (#AP-4948).

I hope that the delay has not caused you any inconvenience.

Sincerely,

Marilyn Stephenson
Accounts Payable

Enclosure

- Be sure to state the number and amount of the check enclosed.

- Apologize for the delay and explain it briefly.

Company Name
Address
City, State Zip

Date

Mrs. Helena Purcell
Creative Custom Catering
26 Muzzey Street
Lexington, MA 02173

Dear Mrs. Purcell:

All who attended the annual fund raising luncheon last Friday remarked on the exquisite buffet. Our thanks to you for providing such a memorable feast.

We received your bill for $4,672.00 (#266084) yesterday. Enclosed is a check for $2,500.00 toward the balance of our account. Because we are entirely dependent on membership contributions for meeting our expenses, we are forced to pay the remaining $2,172.00 next month, when our fund drive has ended.

I regret that we cannot pay the entire amount due today and hope you understand our situation and the reason for the delay.

Sincerely,

Carol Fontana
Vice President

Enclosure

- Express appreciation for good service provided.

- Refer to the invoice by number and propose an alternate payment schedule, giving the reason why you need more time.

- Express regret for not paying more promptly.

Sender's Name
Address
City, State Zip

Mr. Terrence Fisher
Fisher Florals
345 Beach Road
Rehoboth Beach, DE 19971

Dear Mr. Fisher:

I'm sorry that the check I sent you on May 12 (#4409) never arrived. Enclosed is a second check for $545.00 (#4432), which should cover the balance of our account. I've stopped payment on #4409; if it arrives, please return it to me. I apologize for this delay and for any inconvenience that the missing check may have caused you.

Yours very truly,

Edwina Derry
Banquet Manager

Enclosure

- Note the number and date of the first check sent.

- Give the number of the replacement check enclosed and tell the reader what to do if the missing check arrives.

- Apologize for any inconvenience.

Sender's Name
Address
City, State Zip

Date

Mr. Terrence Fisher
Fisher Florals
345 Beach Road
Rehoboth Beach, DE 19971

Dear Mr. Fisher:

Today I received your second bill for the flowers you provided for the Osgood wedding on April 29. I assume that as of May 16 you had not yet received my check #4409 for $545.00 that I mailed you on May 12. If the check does not arrive by Monday, will you please let me know? I'll be happy to stop payment on the original check and send you another. We were quite pleased with the beautiful arrangements you made for the Osgood wedding and want to be sure you receive prompt payment.

Yours very truly,

Edwina Derry
Banquet Manager

- Be sure to note the date when you sent the check (and its number and amount).

- Arrange to send another if the original check does not arrive by a specific date.

- As always, be cordial...maintain a good relationship.

Company Name
Address
City, State Zip

Date

Mr. Royce Flaherty
Renshaw Card Company
60 Horse Hill Road
Purchase, NY 10577

Dear Mr. Flaherty:

I have enclosed our final payment of $310.76 (check #6490) for 29,750 of the cards you shipped to us last year. Please apply the payment against the balance on the original invoice #2308.

As we agreed last year, we are paying for the cards on an as-used basis, returning any unused cards for credit. There are 20,250 cards remaining from the 50,000 you shipped us last year. Please let me know how we should arrange to return them to you for credit.

Sincerely,

Terry Getman

Enclosure

- Identify for your reader exactly what figures you are basing your payment on (if it's different from the balance on the invoice).

- Give invoice number and any other relevant information.

- Ask how to proceed with returns (next steps).

Company Name
Address
City, State Zip

Date

Mr. Arnold Smythe
Nature Collectibles
Box 780
Burlington, VT 05405

Dear Mr. Smythe:

When we examined 2 of the 36 sets of Animal Family Figurines that your carrier, Apex Trucking, delivered last Wednesday, May 4, we were dismayed to find several figurines in two sets had arrived broken. I would like to arrange to have the sets with broken figurines returned to you as proof of damage.

Please credit our account for the two sets that were broken. Apart from this problem, we were very pleased with this new addition to your line and hope to reorder in the near future.

Sincerely,

Ivana Robertson
Collectibles Department

- Specify how many items arrived damaged and describe the damage.

- State how you'd like the matter handled.

- Call attention to any possible billing situation.

Company Name
Address
City, State Zip

Date

Mr. Hank Robinson
Southwest Hardware Cooperative
158 Canyon Rd.
Tucson, AZ 85711

Dear Mr. Robinson:

I would like to arrange to have 8 Home/Office Tool Kits returned to your warehouse on Friday, June 8. These kits were mistakenly included in the order you delivered to our store on May 26. Perhaps they were destined for another customer—our delivery was not short any of the items I ordered (PO# 155062).

Please let me know if June 8 is acceptable and credit our account accordingly if the tool kits were charged to it.

Regards,

Kenneth Buffington
Hardware Manager

- State exactly what you wish to return and why.

- Give all necessary details, including dates and number of merchandise items involved.

- Call attention to any possible billing error.

Company Name
Address
City, State Zip

Date

Ms. Jessica Chasen
Q-Design Art Supplies, Inc.
2600 Mercer Blvd.
Seattle, WA 98124

Dear Ms. Chasen:

Enclosed are 24 pads of Strathmore Parchment Calligraphy Writing Paper that were mistakenly shipped to us on April 2 (invoice #578657). Ordering by phone from Lisa Roberts on March 30, we asked for 24 pads of white calligraphy paper. Please accept the parchment paper for return and send us 24 pads of the white as soon as possible.

Thank you for rectifying this matter promptly.

Sincerely,

Harriet Peters
Office Manager

Enclosures

- Specify what you were sent as well as what should have been sent.

- Include all necessary information: dates, invoice numbers, the name of the person with whom you placed the order.

- Be sure to state how you'd like the matter handled.

Request Permission to Return Shipment, Arrived Too Late (6-37)

Company Name
Address
City, State Zip

Date

Mr. George Blunt
Pro-Com Industries
29-14 Anchor Dr.
San Diego, CA 92119

Dear Mr. Blunt:

We received today the Adobe Project Billing System you shipped to us on May 4 (invoice #2934837). When we ordered this software package by phone on February 11, Doug Tanchum assured us that it would be shipped within two weeks. With that expectation, we looked forward to receiving the system by March 1 to fill an urgent need. When it had not arrived by April 1 and Doug could not guarantee that it would arrive promptly, we ordered a similar system through another vendor.

Please let me know how you would like this merchandise returned and credit our account for $675.00. We value your products and would like to order them again, providing you understand merchandise availability is a priority with us.

Sincerely,

Marta Newman
Office Manager

- Specify the items received and when delivery was promised.

- Include all necessary information: dates, invoice numbers, the name of the person with whom you placed the order.

- Be sure to state how you'd like the matter handled and mention that delivery time is an important issue with you.

Request Permission to Return Shipment, Damaged (6-38)

Company Name
Address
City, State Zip

Date

Ms. Aliza Trocfel
Computer Supply Corp.
415 Main St.
Ridgefield, CT 06877

Dear Ms. Trocfel:

When the Data Defender Diskette File (our PO #698) you shipped to us on March 12 (invoice #2049037) arrived, we were dismayed to find that it had been damaged in transit. The plastic cover was cracked. Please let me know how you would like it returned and send us a replacement as soon as possible.

Thank you for handling this matter promptly.

Sincerely,

Osborne Stallings
Vice President

Enclosures

- Specify what item(s) you were sent and exactly how it was damaged.

- Include all necessary information: dates, purchase order and invoice numbers.

- Be sure to state how you'd like the matter handled.

Company Name
Address
City, State Zip

Date

Mr. Arthur Brownlee
Rapidoprint Inc.
1404 Beasley Rd.
Jacksonville, FL 32219

Dear Mr. Brownlee:

I would like to return the Rapidoprint DD3700 Processor (invoice #59302483) that was delivered last week. Fire destroyed our office on May 24. We are in the process of rebuilding our facility and cannot use the processor at this time. I am shipping the unit back to your warehouse. Please credit my account accordingly.

Thank you for your understanding.

Sincerely,

Phyllis Evans
Office Manager

- Specify what item you were sent and when it was ordered.

- Explain why you no longer need the merchandise.

- Be sure to state how you'd like the matter handled.

Personnel Relations 7

Many people have become so fearful of employer-employee relations that they avoid putting anything in writing because they feel it may come back to haunt them. But all the same reasons for putting things in writing discussed in the introduction to this book apply equally to writing in the personnel area. Acrimonious disputes can be avoided if everyone understands hiring practices, job evaluation practices, and other policies and procedures that the company follows. Avoiding these disputes saves immense amounts of time and emotional capital.

The trade-off, of course, is that written practices do constrain employers, even though any policy can be changed at any time with appropriate notice. In practice, changing a "perk" is difficult to do. One entrepreneur cites the story of giving everyone a turkey for the holidays in his first year of business and the nightmare it grew into some years down the road when he found himself with several hundred employees, each waiting for his or her turkey. The moral here is to try to envision your company as it will be in a few years when you think about appropriate policies and procedures.

Hiring and references. From posting a job opening to writing a job confirmation letter, writing is part of the hiring process. Your first step is to think through what the job entails in terms of responsibilities and duties and then to develop a list of the skills necessary to do that job. Many people list very high qualifications (typing speed, college degree) as a way of screening people. One office manager says, "If a person has the discipline to learn to type 75 words per minute, I can teach him or her to do anything else required on the job." A good way to appraise realistically what the job involves is to talk with the person who currently holds the job, or to others in firms similar to yours if the position is new. Doing this preliminary spadework will allow you to write an announcement of a job opening or a job description. If you don't want to get the protest "but that's not in my job description," you may want to add "and other duties as assigned" to cover yourself.

Most managers hate the interviewing process. An interview outline can help immensely because it provides structure to the conversation and helps keep the interviewer in control.

A letter confirming or revising a job offer has contractual implications and should be looked over by an attorney. Be careful not to stipulate anything more than the salary and the starting date. If you have discussed a probationary period, you may also wish to include that in the letter. However, put nothing in the letter that has not been discussed in person. If you do, you're likely to poison the atmosphere of trust you have presumably tried to establish.

References should be handled with finesse. Sound too glowing and you're likely to be disbelieved, too negative and you might seem bitter or personally involved. Keep a reference factual, but if an employee was less than satisfactory, what you don't say can take on as much meaning as what you do say.

Problems. If you have a problem employee, your first step is to talk with the person. Discuss how performance has been falling short of expectations and agreed-upon goals. You may want to refer to the employee's latest performance appraisal. If the employee has personal problems, these can be dealt with on a case-by-case basis.

After each conversation, dictate a letter to the files giving the gist of the conversation. You may want to have the employee initial it so you have a record that the employee understands that he or she is not performing up to standards. If conversations do not achieve the desired result, you may want to write a warning memo.

There are several key things to remember in writing letters and memos that deal with personnel matters. Deal with facts (rather than opinions) as much as possible. Have an attorney check anything that has contractual implications—a statement of benefits, for example. And always adopt an objective rather than adversarial tone—people will simply respond better.

Company Name
Address
City, State Zip

To: All Staff

From: Donald J. Johnson

Date:

Subject: Opening for Secretary/Sales Assistant

As you know, Nina Kamchatka will be leaving us in two months to relocate to San Diego. Her position as Secretary/Sales Assistant will therefore be open. We always prefer to promote from within, and we welcome applications from anyone interested.

Duties include (but are not limited to):

- Providing secretarial support for Vice-President of Sales
- Typing all correspondence
- Managing extensive phone contact with clients
- Maintaining sales and records
- Making travel arrangements

Skills required are:

- Typing at 65 wpm
- Six-months' familiarity with PC and spreadsheet programs

Nina has offered to discuss her duties and the nature of her job with anyone who has an interest in succeeding her. Please call Joe Doddsworth in Personnel if you would like additional information.

- Announcing a job opening should be done in memo format.

- Use a positive tone and be very specific about the skills required.

- Saying that the list of duties is not complete covers you later on and avoids having the new hire saying "that's not my job."

Request for Help in Recruiting New Employees (7-02)

Company Name
Address
City, State Zip

To: All Employees

From: William Winston

Date:

Subject: Recruiting New Employees

The unemployment rate in our area is now 3% and dropping. As a result, we're having difficulty finding and recruiting new telemarketing hires, despite the fact that our wages are above average and we offer flexible hours for students and mothers.

Because we want the very best people available, we want to enlist your help in finding people who are as qualified as you. We'll give you $100 for each person you recommend that we ultimately hire, and we'll give you an additional $500 if that person stays with us for three months. Remember that the people we want must have superb telephone skills and an extremely responsible approach to working.

Please call me directly for further information (and please be sure anyone you refer to us mentions your name as a referral).

- Your own employees are a valuable source of leads. Businesses live and die on the quality of their people, and it's worthwhile to reward referrals.

Company Name
Address
City, State Zip

Date

Mr. Craig Stern
23 Dolphin Way
Port Washington, NY 11050

Dear Mr. Stern:

Thank you for sending your resume.

At this time, we do not foresee any branch manager openings with our firm during the next six months to one year. Generally, these positions are filled internally. No one can anticipate the future, though, and we'll gladly call you if we expand even more rapidly than anticipated.

Thank you for your interest in New Age. Please keep us in mind as you progress in your career.

Yours truly,

Walter Parker
Vice President, Sales

- Don't ignore an unsolicited resume even if you have no instant need for the person. There's always the future to consider.

- Consider your letter another opportunity to "sell" your firm and indicate that your firm is a good place at which to work.

Company Name
Address
City, State Zip

Date

Mr. Mark Canter
1650 Handler Drive
Fort Worth, TX 76125

Dear Mr. Canter:

I enjoyed talking with you on the phone Tuesday. We appreciate your promptness in sending along your resume, and, naturally, we give a great deal of weight to Phil Beckwith's recommendation.

As I mentioned on the phone, we expect to have openings for sales representatives in the spring. We will keep your resume on file and call you for an interview at that time.

If you do not hear from me by April 30, please call and check on the status of our hiring process.

Best,

Thomas H. Stanley
Personnel Manager

- Always respond immediately to job inquiries, even if you do not have an immediate opening. A job applicant is a potential member of your team and should be treated with courtesy.

- Provide an opportunity for the job seeker to re-establish contact, if appropriate. Leaving the ball in the job seeker's court will ensure that you aren't viewed as neglectful in the future.

Company Name
Address
City, State Zip

Date

Mr. Howard Fitzgibbons
567 Parakeet Way
Houston, TX 77034

Dear Mr. Fitzgibbons:

Thank you for taking the time to come in and fill out an application for the position of night store manager. Although we were certainly impressed with your qualifications, and the hours you were available were consistent with our requirements, I'm sorry to tell you that we'll have to put you on our waiting list.

While we currently do have a full roster of night managers, openings do occur from time to time. Please let us know if you change your address so that we may locate you if an opening does occur.

Sincerely,

Henry Carradine
Vice President, Personnel

- This letter is a bit more encouraging than a "we'll keep you on file" letter because it asks for notification of an address change, which is outside normal "form-letterese." It's always better to offer job seekers some hope (if it exists). It doesn't cost anything, and it leaves a very positive impression of your company.

Company Name
Address
City, State Zip

Date

Mr. Charles Plowright
150 Valentine's Lane
Old Brookville, NY 11511

Dear Mr. Plowright:

Mike Stamp tells me that you are interested in talking with financial
planning firms like ours about the possibility of working as an associate
with the expectation of ultimately being made partner. Mike speaks very
highly of you, both as a solid person to work with and as a high
producer with a substantial client base. We're very interested in both
aspects of your experience.

Our firm has expanded rapidly in the past five years—we now have four
partners and ten associates—and we have every expectation of
continued growth as financial planning becomes more important to
individuals and as our Long Island community grows.

We'd very much like to talk. Please call me at your earliest convenience.

Sincerely,

Thomas C. Calandra
Executive Vice President

- A letter to the person's home is a good way to approach someone who can't be or shouldn't
  be reached on the job. (Calling at home may be viewed as intrusive.)

- "Sell" your firm in the letter.

Interview Outline (7-07)

Company Name
Address
City, State Zip

1. Tell me about your present job.

2. Tell me how your boss and/or co-workers would describe you.

3. Describe your greatest work-related accomplishment within the last five years.

4. Describe your most frustrating work-related experience in the past five years and why it was so.

5. When given a new assignment or project, how do you approach it?

6. In what type of position are you most interested?

7. Do you prefer working with others or by yourself?

8. What led to your interest in our company?

- These questions should yield useful information about the applicant's strengths, weaknesses, working style, and self-perception. Good interviewers allow the applicant's own questions and responses to drive the interview.

- Do not ask questions that are either illegal (discrimination by race, creed, or sex) or highly personal.

Company Name
Address
City, State Zip

Date

Mr. Brian Poor
28 Trumbull Street
New Bedford, MA 02740

Dear Brian:

We were quite impressed with your qualifications, and after some consideration, we have decided that you are the ideal choice for the position of Unit Manager at Wesley Video Productions. Congratulations, and welcome aboard!

The terms are as we discussed in the interview. The salary is $30,000 a year. You'll have three weeks vacation per year and Blue Cross/Blue Shield health insurance. All employees at Wesley Video get five personal days and 10 sick days per year. We have a pension plan that you can sign up for after working at Wesley Video for one year.

We would like you to start on Monday, April 23. If you have any questions, please call us. If not, we'll see you on the 23rd!

Very truly yours,

Peter Vaughn
Vice President, Production

- Don't get into the specific responsibilities of the job. The point of this letter is to have a written record of the terms of employment. It's really a confirmation of previous discussions, so keep it simple and to the point.

Company Name
Address
City, State Zip

Date

Mr. Richard Pearle
41 Hallen Drive
Pace, FL 32570

Dear Mr. Pearle:

Thank you for responding to our job offer so promptly. We understand that there are some details to be worked out, but none of them appear to be insurmountable.

I spoke with the President of Kidsworks, Alan Weiss, and we both feel that we cannot increase the base salary we offered beyond $52,000 per annum. However, we can include a performance bonus of 15%, subject to review of both Mr. Weiss and myself. We will also include $5,000 to cover your relocation expenses.

If you have any further questions or comments, please call my office.

Sincerely,

Elaine Drile
Vice President

- Pretty self-explanatory. Keep things congenial because everybody will soon be working together, and you should therefore reduce the potential for bad blood developing.

- Make your offer and be sure to keep the lines of communication open.

Company Name
Address
City, State Zip

Date

Mr. Jason Clarides
P. O. Box 177
Sylvia, KS 42923

Dear Mr. Clarides:

It was a pleasure to meet with you last week in our offices at Senior Care, Inc. Your training in social work and business administration gives you a combination of skills that will be useful in any gerontology-related field.

As we discussed during the interview, Senior Care is looking for a person with at least five years of management experience in a residential facility for senior citizens. Because of your limited managerial experience, we are unable to offer you the position.

I wish you all the best for a successful career working on behalf of senior citizens.

Sincerely,

Carla Schultz
Vice President, Personnel

- Begin your letter by acknowledging one of the interviewee's areas of strength that you learned about during the interview.

- Let the applicant know why he or she doesn't meet your requirement by stating your unmet need.

- Close your letter with cordial good wishes for the future.

Company Name
Address
City, State Zip

Date

Mr. Frederick Hartland
56 Long Ridge Lane
Hartford, CT 06110

Dear Mr. Hartland:

I am sorry to tell you that, since we did not hear from you in response to our job offer, the offer expired as of last Friday.

I understood, when we spoke three weeks ago, that you were considering other opportunities, and we agreed that our job offer would be time-limited. I am, as you can imagine, personally disappointed that you won't be joining us as my Executive Assistant, but I hope that you will remember our conversations and consider Thomlinson Antique Auction Gallery if you decide to reevaluate your career in the future.

Best of luck in your new job.

Sincerely,

Allan J. Klein
Vice President

- Even if someone has been impolite (letting a job offer expire, rather than calling or writing, is quite rude), do not let your impatience be reflected in your tone. Something tragic may have happened, or the mail may have gone astray.

- Always keep the door open for future contacts.

Company Name
Address
City, State Zip

To: James Murdock

From: Timothy Nixon

Date:

Subject: Hours of Work

As we discussed in our meeting on October 10, it's important for you to reach the office on time. No one objects to an occasional slip. In fact, with the difficulties of commuting these days, being late once in a while is quite understandable.

Here's the problem, though. In the last month, even though we had already discussed the company's expectations at our October 10 meeting, you have been from 30-45 minutes late on seven (7) days, specifically October 14, 17, 18, 20, 26, 27, and November 1. This kind of performance is unacceptable—it sends me the message that you don't care about the job, and it certainly sets a bad example for your secretary, who is always here on time, even early most days.

There may be something that prevents you from getting to work on time. If there's anything I need to know, let's talk. However, you must improve your on-time performance to no more than one day late during the next month or I'll have to send you a formal warning which will be placed in your personnel file.

- It's only fair to tell employees when their performance is inadequate. Usually, you tell them first face-to-face. Then, if they don't improve, you should notify them in writing.

- Be specific about what you want improved and state a deadline. In serious cases, this becomes part of a written record to justify termination.

Company Name
Address
City, State Zip

To: Richard Candy

From: Bob Rolfe

Date:

Subject: Excessive Sick Days

In my memo of March 3, I stated that you had already used 10 sick days this year—the number of sick days allowable for the entire year. During March, you called in sick an additional three days— March 17, 18, and 21.

We value all our staff members, but we must warn you formally that any additional sick leave this year will be unpaid. Please schedule a meeting with me to discuss this problem as soon as you can.

- This memo reflects a personnel situation that has already deteriorated and may be unsalvageable. It represents a formal warning. The plea for a meeting is a last-ditch attempt to save the situation.

- Be specific as to the action expected and the time period involved.

Termination of Employee (7-14)

Company Name
Address
City, State Zip

Date

Mr. Joseph P. Duffy
60 Sachem Street NW
Washington, D.C. 20332

Dear Joe:

As we discussed on Monday, the downturn in the market for industrial fans in the Washington region has led the company to close the regional office. As a consequence, your position has been eliminated.

To confirm our conversation, you will terminate your employment on June 22 and receive severance pay equal to three months' salary. The company will pay your medical insurance for the remainder of the year. In lieu of profit sharing for this year, you have agreed to accept a one-time payment of $5,000. Your retirement benefits will be retained by the company until we receive instructions from you.

Sincerely,

Thomas Sweet
Vice President, Personnel

Attachment

- Terminating an employee, for whatever reason, is a delicate subject and should be discussed first in person, then followed-up with a confirming letter like this one.

Company Name
Address
City, State Zip

Date

Mr. Melvin Jobs
President
Grove Water Distributors
40 Isleboro Walk
Augusta, ME 04330

Dear Mr. Jobs:

I'm delighted to respond to your request for a reference for Bonnie Bronson, who was our office manager for the past two years.

We were extremely disappointed to lose Ms. Bronson because of her relocation to Maine. She was almost entirely responsible for organizing the office systems here at Mechanical Systems, Inc. In short, she took us from an office in which we were constantly on a catch-up basis to one in which our systems for billing, collections, and personnel were sensible and controllable. Furthermore, her management skills were evident through her relations with our part-time clerical staff. She was totally responsible for hiring and training these three individuals, and a conversation with any of them reveals that she dealt with them fairly and professionally.

If you need an office manager who is responsible, is skilled, and has potential for advancement, you should hire Ms. Bronson.

Sincerely,

Melissa Anderson

- This is an easy letter to write—it's a rave review, and you can send a blind carbon copy to Ms. Bronson herself.

- Note, though, that the good reference is backed up with specific details.

Company Name
Address
City, State Zip

Date

To Whom It May Concern:

During the past two years, I have had the distinct pleasure of having Caryl Adams work for me at Bilcott Industries. As she leaves to accept new challenges, I welcome this opportunity to provide a recommendation on her behalf.

In my association with Caryl, she has been an integral part of the Operations Research Department as an Operations Analyst. Her work has been exemplary. She has provided timely, accurate, and insightful analyses to our clients across all industries.

Her writing and analytical skills are sharply honed. She is industrious and dedicated. Caryl's approach to her job can be characterized as truly professional. I wish her my very best as she seeks new frontiers.

Sincerely,

Phillip George
President

- When a good employee leaves for "greener pastures," it's not uncommon to be asked to write such a letter.

- To provide context, mention where, in what relationship, and for how long you knew the candidate.

- Stress the person's strong points, and how they might fit in with the individual's career objectives.

Company Name
Address
City, State Zip

Date

Ms. Sylvia Toth
Personnel Director
Scientific Investigations, Inc.
40 Washburn Street
Sandusky, OH 44870

Dear Ms. Toth:

We received your letter asking for a reference for Jane Howell. I have
reviewed our personnel records.

Ms. Howell worked for Atlee Industries for just under two years. She
started out as a receptionist and became a secretary for our Marketing
division after one year. Her salary when she left was $19,200. She left
Atlee because her husband had been relocated. Ms. Howell was well
liked by her co-workers.

If you have any further questions, please call my office.

Sincerely,

Janet Birkowski
Vice President, Personnel

- Comments should be restricted to work-related matters. Personal criticisms should be
  avoided. You are being asked what kind of worker this person is, not whether you like him
  or her.

Company Name
Address
City, State Zip

Date

Mr. Stephen Montgomery
Institute of Management Research
2101 L Street NW
Washington, D.C. 20037

Dear Mr. Montgomery:

Edward Potts has given your name as a reference for an associate's
position with Toombs, Hardy and Foulkes. Would you provide for us
your impression of Mr. Potts' talents and strengths as a professional
and as a team player, as well as any other thoughts that you feel would
aid us in making a decision.

Thank you.

Sincerely,

Harvey Simpson
Partner

- Give the name of the person and the position for which he or she is being considered.

- Give an idea of the kind of information you want, while also soliciting any additional facts that might prove helpful.

Request for Verification of Employment (7-19)

Company Name
Address
City, State Zip

Date

Mr. Harold Ramones
Calhoun Trucking Company
270 Cottage Street
Springfield, MA 01104

Dear Mr. Ramones:

We wish to verify that Bryan Constantine (SS #021-36-8080) was employed by your company as a driver from December 2, 1983, to April 4, 1988. We are considering Bryan for a position as a driver and would like this and any other information you have regarding his value as an employee.

Thank you.

Sincerely,

Lloyd Daniels
Vice President, Personnel

- Give the candidate's full name (and social security number if you have it) as well as the period of employment on which you're checking.

- Take advantage of the opportunity to ask for additional information you might need.

Response to Request for Employment Verification (7-20)

Company Name
Address
City, State Zip

Date

Mr. Clarence Goodwin
Picnics Unlimited
55 Eastern Meadowlark Drive
Atlanta, GA 30305

Dear Mr. Goodwin:

You asked us to confirm certain information from Harley Stone's employment application in writing.

Harley Stone worked for Catering Around, a division of our firm, from June 1985 to July 1988. He began as a driver, a position he held for 6 months. For the rest of his employment period, he was a bartender and waiter. He left our company to move to Atlanta, where his wife had taken a new job. This information agrees with that given on Mr. Stone's application.

If we can help you in any other way, please call or write.

Sincerely,

Ann Richardson

- If you're asked to verify facts of employment, do just that and no more. Launching into unsolicited opinions may get you into trouble.

Description of Employee Benefits (7-21)

Company Name
Address
City, State Zip

To: All Employees

From: Hoyt Murdock, Human Resources Manager

Date:

Subject: Description of Expanded Health Insurance Coverage

Our department is constantly reviewing employee benefits to provide improvements. Most recently, we focused on our psychological benefits package in response to requests from employees and with a view to general trends among other major regional employers.

As a result of our evaluation, we are pleased to announce that as of June 30, the lifetime limit on reimbursements for in-patient psychiatric treatment has been increased to $50,000. In addition, GHCP will now reimburse out-patient psychological counseling at $40 per visit; annual limits on out-patient visits have been increased to $1,000 per year. The lifetime limit for out-patient psychological counseling has been increased to $10,000.

These new benefits will be described in our annual benefits brochure, but you may wish to keep a copy of this memo on file for reference.

- Benefits are important to employees, but the specifics may be ignored until the benefit is actually necessary. If you've made a major advance in benefit coverage, announcing it in a separate memo will encourage those concerned to pay attention and will give the personnel folks some welcome public relations help.

RESPONSIBILITIES OF A RETAIL CLERK

Retail Clerks in an Apple Pie Video Rental Store are primarily responsible for taking care of customers by receiving and renting films. Other duties may be assigned by the store manager.

Time Spent	Duties
75%	Handles customer requests in person and by telephone. Rents videos, receives returned videos. Completes paperwork for new memberships. Operates the store computer. Receives payment, makes change.
15%	Files returned videos. Returns display boxes to shelves. Keeps shelves orderly.
10%	Puts labels on promotional mailers. Dusts shelves. Receives shipments. Logs special requests. Checks drop box. Performs other duties as requested.

Skills Required

1. Must have good public relations skills.
2. Must be able to maintain the store's filing and shelving systems.
3. Must be able to learn and effectively operate the store computer.
4. Must be able to make change accurately.
5. Must be willing to perform other assigned duties.
6. Must be available and dependable for flexible scheduling of work hours, including holidays.
7. Must be able to work independently and without regular supervision.

Apple Pie Video Rental Stores, 2 Celluloid Square, Americus, GA 35291

- Time allotments help to explain both the nature of the work and the employer's priorities.

- Be sure to include special expectations in the job description, such as availability to work on holidays. This can deter the "but that's not in my job description!" blues for both employer and employee.

Summertime Concessions, Inc.
23 Sugar Mill Lane
Buhler, Kansas 49387

<u>JOB DESCRIPTION</u>

TITLE: Office Manager

GENERAL DESCRIPTION: This is a full-time position in which the person has responsibility for managing the office, handling assigned duties, supervising employees, and assisting the company president as needed. Because Summertime Concessions, Inc. is a small, family-owned business, the Office Manager has a broad range of duties. These vary from standard secretarial tasks to making sound judgment calls in the occasional absence of the president. The position answers to the company president.

SKILLS AND QUALIFICATIONS:
- Minimum of two-years experience as an office secretary with experience in supervising employees.
- Competence in use of the Macintosh computer for wordprocessing.
- Knowledge of food services and concessions management is highly desirable.
- Ability to work effectively with minimal supervision and to take initiative in problem-solving.
- Willingness to assist other office employees when needed and to perform other duties as required.
- Availability to work overtime to assist with inventory (usually one week per year).
- Ability to complete assigned workload satisfactorily.
- Ability to supervise and motivate employees effectively.

- A good job description is specific without being compulsively detailed. It should give the reader a clear idea of what the job entails and what is necessary to be successful at it.

- When writing a job description, think in terms of the qualities you desire in an employee (e.g., willingness to pitch in) as well as the skills required to get the job done.

Pygmalion Consultants, Inc.

PERFORMANCE APPRAISAL FORM

Use the reverse side if necessary

Date _____
Employee _____ Position _____
Evaluator _____ Position _____

COMPETENCIES/AREAS OF STRENGTH:

Brad, your skills as a training specialist and consultant are excellent. You are a very strong teacher and group facilitator. Your recent workshop for agoraphobics is a fine example of your abilities in this area, especially your ability to be sensitive to both individual and group needs.

I am pleased by your ability to research and design workshops and seminars. Your designs are practical, thorough, and suited to the knowledge level of the participants.

You have also been an asset to Pygmalion Consultants in your ability to network and generate referrals for the company. The increased business (and bonuses!) have made everyone happy.

CONCERNS/AREAS FOR IMPROVEMENT:

As we have discussed before, your tendency to produce results at the eleventh hour has been problematic. An example is the way several of the staff were forced to work overtime to finish the Golden Valley Public School Teachers project. Your expectation that the support staff can and will set aside their work at the last minute is unreasonable. As you know, good working relations between the staff and the consultants are a necessity. How can we work together to solve this problem?

Although you always dress neatly, your preference for casual dress in the office has become inappropriate. The company considers its image to be important both "at home" because of visiting clients and in public because of general professionalism. We expect you to wear business suits in and out of the office and to keep the tie tied and the sleeves buttoned.

- Make your evaluations specific. Back them up with examples.

- When evaluating undesirable performance, state clearly what you find unacceptable, why it is problematic, and what changes you expect the employee to make.

Summertime Concessions, Inc.

PERFORMANCE APPRAISAL FOR _____

This appraisal is based on the list of responsibilities, skills, and qualifications listed in the job description for an Office Manager. The evaluator should rate the employee in each category and use the adjacent space for explanatory comments.

Rating System
  1 = Needs improvement/Not adequate
  2 = Fair/Minimally adequate
  3 = Good/Adequate
  4 = Excellent/More than adequate

1. Competence in use of computer/word processer: 1 2 <u>3</u> 4
   Your skills have been steadily improving.

2. Knowledge of food service and concessions management: 1 2 3 <u>4</u>
   *What you didn't know when you started you've
   learned quickly!*

3. Ability to work effectively with minimal supervision: 1 2 <u>3</u> 4
   *Although you still need some coaching on the
   Macintosh, you do fine otherwise.*

4. Ability to take initiative in problem-solving: 1 2 <u>3</u> 4
   *I expect this will increase as you learn the business
   more thoroughly.*

5. Willingness to assist other employees: 1 <u>2</u> 3 4
   *Could use improvement here, especially when
   facing deadlines.*

6. Willingness to perform other duties as required: 1 2 3 <u>4</u>
   *It's good to know we can count on you to get the
   job done—whatever it is!*

7. Ability to complete assigned workload satisfactorily: 1 2 <u>3</u> 4
   Your work is high quality but is sometimes
   completed late (usually because you are a
   perfectionist!), so time management is an issue here.

8. Ability to supervise and motivate employees effectively: 1 2 <u>3</u> 4
   My concern here relates to #5. Your supervision is
   generally good, but it's hard for you to stop what
   you're doing to help others during a crunch.

<u>Additional Categories and Comments</u>

Overall, we're very pleased with your work. You are dependable,
a hard worker, and able to manage efficiently several demanding
tasks at once.

Your work could be improved by better monitoring of office
expenditures to keep from going over budget again.

Another area of concern is your occasional tardiness. Although
you make up your time, it is important that you arrive promptly
at 8:30.

Signature of Evaluator   Position   Date

I have read and discussed this performance appraisal with the
evaluator. My comments, if any, are on the reverse side.

Signature of Employee   Date

- A standardized form helps you to evaluate performance based on the actual job description. This style enables you to elaborate on your ratings.

- Leaving space for additional feedback allows you to include other points of praise or criticism and serves as an opener for discussion.

Company Name
Address
City, State Zip

Date

Mr. Grant Savage
40 Mayflower Street
Niagara Falls, NY 14304

Dear Grant:

I'm delighted to confirm your promotion to Director of Parts & Service. When we interviewed internal and external candidates for the position, your five years of loyal service and progressively more responsible positions with the company weighed heavily.

I understand you're planning to take two weeks vacation and assume your new position April 18. At that time, your salary will be $30,000 a year. Your benefits, which we discussed earlier, are described in the attached customized printout.

Since Parts & Service is a major profit center for our dealership, we're very pleased to have you in charge.

Sincerely,

John Brody

Enclosure

- Promotion letters are easy to write, especially since the promotion has already been discussed in person. Strive for a warm but not effusive tone.

- Make sure all details—salary, starting date—are clear.

Company Name
Address
City, State Zip

Date

Ms. Linda Wellington
45 Grand Avenue
New Haven, CT 06513

Dear Linda,

I'm pleased to tell you that your salary for next year, starting on the anniversary day of your employment, will be increased 5% to reflect the cost-of-living increase, plus an additional 8% merit increase based on the achievements and increased skills we discussed at your appraisal meeting. This brings your salary to $37,500 next year.

We're delighted to have you with us and look forward to another productive year.

Best wishes,

Susan Makepeace
Vice President, Personnel

- Because salary issues are sensitive, these letters are usually sent home.

- Be very specific about the salary figures. Don't let the reader puzzle over the impact of the percentages.

Company Name
Address
City, State Zip

Date

Mr. Frank Peabody
Microchips Etc.
1345 Eglin Avenue
Dublin, OH 43017

Dear Frank:

Thought I'd drop you a note to let you know how well you handled the presentation to Datastar yesterday. I tried to get to you afterward, but you were in deep conversation with John Truman and I had to dash for the plane.

The presentation was great. You really zeroed in on their main issues—turnaround time and capabilities. Even more impressive was the way you handled the question and answer session. You were brief and to the point. You refused to argue with our always contentious client, Mr. Ackerman, and you brought everything to closure after you wrapped up the question and answer session. Keep this up and we'll be giving you more of these kinds of assignments.

Best,

Simon Schotts
Executive Vice President

- This should be a very informal, handwritten note—sent to an employee you don't see daily.

- People are far more motivated by sincere praise than by blame, and the remarks are most effective when they are very specific.

Managing Your Business 8

Despite the fact that most of us would prefer to spend all our time on the creative or income producing aspects of our businesses, the reality is that no business can run itself—that is, operate efficiently without coming to grips with the day-to-day logistics of carrying on operations.

Inquiry letters are vitally important because even though you may have adequate financial backing or a large departmental budget, even if you are noted for your technical competence, you still need information on *how to run your business.* Given the complexity of the modern business environment, you have a much better chance of getting the information you need if you put your request on paper and you ask the reader to reply in writing. People may give you a glib answer over the phone, but they'll think twice about misinforming you in writing. In addition, because it takes time to write, you can use these letters to separate those who truly want your business (and therefore are likely to give you good service) from those who take a lackadaisical approach to their customers.

To get the maximum benefit from inquiry letters, be very specific about the result you want from the interchange. Even when your intent is to buy something, don't waste the reader's time and your own by making a vague request. Think about what your needs are before you write. If you can, lay out the precise criteria you intend to use to make the purchase. If you simply cannot pay more than a certain amount of money, for example, telling the vendor what your limits are may forestall his all-too-human tendency to suggest more elaborate and pricier products or services than you can afford.

Inquiries and confirmations concerning travel arrangements and meetings must be very exact. Anyone who has ever found himself in an inadequately curtained meeting room at high noon with the wrong slide carousel for a 35-mm slide presentation can attest to this. Getting all logistical arrangements in writing can save endless time and aggravation. It is also only fair to hotel or rental service personnel, who may be juggling numerous requests and demands for the same facilities on the same day.

If asking for exactly what you want is half the battle, using the appropriate tone is the other half. People can be better judged by the way they treat subordinates and service people than by the way they treat their bosses. If you have any question about the way you come across when you communicate with others, have someone else read your correspondence and give you some feedback.

Company Name
Address
City, State Zip

Date

Mr. Dennis Stimson
River Development Association
3084 U.S. 33 North
Benton Harbor, MI 49022

Dear Mr. Stimson:

We would like to renew our office lease for an additional two years. We are very pleased with the office and the maintenance of the building itself.

When we re-read our lease, we noted that there was no automatic renewal clause. We would be willing to increase the rent by 5%.

Please call and let us know if this is acceptable.

Best regards,

Noel Johnson
Managing Partner

- Usually, you can initiate a matter like this with a phone call. Landlords are notoriously difficult to reach, however, so a letter is justified, particularly if the relationship has been relatively good in the past. More importantly, a written record will help avoid future misunderstandings about financial arrangements. You do *not* want to write if you are in a hostile, confrontational mood.

Company Name
Address
City, State Zip

Date

Mr. Samuel Webster
Commercial Loan Division
Nornova Bank & Trust
One Nornova Square
Boise, ID 83728

Dear Mr. Webster:

I need to know the fate of our application for a $50,000 line of credit
which, according to McGregor Carlton, your assistant, has been given
file number 20-4326112.

When we first discussed this matter, I stressed the need for access
to this credit because of our seasonal cash requirements. We are now
ordering for the Christmas season, and many of our overseas suppliers
require cash deposits before making production commitments.

According to Mr. Carlton, all problems in granting our request were
trivial, yet we have not yet received approval. We have had an account
with Nornova for three years, and we feel we are not being treated with
the consideration we deserve. Please call me as soon as you receive
this letter.

Sincerely,

John T. Riker
663-4499

- Banks, like all bureaucracies, are sometimes frustrating to deal with. If you can't get
  satisfaction with a phone call, write a letter. (To ensure the letter gets prompt attention, you
  may have to send it by messenger or overnight delivery service.)

- Say *why* your request is urgent in very specific terms. (Everyone says they needed it
  yesterday—give proof.)

Inquiry about Business Credit Card (8-03)

Company Name
Address
City, State Zip

Date

New Accounts Manager
Mega Credit Card Company
4252 Three Mile Road
Dallas, TX 75261

Dear New Accounts Manager:

Please send us an application for business credit cards. In addition, please write us with the answers to these questions:

- What are your annual fees?

- How is the interest rate calculated?

- Do you provide a computerized end-of-the-year statement broken down by individual user?

- Can we impose different charge limits for different users (specifically, $5,000 for partners; $1,200 for associates)?

We look forward to hearing from you soon.

Sincerely,

James S. Levy
Vice President

- Don't be intimidated by the size of the firm you're dealing with. If you're comparison shopping, and you should, get answers to the same questions from each firm so you can make an informed decisison.

Company Name
Address
City, State Zip

Date

Mr. James C. Jagoe
Custom Business Plans, Inc.
4322 Pendragon Boulevard
Rocklin, CA 95677

Dear Mr. Jagoe:

As I mentioned in our phone conversation, Kirk Specialty Products has expanded rapidly in the last year and now has 20 employees. We want to put together a comprehensive insurance plan for our employees and for the business. Three local firms have been asked to submit proposals.

Please consider the following possible types of coverage when structuring your proposal:

- Health insurance, including hospitalization and major medical.

- A SMP (Special Multi-Peril Policy) for on-premises liability.

- Surety bond that will cover both general employee honesty and our payroll people.

- An OLT (Owners, Landlords, and Tenants) policy for ourmachinery and other equipment.

- A Business Automobile policy for the company-owned cars driven by myself and our three sales representatives.

Please submit your proposal and quote as soon as possible. We want to make our decision on insurance coverage by the end of the month.

Sincerely,

John F. Kirk

- Shop around when planning a major expenditure.

- Be as specific as possible about your needs so you will be able to compare proposals easily.

- Insist on a written proposal. You want to decide, not be "sold." You can always talk later.

Inquiry about Accounting Services (8-05)

Company Name
Address
City, State Zip

Date

Mr. John Benisch
Dunning, Hawkes, and Benisch
301 Silver Oak Street
Deerfield, IL 60015

Dear John:

Since you've done our partnership tax return for four years now, you're the obvious one to advise us on accounting services. Now that we're expanding, we can no longer take the time to keep the books. I assume Dunning, Hawkes, and Benisch will take these tasks off our hands for a fee. Please let us know what you would charge under the following conditions:

- You would provide the software consultation and training necessary to automate the process with additional help as needed.

- You would provide one of your bookkeeper's services on a monthly basis (no automation).

Please call if you have any questions.

Sincerely,

Jeff Roberts

- It's always better to deal with someone you know, but you should also price alternatives.

- Putting it in writing makes it clear that you intend to be businesslike about the issue.

Inquiry about Office Equipment (8-06)

Company Name
Address
City, State Zip

Date

Faxright Corporation
30 Canner Park Road
Melville, NY 11746

Dear Faxright:

Our firm, with 20 professional consultants, is interested in purchasing a facsimile machine to communicate more quickly with our clients.

Our criteria are:

- lowest possible price
- ability to delay transmissions until lowest phone rate periods
- good resolution of both text and photographs
- minimum service problems, preferably with self-diagnostics system

Please send me written information on how well your line of fax machines meets these criteria. (We will not respond to phone calls unless we have written information.)

Sincerely,

Jane Redmond
Purchasing Department

- If you're seeking information, help the salespeople out by stating your criteria.

- Insisting on written information helps you screen vendors. Those who don't bother to respond in writing don't care enough to deserve your business.

Inquiry about Car Leasing (8-07)

Company Name
Address
City, State Zip

Date

Double R Automobile Leasing
2477 178th Street South
Omaha, NE 68130

Dear Manager:

Our company is considering leasing 12 automobiles rather than buying them outright. Because it is important for us to present a favorable (and prosperous) image to our clients, we are interested in luxury cars only.

We have been talking with those of our colleagues who run similar businesses, so we have a rather specific view of what we need. We are interested in an *open end,* 36-month lease with a 20% down payment. Please let us know what our costs would be for a current-year model Mercedes, and provide a detailed explanation of the other terms of the lease, including our obligation and/or right to buy at the end of the lease term and the price we would pay for each vehicle.

We look forward to hearing from you soon.

Sincerely,

T. Arthur Post
Vice President, Operations

- You'll naturally consult your tax advisor on any decision of this magnitude.

- The more specific your request for information, the more knowledgeable you appear, the better the facts you will receive, and the better bargaining position you will have.

Company Name
Address
City, State Zip

Date

Mr. Russell Puhl
Computertime, Inc.
191 San Marcos Avenue
Mill Valley, CA 94941

Dear Mr. Puhl:

We recently noted in the *Mill Valley News* "Business Talks" column that you offer consulting services to small businesses. We have a public relations firm, and we need help interconnecting our current systems. We have three Mac Pluses and a Laserwriter, plus two very old IBM PCs and a NEC Daisy Wheel printer.

We would like consulting help to decide whether we should (or could) network our various systems, whether we need to purchase some software to port data between the two systems, and what kind of software we need to support our substantial business in presentation visuals.

Please call us and let us know your background and hourly rates.

Sincerely,

Tom Robinson
Office Manager

- It's helpful to tell people where you heard of them.

- Make sure you tell the reader what you want help with in the first paragraph.

- Don't overlook asking for background information.

Inquiry to Franchisor (8-09)

Sender's Name
Address
City, State Zip

Date

Ms. Delores Calhoun
Picture Perfect
1220 Morris Road
High Point, NC 27266

Dear Ms. Calhoun:

I am interested in buying a Picture Perfect franchise in Warwick, Rhode Island, and would like to know if you offer your franchisees:

- location analysis
- help in constructing facilities
- ongoing staff training
- discount on supplies
- national advertising

I would also like to know your requirements of franchisees regarding:

- start-up costs and fees
- royalties
- advertising and promotion contributions

Please send me whatever information you have for franchisees as well as details about each of these specific areas. I look forward to learning more about owning a Picture Perfect franchise.

Yours truly,

Keith Radell

- It's important to understand each party's (yours and the franchisor's) obligations before you contract to buy a franchise.

- Know what the franchise will provide you in support (critical to your success) as well as what the start-up and operating costs will be.

Company Name
Address
City, State Zip

Date

Mr. Peter Charles
Atlas Communications
4938 National Way
Tucker, GA 30084

Dear Pete:

We are interested in purchasing six telephones for our new office, five to be used on desks and one that will be on the wall. We need a total of seven jacks. As you may remember, we have four lines coming in, three that roll over and one individual line that services our facsimile machine.

We'll be moving January 2, and we must have the phones installed and operating by that date.

Please call me at 632-7777 (I'm most easily available between 8:30 and 9:30 a.m.) and let me know what you would charge me for the phones and jacks and what your terms are. As usual, we're trying to conserve cash.

Sincerely,

A. L. Cooke
Vice President

- Try to be explicit in your requirements—even if you are just starting the process.

- Always give the person the best time to call.

Company Name
Address
City, State Zip

Date

Mr. Samuel Smith
Town Engineer
Town of Kokomo
Kokomo, IN 46901

Dear Mr. Smith:

We are interested in locating a small manufacturing plant at 7 Locust Square. According to our current plans, the manufacturing process in this plant will use a maximum of 5,000 gallons of water per hour during peak periods. In order to get a construction loan, we need written confirmation from you, by the end of the month, that the sewer system in this light manufacturing zone can, in fact, handle that gallonage and that this quantity of water is available from the town's water system.

If you need further clarification of our needs, please write or call me at 652-4411.

Sincerely,

Paul Matsen
President

- Even town officials need to know why you're asking for information and when you need it.

- Resist the urge to be abrupt, even if you've become irritated by the slowness of the bureaucratic process.

- Show that you're flexible and cooperative.

Company Name
Address
City, State Zip

Date

Mr. Harold M. Nixon
Zoning Commissioner
Town of Ridgefield
Ridgefield, CT 06877

Dear Mr. Nixon:

We are contemplating a third-floor addition to our boat dealership, which will include 10 office suites. (I've attached the architect's initial sketches.) Before we invest additional money in blueprints, could you please confirm that our location at 23 Birch Road (please see attached plot plan) is indeed zoned for "any industrial use" or whether we will have to seek a variance.

Please call me at 431-9622 and let me know as soon as you can so I can tell the architect to proceed.

Sincerely,

Chris M. Forbes

Attachments

- Frequently, a letter provides the best way to deal with technical issues. In this case, providing sketches and plot plans makes it easy to respond.

Company Name
Address
City, State Zip

Date

Ms. Regina Baker
President
Meetings Unlimited
602 Third Avenue
New York, NY 10017

Dear Ms. Baker:

I would like to have a holiday party on December 15 for 50-60 of our firm's most important clients and their guests. The atmosphere should be friendly and sociable, as this is our way of thanking the people who do business with us.

I understand that you have access to caterers, facilities, musicians, and florists that I could not duplicate if I worked at it for months. Please call me at 742-6699 to set up an appointment to discuss how you would handle organizing this event and what your fee schedule is. As you'll notice, time is getting short, so I hope to hear from you soon.

Sincerely,

Yvonne S. Mann
Office Manager

- If you're unfamiliar with the involved logistics of setting up events or meetings, you may wish to consult a meeting or event planner. The details, after all, can make or break an event—such as failing to have non-alcoholic beverages available for a health-conscious crowd or lack of extra bulbs for overhead projectors, for example.

Company Name
Address
City, State Zip

Date

Mr. Paul Griswold
Manager
Computer Universe Incorporated
2602 85th Avenue SW
Fort Lauderdale, FL 33300

Dear Mr. Griswold:

As newcomers to the Fort Lauderdale area, we are seeking a source of computer supplies. We have 11 computers in house (9 Mac's and 2 IBM PCs), plus 3 printers (2 laser printers and 1 daisy wheel printer). As you can imagine, we require a quantity of ribbons, disks, and cartridges.

In our old location we dealt with a store that gave us a 20% discount off list for all equipment. We are asking you and two of your competitors about their usual discount for regular customers. Please call me at the number listed below as soon as possible to discuss our opening an account with you.

Sincerely,

Mort Danbury
Office Manager
537-2324 extension 32

- If you want the best deal possible, indicate that you will be a loyal and substantial account—and that you are shopping around.

- Do the heavy negotiating by phone.

Company Name
Address
City, State Zip

Date

Mr. William Critelli
Wicklow-Critelli Associates
2699 Wharton Street
Fort Smith, AR 72901

Dear Mr. Critelli:

As we discussed, we're interested in health care and possibly disability coverage for our four employees, all nonsmokers, including:

- office manager, female, married, one child (age 35)
- marketing representative, male, married, no children (age 26)
- marketing representative, male, single, no children (age 24)
- senior marketing associate, female, married, adult children who would not be covered by this policy (age 50)

You also offered to price a $10,000 life-insurance policy and a basic dental policy for these employees.

Please send me a letter with the detailed options. We can set up a meeting after I receive it.

Sincerely,

Barbara Manford
Partner

- Dealing with insurance complexities is tiring. Give the insurance representative enough information to provide a quote. Insist on a letter. It preserves your time, and the length of time it takes the person to respond is an indication of how well you'll be served in the future.

Company Name
Address
City, State Zip

Date

Optistar Bank
Commercial Banking Division
4200 South Wright Boulevard
Dayton, OH 45479

Dear Optistar Bank:

We are a local gourmet pet food store with $1.1 million in annual sales. We have become dissatisfied with our current bank's service and feel its charges are excessive. We are therefore writing to other area banks to see what services they provide to retail businesses of our size.

Please reply in writing with a complete description of your services and include a schedule of fees. You are welcome to call me if you need further information. After I have researched this issue, I will call to set up an account with the bank we select.

Sincerely,

Arnie L. Lindstrom
President

- If you don't know anyone who can provide a personal recommendation of a good bank (and an introduction to a responsive banker), you'll have to write.

- Try to get banks to respond first in writing. Whether they do so, and how soon, provides some indication of how badly they want your business.

Company Name
Address
City, State Zip

Date

Mr. P. Henry Trotter
Trotter, Trotter, and Gambardella
432 Nicholas Circle
Omaha, NE 68154

Dear Mr. Trotter:

Sarah Cahill has suggested that your firm has the expertise in
intellectual properties law to assist me with a software copyright
problem. Could you send me resumes of your firm's software copyright
law experts, as well as a fee schedule? Because of the frequency with
which these issues have arisen in the last two years, I might also be
interested in a retainer agreement.

I will call you after I have had a chance to look at your materials.

Sincerely,

Lawrence Dewhurst

- Be specific about what kind of legal services you're interested in.

- Use the name of the person who referred you to get the reader's attention.

Company Name
Address
City, State Zip

Date

Membership Chairman
Association of Sole Proprietors
432 Lindy Avenue, Suite 2
St. Louis, MO 63164

Dear Membership Chairman:

My good friend Bret McCumber tells me that your association has
provided him with an "instant network" of like-minded people to share
the pleasures and problems of sole proprietorship. I am interested in
joining your organization and would like to receive information and a
membership application as soon as possible.

Sincerely,

Susan L. Richards
President

- Indicate why you are interested in becoming a member.

- Ask for action by requesting an application.

Company Name
Address
City, State Zip

Date

Mr. John P. Duke
Wheel-Duke Venture Capital
3288 Buena Vista Drive
Rocklin, CA 95677

Dear Mr. Duke:

George Welles tells me that your firm provides financing for start-up ventures. Before I submit a formal application, I'd like to know in more detail what types of situations you prefer, what kind of participation you usually require, what time limits you generally stipulate, and your collateral requirements.

I will call you on September 10 to discuss these issues.

I look forward to our conversation.

Sincerely,

Merle C. Davies
President

- In this kind of stiutation, writing should get you a bit further than a phone call since it's formal and shows serious intent.

- It's vital that you get the details requested. The more similar your financial request is to those that the firm has favored in the past, the more likely you are to get funding.

Sender's Name
Address
City, State Zip

Date

Mr. Tolbert Holmes
U. S. Department of Commerce
Washington, D.C. 20037

Dear Mr. Holmes:

I am planning to open a restaurant in Guilford, Connecticut, within a few months and need information regarding regulatory requirements for new business owners (particularly new restaurant owners). Would you please send me whatever information you have on:

- tax regulations
- food service regulations
- regulations of any agency under whose purview restaurants fall

If necessary, please direct me also to any other federal agencies that you feel I should contact.

Sincerely,

Milton Twomey

- Specify the kind of business you're opening.

- State the information you need as specifically as possible, while leaving the door open for additional information.

- Be prepared to follow up; bureaucracies are often slow.

Sender's Name
Address
City, State Zip

Date

Ms. Irene S. Fountain
Connecticut State Department of Taxes
185 State Street
Hamden, CT 06517

Dear Ms. Fountain:

I am planning to open a beauty salon in a small shopping mall within the next few months and would like information regarding:

- state tax filing requirements
- liability insurance requirements
- state regulations affecting beauty salons

Please send me whatever information you have available on the above (or other regulations that will affect my business) and direct me to the state agencies that I should contact before I begin my venture.

Sincerely,

Rose Farentino

- Specify the kind of business you're opening.

- State what kind of information you need and ask whether there are any other regulations of which you should be aware.

- Follow up if you do not get a prompt response.

Request for Help from Elected Representative (8-22)

Company Name
Address
City, State Zip

Date

The Honorable Richard Marcus   Re: Waiver—Low Sulfur Fuel Oil
District Office
7 Dover Park
Independence, MO 64050

Dear Mr. Marcus:

I understand from Thomas Lexington that Senator North has forwarded our correspondence to you. As you have seen, it concerns our interest in having the Environmental Protection Agency grant us a waiver that will allow our factory to burn low sulfur fuel oil.

We understand from Mr. Lexington that the EPA may not act on our application for several months, even a year or more. If so, our factory, as well as the others in our area, will lose the savings that would accompany use of this much less expensive fuel oil. For our factory alone, the savings would be in the $62,000 range, and I'm sure that the all-around savings in the area might be up to $1 million or even more.

As I explained in my letter to Senator North, I have called Mr. Fred Downey, who is a member of the House Subcommittee on Health and the Environment, to ask his help in urging the EPA to act on this matter as quickly as possible. I have not yet heard from his office. I imagine, however, that he has heard from many other businesspeople in this area on this matter.

We would very much appreciate your help in this matter. Because of the relatively shaky condition of the economy in our area, I know that we have a mutual interest in getting the kind of savings that will allow businesses like ours to survive.

Sincerely yours,

Dennis R. Kendall

• Putting these matters before elected representatives is an extremely important part of an executive's job. This letter provides the reader with a sense of the bases that have already been covered, as well as the reasons for doing what the writer suggests (because the consequences otherwise might include closing a plant, with a loss of jobs, in his district).

Company Name
Address
City, State Zip

Date

Mr. Cecil Tompkins
Westport Town Engineer
Westport Town Hall
Westport, CT 06880

Dear Mr. Tompkins:

During the last four months, the Town has undertaken various improvements related to the sewer installations in the Rockland Park area. During the course of these improvements, a landfill dike was constructed across the inlet that runs from the Sound to our property line.

My primary concern is that the dike has created a large area of trapped brackish water and mud between the dike and our property. The resulting stagnant pools are a nuisance that is both unsightly and unhealthy. Sewage drainage from several businesses is now trapped. This problem will continue until the final extension of the sewer line. Inquiries at your office last week indicate that this project may not be funded for some years.

We request, then, that the area between the dike and our property be filled to a sufficient height to eliminate the water/swamp problem. The attached map indicates the area of concern.

I would be pleased to accompany you, or someone from your department, on a site visit. If you prefer, please review the situation and let me know as soon as possible if my proposed solution is workable.

Sincerely,

James A. Sterling

Attachment

- Create a sense of government responsibility for the problem in the first paragraph.

- Offer a solution or alternate solutions.

Company Name
Address
City, State Zip

Date

Personnel Resources, Inc.
32 Newman Square, Suite 340
Stamford, CT 06497

Dear Personnel Resources Staff:

We've noted with interest the bulletins on secretarial and administrative help that you send us on a regular basis, and we would like to inquire about your method of operation and your fees. Specifically, we would like to know whether you charge a percentage of the person's salary or a flat fee. We would also be interested in your guarantee. If the person leaves after a month's employment, is the fee refundable?

We would very much appreciate receiving your brochure and a current client listing.

Sincerely,

Benjamin O. Whitney
Vice President, Personnel

- It's always helpful to tell people where you heard about their firm. It establishes a more personal relationship immediately.

- Ask for a representative client listing so you can do a check of their competence and the types of businesses served.

Company Name
Address
City, State Zip

Date

Mr. Martin Silva
ExecuSearch, Inc.
2200 Maple Avenue
Baltimore, MD 21215

Dear Mr. Silva:

Your firm has been recommended to me by Howard Davies at Thompson, Thornberg and Reiss, who speaks very highly of the candidates you placed at his firm.

Newton and Marcus has recently reorganized, leaving us in need of three product managers. I'd like information regarding your firm's services, particularly:

- fee structure
- guarantees
- approach

I'd like to talk with you personally about the type of people we're looking for as well as how your firm can help us with our staffing needs. Please call so we can arrange a mutually convenient time to talk.

Sincerely,

Taylor Noublom
Executive Vice President

- If the firm has been recommended, state by whom.

- State what your company's needs are and what information you want.

- Ask the consultant to speak with you personally (he'll be happy to).

Company Name
Address
City, State Zip

Date

Mr. Alex Groton
Xerxes Temps, Inc.
Tacoma Financial Center
1145 Broadway Plaza
Tacoma, WA 98402

Dear Mr. Groton:

Gerry Hought of Hought, Layton, and Steele suggested that you were the best person in the area to talk to about accounting temporaries. Our firm is not quite as large as Gerry's, but it is similar in most other respects, including our need for temporary help in the traditional peak seasons.

Gerry has given me some information about the way you work, but I would appreciate a detailed description of your rates, your guarantees (for example, what happens if we are dissatisfied with a particular temp?), and the fees you charge if we decide to hire an individual on a full-time basis.

I look forward to hearing from you soon.

Sincerely,

Harriet Sitka
Office Manager

- If you have talked to a client of the temporary agency, make that very plain in the letter. You will get better service.

- The more specific your request for information, the better. For example, asking about the policy if you decide to hire someone full time indicates that you've dealt with temporary agencies before and are therefore relatively knowledgeable.

Company Name
Address
City, State Zip

Date

Mr. Martin Brien
Tax Assessor
Town of Robindale
Robindale, FL 33497

Dear Mr. Brien:

I have checked the record of the assessment of my property at 2033 Buckskin Trail, and I believe I have found two errors: the assessment is calculated on a square footage of 100,000. In fact, the dimensions of the lot are 150' by 100', or 15,000 square feet. In addition, the "single-family dwelling" referred to in the assessment is a storage shed. In order to stay on good terms with the neighbors, we added a false front and landscaping. I would be pleased to meet you or someone from your office to show you the interior of the shed.

I understand that such problems arise in any major reassessment. I do hope, however, to resolve the matter as soon as possible as taxes based on this assessment represent a real burden to my business.

I will call you next week to set up an appointment.

Sincerely,

Elliott J. Walker
President

- Mistakes can happen. Recognizing this, and taking a reasonable tone, will get you farther than ranting and raving.

- It's always wise to evaluate your assessment by comparing it with that of similar properties. If you believe it is high, check the assessment itself for errors.

Company Name
Address
City, State Zip

Date

Ms. Rachel Dornfield, President
Public Relations Strategies, Inc.
251 West 57th Street
New York, NY 10107

Dear Ms. Dornfield:

We've very much enjoyed having your firm as tenants for the past two years and hope to continue the relationship. As you know, your lease ends August 31, and you have an option to renew for an additional two years with a 10% escalation in rent, as before.

Please call or write and let us know what you intend to do. We hope for a positive answer.

Sincerely,

Andrew T. Forge
Vice President

• If it's hard to reach someone by phone, a note may get his or her attention. But sending a letter by itself isn't enough. Make a note to call within a week or so as the mails can be unreliable.

Company Name
Address
City, State Zip

Date

Mr. George Haight
Vivian Development Corporation
200 First Avenue
Des Moines, IA 50322

Dear George:

I'm happy that we've cleared up the misunderstanding about our renovations to our office space at 60 Ferry Street.

To recap, we are not making any changes to the building that will affect the load bearing capabilities of the existing structure. As you can see from the attached plan provided by our contractor, all new walls are non-load-bearing, and we plan no demolition of existing partitions or walls.

As we discussed yesterday, these changes are within the provisions of our lease. I'm glad you agree that these renovations will significantly improve the space.

Sincerely,

F. Anthony Cipriano

Attachment

- If there's any possibility of misunderstanding, put it in writing. (If the details imply any contractual obligations, you'll probably want your attorney to look at the letter.)

- Make sure your tone is reasonably informal and neutral. An adversarial tone almost never serves your needs.

Company Name
Address
City, State Zip

Date

Chief Clerk
Superior Court
Judicial District
235 Church Street
New Haven, CT 06500

Dear Chief Clerk:

Ms. Jodie L. Forbes has been notified to appear in the state court on July 2 for jury duty. Ms. Forbes is the sole secretary/administrative assistant in Watley and Carling's three-person office, and she is essential to the operation of the business. This is our busiest season and we could not process our orders if Ms. Forbes were to serve at this time.

Please excuse her from jury duty.

Sincerely,

William Watley
President

- Serving on a jury is a civic duty, and no one should be excused unless there is real hardship. If the person is an essential employee, providing evidence of the hardship may help.

- In some states, where the obligation for jury service involves "one day or one trial," it's probable that only a medical excuse from a physician will get the person excused.

Executive Summary

The Concept House, Inc., an innovative desk-top publishing company, seeks $500,000 in venture capital to fund initial start-up costs and to acquire a database of high-quality conceptual graphics for executive presentations.

The current desk-top publishing market has five relatively large firms, but none of them provides conceptual graphics by top artists. The major problem is the antiquated retrieval system, which makes turnaround time excessively long. As a result, most executives hire outside artists at very high rates. The Concept House will create a database using only top artists by paying them top prices on a per use basis.

The Concept House's management team, T. L. Williams and Joseph Frey, are both experienced. Williams has created the top-selling conceptual graphics computer program in the industry; Frey is an award-winning artist with extensive connections. Frey's task is to sign artists to exclusive contracts.

Sales and marketing forecasts project that investors will have a significant profit within the first two years. The partners, who have invested a very substantial percentage of their personal assets, project that they will buy out the venture capitalist interest in Year 4.

The Concept House provides a much needed service in a growing market.

Full information on this opportunity is available from Kyle Benson, President, Benson Associates, 1400 Manorhaven Boulevard, Port Washington, NY 11050, who is representing The Concept House.

- The executive summary should provide enough information to "sell" the venture capitalist on the need to talk further, without giving everything away.

- Naturally, if you are representing yourself, you will give your own name and address.

Company Name
Address
City, State Zip

Date

Lowell Y. Isaacson
Isaacson Ventures
Staten Island Development Center
2760 Victory Boulevard
Staten Island, NY 10314

Dear Mr. Isaacson:

I've attached an executive summary of a business plan for The Concept House, Inc., Inc., an innovative presentation graphics development company whose principals are seeking $500,000 in venture capital for a start-up situation.

If the financing arrangements interest you, I would be happy to send you a complete business plan. Please write or call me. I look forward to talking with you soon.

Sincerely yours,

Kyle Benson
President

Attachment

- To save everyone's time, it's better to get someone's attention by sending an executive summary with a cover letter rather than sending the entire business plan. With this method, you can determine who is interested in the concept and the general financial arrangements, without letting everyone know your competitive secrets.

Company Name
Address
City, State Zip

Date

Mr. Thomas P. Smith
Trident Bottling Company
78 King Street
Burlington, VT 05401

Dear Tom:

How are you? I hope you and your family are fine and that business is treating you well.

Since I last saw you at the reunion, I've developed a new line of tamper-proof packaging for bottles. Do you know of any distributors in the food machinery business who would be interested in representing me? I'd greatly appreciate any contacts you could pass along. Please call if you have any questions; otherwise, I'll call next week.

Thanks for your help.

Sincerely yours,

Hank Tompkins

- Be specific as to the information you want.

- Take the responsibility of getting back to them for the answers rather than waiting for them to get back to you.

- Express appreciation for their anticipated help.

Company Name
Address
City, State Zip

Date

Norman M. Ladue
Ladue Legal Services, Suite 45
1200 Six Mile Road
Battle Creek, MI 49017

Dear Norm:

Thanks for answering my question the other day. I understand that there may be more to the issue than meets the eye, but I appreciate your giving me some sense of my legal obligations. If my informal negotiations aren't successful, I'll call you immediately to set up an appointment.

Again, thank you for helping me out. You know you can always count on me to serve as your "tax hotline."

Give my best to June.

Best wishes,

Rochelle K. Waters
CPA

- Professionals are in the business of charging for their expertise. Don't abuse a friendship by asking for detailed (and free) advice. In this situation, there is clearly reciprocity—the writer and the reader trade information and advice freely.

Company Name
Address
City, State Zip

Date

Mr. James Hallogan
Small Business Administration
[Address is listed in
Blue Pages of your
phone book under
U.S. Government]

Dear Mr. Hallogan:

We've attached an application for a $100,000 business loan. You will
note that there are three attachments explaining our financials and
credit history. You should also know that we have someone interested
in buying any portion of the loan that the SBA chooses to guarantee.

We look forward to your response.

Sincerely,

Jack H. Colburn
President

Attachments

- If you need to explain anything and there's no room on the application, provide attachments.

- If you have someone interested in buying the guaranteed portion of the loan, say so. (You need not give a name.)

Company Name
Address
City, State Zip

Date

The Annual Meeting of stockholders in Lidditz Corporation will be held in the Grand Ballroom of the Inn at Big Mountain, 7777 South Big Mountain Parkway, Phoenix, Arizona, on June 15, at 10 a.m., for the following purposes:

- to elect six directors

- to approve and ratify the appointment of John Oldfield and Company as auditors

- to act upon stockholder proposals

- to transact such other business as properly may come before the meeting

Your vote is important!

- It's always a good idea to list the topics to be subject of the meeting, as well as the time and place.

Company Name
Address
City, State Zip

To: Board Members

From: Jacob E. Walton

Date:

Subject: Quarterly Board Meeting

The Executive Board of the Regis Corporation will hold its quarterly meeting on Monday, October 17, at 10 a.m. in the Executive Conference Room at Regis Corporation Headquarters, Denver, Colorado. The attached agenda outlines the issues we have scheduled for discussion. Please call Celeste Talbott at (303) 529-6431 x6209 to indicate whether or not you will attend and if you wish to add additional items to the agenda.

Attachment

- Give all important data: date, time, location.

- Attach agenda.

- Provide an easy way to RSVP (you'll get a better response).

Request for Hotel Rates (8-38)

Company Name
Address
City, State Zip

Date

Reservations Director
Silver Sands Hotel
1420 Palm Avenue
Tampa, FL 33601

Dear Reservations Director:

Please send us your room rates for long-term arrangements. We need four single rooms for two months starting October 1 and ending November 30. I understand you have only suite-style rooms, which our employees prefer. They must also have non-smoking rooms.

We are asking two of your competitors to tell us their rates. We do have a preference for your hotel, since it comes highly recommended and is located only four blocks from our client's headquarters. Price, however, is a factor, especially considering the lengthy stay.

Please respond in writing at your earliest convenience.

Sincerely,

Tony Audette
Vice President

- Normally, hotel reservations are made on the phone. If you want to negotiate, ask the reservations people to respond in writing.

- "Dear Sir or Madam" is a bit archaic, but it's another possibility when you don't have a name to use in the salutation.

Company Name
Address
City, State Zip

Date

Mr. Torrance C. Wayne
Conference Facilities Manager
The Proxmire Inn
32 Gathering Hill Lane
Amana, IA 52203

Dear Mr. Wayne:

I enjoyed talking to you Tuesday. The Proxmire Inn does indeed have the facilities we require for our firm's quarterly planning meeting.

I'd like to confirm that we've agreed to book "the cottage," which includes a large meeting room for our entire department (25 people), as well as two smaller conference rooms for committee meetings (8-10 people each). The date we agreed on was June 25.

We need the following A/V equipment:

    In the large meeting room:
        An overhead projector and screen
        A VCR and monitor

    In each of the smaller rooms:
        An overhead projector and screen
        Two flip charts

The fee for the cottage will be $800, to include the A/V equipment and lunch. I will be calling June 5 to check on these arrangements. In the meantime, please send me a written confirmation.

Sincerely,

Horace Hawkins
Vice President, Marketing

- It doesn't hurt to treat hotel personnel as if they were human beings. If you did enjoy talking to them, say so.

- Conferences can be scuttled by insufficient attention to logistics. Put it in writing and get a written response. Then follow up with a phone call.

Confirmation of Equipment Rental (8-40)

Company Name
Address
City, State Zip

Date

Ms. Linda Nistrom
A/V Concepts, Inc.
3487 Half Moon Street
Wilkes-Barre, PA 18705

Dear Ms. Nistrom:

As we discussed on the phone yesterday, you have agreed to rent us the following equipment on July 12 from 8:00 a.m. to 1:00 p.m.:

- black and white monitor
- VCR
- camera

In addition, you have agreed to have one of your staff set up the equipment by 7:30 a.m., and to run the equipment for the duration of our interviewing workshop. We will be holding the workshop in our fourth floor conference room.

According to your quote yesterday, the cost for the rental of the equipment and the assistance of your staff person will be $255.00 inclusive.

As I mentioned to you yesterday, your firm came highly recommended, and we look forward to working with you.

Sincerely yours,

Carolyn Bond
Administrator

- Even if you've detailed everything thoroughly in a phone conversation, putting it all down on paper will avoid difficulties later. Be sure to refer to the cost that the firm quoted you and be very specific about the equipment.

Appreciation to Hotel/Facility for Help/Good Service (8-41)

Company Name
Address
City, State Zip

Date

Manager
The Gathering
3642 Autumn Street
Santa Monica, CA 90405

Dear Manager:

Our firm, Bowden, Inc., had an offsite meeting at your facility on May 11. We were greeted by Gus Menzies when we arrived, and we found his assistance invaluable for the rest of the day. He checked on our needs frequently but unobtrusively, handled our crisis with the overhead projector (which we had supplied) with good humor and swiftness, and, all in all, gave us an enormous amount of confidence that our every need would be met.

Please thank him for us.

Sincerely,

Joseph C. Trowbridge
Vice President, Sales

- Good service should be noted, and writing to the manager shows your gratitude, provides tangible recognition of the person, and helps assure that your company will get good service in the future. (People complain of the decline in service while failing to recognize that the decline in customer courtesy has accelerated it.)

Company Name
Address
City, State Zip

Date

Mr. David R. Rivers
Manager
Trail Drive Inn
2 Whipoorwill Way
Boise, ID 83709

Dear Mr. Rivers:

I have stayed at the Trail Drive Inn every September, December, and May for over 7 years. In every instance, I have been more than pleased with the facility and service.

Last week, however, I was horrified to return to my room to find that the maid had discarded (and, it ultimately transpired, incinerated) an entire carton of confidential papers that I had left on the credenza in my room. I spoke to the front desk clerk, who kindly tore up my bill. Nevertheless, I wish to make sure this costly and personally embarrassing episode is not repeated. Please note in your records that on subsequent stays, my room is to be cleaned, but that nothing, including the contents of wastebaskets, is to be removed until I check out.

Sincerely,

Owen Willis

- If you're a steady customer, say so up front; it makes a difference.

- If you want something to happen, you'll have to ask for it. Giving a facility an opportunity to make good on a loss allows them to keep a valued customer and gives you a greater feeling of security. Writing to the hotel manager is a good way of ensuring that you'll get what you want.

Special Travel Requirements for Company Employees (8-43)

Company Name
Address
City, State Zip

Date

Mr. Terry M. Sliney
Wonderland Tour and Travel
2720 Cypress Creek Boulevard
Winston-Salem, NC 27156

Dear Mr. Sliney:

Until further notice, please make these arrangements when booking airline reservations for the following employees:

> Paul Gordon: aisle seat, vegetarian meal
> Tonya Marinelli: bulkhead seat, low-calorie meal
> Lindley Chitters: aisle seat, low-calorie meal

As you have already noted in your file, all these employees are non-smokers.

Thanks for your help.

Sincerely,

William Thomas

- Travel agents are among the most harried people on earth. Make it easy for them to serve you by putting special requirements in writing.

Internal Communications 9

Written communications were once the major method of communicating internally. As management styles became more participative and less directive, however, internal communication tended to be more in the form of a quick "huddle" in the hall, a short meeting, or a phone call rather than the standard memo. Now, with the advent of people operating in widely dispersed locations, the written word is once again assuming more importance.

A well run business or department demands writing. Take agendas, for example. Agendas have an action bias—they not only stipulate what actions are required, they also specify who is responsible for taking action. The person who writes them, therefore, has a much greater chance of getting decisions implemented than someone who runs a meeting by the "seat of his pants."

Recommendations and reports. A memo that makes a recommendation saves everyone time by highlighting the reasons for the recommendation. Many decision makers actually think better when they have something in writing (these are the people who say "send me a memo so I can react to it"), and creating a cogent, logical argument on paper may be all you need to do to convince the reader.

The report is a dying breed. It used to be considered a "product," an end in itself, but more and more the product is the decision, the action, or the plan rather than a tome gathering dust on the shelf. Whether or not reports are produced depends on the decision maker—some decision makers want reports to reassure them that all the bases have been covered; some only want a presentation that shows (rather than tells) them that the recommendation is based on tight reasoning and extensive research. In any case, the decision maker usually reads the executive summary. Perhaps he or she will read *only* the executive summary, especially if the writer has high credibility and a "good news" message. The executive summaries included in this section follow all the rules. They attract the reader's attention by telling him or her why it's important to read on, and then they tell the main point and summarize the organization of the report itself. To write a lucid executive summary, you must have good organization. Otherwise, you'll find yourself writing things like this: "This report begins with an introduction (what else would it begin with?) and continues with an analysis of the problem...I then discuss..." That approach, which may sound frighteningly familiar, is deadly dull.

Policies and procedures. Great care should be taken with any written explanation—whether it is a new policy or procedure or a clarification of an existing policy—because staff members often feel threatened by change. Take the time to detail why a change has been made or why a clarification is required. This will reduce needless speculation (often erroneous) by employees, and will help them understand the reasoning behind company decisions.

Announcements. Managers tend to speed through the writing of announcements, but that's a mistake. Even if a decision has already been made, and a change is already in the works, treating the staff as if they were uninvolved is insulting. Most efficient managers consult the people affected before making any major change, to get their comments and suggestions, so announcements of new procedures are surprise-free; that is, they merely confirm what has already been agreed upon. Similarly, promotions and resignations should be announced first in staff meetings, with memos following in case people haven't heard the news directly. Once again, the purpose of writing it down in these cases is to solidify and make real to people news that is already "old."

If an executive or manager must impart bad news to the entire company, a written communication is essential. A memo dealing with difficult conditions should be direct and should say clearly what problems must be faced. If there are potential solutions, of if employee cooperation can help in specific ways, the details should be spelled out.

Company Name
Address
City, State Zip

To: All Sales Representatives

From: Thomas Lavel

Date:

Subject: Quarterly Meeting

In response to the feedback session at the last quarterly meeting, our fourth quarter meeting will be held offsite—at the Huckleberry River Inn in Blackthorn on January 30. I've enclosed a simplified map and an agenda. As usual, the meeting will start at 9 a.m. and end at 4 p.m. I look forward to seeing you there.

- Meeting notices should be complete, including references to who, what, when, and where. Enclosing a map is essential for offsite meetings, and an agenda is also vital.

- If you have responded to staff suggestions, make sure you point it out.

Agenda (9-02)

Company Name
Address
City, State Zip

Date:

Time: 2:00 P.M. - 3:00 P.M.

Location: Conference Room

Objective: Revise vacation policy

Attendees: Lon Beardsley
Tony Marinelli
Sam Skryzak

Agenda Item	Purpose	Time	Presenter
Review vacation policies of competitors	Background	5 mins.	L.B.
Discuss feedback from staff	Establish criteria for change	10 mins.	L.B.
Review cost considerations	Establish cost criteria	10 mins.	L.B.
Brainstorm solutions	Generate alternatives	10 mins.	T.M.
Make decision		10-15 mins.	T.M.

- For major decisions, make sure you allow time to set criteria *and* brainstorm solutions.

- If you say you'll decide, you *will* decide.

Company Name
Address
City, State Zip

Date:

Time: 10:00 a.m. to 11:30 a.m.

Location: Meeting Room A

Objective: Decide whether to increase in-house production
capacity in printing

Attendees: Christopher Covale
Michael Endolf
Simone Martens
Jud Powers
Jillian Stabley
Heather White

Agenda Item	Purpose	Time	Presenter	Material To Be Read in Advance
Establish criteria for making decision	Consensus	15 mins.	—	—
Review 5-year production figures	Information	10 mins.	J.S.	Figures
Estimate long and short-term demands	Decision	20 mins.	S.M.	—
Review cost estimate	Information	15 mins.	J.P.	Estimates
Consider potential short-term use of excess capacity	Decision	20 mins.	C.C.	Estimates

- Always indicate your objective and plan of action to give participants a sense of comfort that their time won't be wasted.

- Assign tasks to people to make sure they are involved and prepared.

Company Name
Address
City, State Zip

To: Printing Capacity Committee

From: Michael Endolf

Date:

Subject: Assingments for Facility Addition Presentation

Action	Person Responsible	Completion Date
Develop new exhibits showing demand by sector.	J.P.	July 18
Create chart for senior management, showing best, worst, and most likely printing demand trends; support with text attachments.	H.W.	July 16
Gather cost estimate for 2,000 and 4,000 square foot print shop additions.	C.C.	July 16

Next meeting scheduled for July 21.

- When you reach agreement on an item requiring action, write out the action and identify the person responsible.

- Distribute assignments as soon as possible after the meeting so those concerned can be aware of everyone's tasks and will know where to direct their own input.

Company Name
Address
City, State Zip

To: S. T. Alexander
          Director, MIS

From: L. M. Wellington

Date:

Subject: Sale of FORMATS

Microware, Inc., a commercial software firm, has expressed interest in
purchasing a license to market FORMATS, an interactive computer
program we've developed in-house. It is essential that we act promptly
because one of the two programmers who developed FORMATS has
already left us and the other will be leaving in two months. No one else
in the firm can develop the program for the commercial market. As a
result, we may both lose a useful tool and miss the opportunity to sell
the program, since Microware has indicated it will not purchase the
program unless we provide training.

There are two ways to sell FORMATS to Microware: The company can
either agree to let Microware market FORMATS in exchange for
royalties, or it can sell the rights to Microware for a one-time fee. I
recommend the second option because the paperwork will be
completed and tax problems resolved all at one time.

Microware and our remaining programmers have tentatively agreed
both on the training schedule and on the one-time licensing fee. I will
call you to set up an appointment to make final arrangements.

- If it is urgent to act, say so.

- If the decision-maker wants both options, give them to him, but also say what you want to
  have happen and why.

- Move towards action by asking for an appointment.

Company Name
Address
City, State Zip

To: Cyril Schiller, President

From: Dolores Ofner

Date:

Subject: Media Strategy for Sunday Openings

At our February 20 meeting, we decided to open all suburban branches of the bank on Sundays in order to serve our existing customers better and to attract new accounts. I've met with Stiller and Orlando, our advertising agency, and they suggest a 12-week advertising campaign, using newspapers as the umbrella media.

In brief, they recommend the following:

Newspapers. Place one full-page ad each week in the four regional weekly newspapers for the first four weeks of the campaign. Run a half page each week in the two urban newspapers during the same period. To sustain awareness of the Sunday opening, a third, smaller ad should run in all newspapers for the remaining eight weeks.

Statement Stuffers. Supplement the newspaper ads with 70,000 statement stuffers to reach existing bank customers. The stuffers will use the same creative theme as the newspaper ads and will also be available as "take ones" in each branch office.

Drive-In Window and Lobby Posters. Place color posters at drive-in windows and lobby entrances at each of the branches.

Outdoor Advertising. Change the copy on our 24 billboards and put up a new billboard sign advertising the Sunday opening on 16 additional billboards. (See attached example.)

So far, S & O has not provided the specific reasoning behind their strategy. I feel strongly that we should not go ahead with this plan until they provide the back-up. Neither you nor I have enough expertise to evaluate their recommendations without it. In addition, I have told them that they must provide a budget as soon as possible.

Attachment

- Remind the reader of the reason for the memo—always a good idea.

- Highlight the main points with headings.

- Outline clearly the next steps to be taken.

Company Name
Address
City, State Zip

To: Brody Newhouse

From: Gus Marwick

Date:

Subject: Word Processing Work-flow

Thank you again for your recent suggestion about reorganizing the work flow in the word-processing department. We had a meeting with the people concerned last week, and they enthusiastically accepted your idea for assigning individual word processing operators to specific departments so that the operators can become familiar with the dictating styles of the individual managers and the technical subject matter. Naturally, we'll reassess the new system after a month or so to see how it's working, but we expect that it will be a great improvement over our current system, which has been the source of endless complaints.

John Harvey and I discussed this improvement in a recent meeting, and he wanted to make sure I thanked you for him as well.

- A steady flow of suggestions and recommendations is vital to a well-run business.

- Encourage communication by responding promptly, telling the specifics of the implementation, and making sure the word gets to higher-ups in the firm.

Company Name
Address
City, State Zip

To: Sally Williams

From: Whitcomb Ellsworth

Date:

Subject: Quota Club Meeting

Thank you for suggesting that we hold this year's Quota Club meeting at Marco Island, Florida. I've visited there myself, and the spot certainly is idyllic. We are already committed to holding this year's meeting at Sea Island, Georgia, however, and cannot change at this late date. I will keep Marco in mind when I schedule next year's event, though, and will seriously explore finding a suitable facility there.

- Make your thanks sincere.

- Give a reasonable (and truthful) reason why you can't act on the suggestion and offer hope for future consideration, if it exists.

Company Name
Address
City, State Zip

To: Elmer K. Lepisko

From: William Harris

Date:

Subject: Change in Soldering Iron Design

It was great to hear in the Tuesday meeting that the design of the new soldering iron is almost complete. Unfortunately, something came up yesterday that will cause us a bit of a problem. As you know, Don Getman returned this week from India, and he's just now had an opportunity to look at the specs. His major issue is the placement of the logo. He wants the soldering iron to "fit in with the appearance of the entire product line," which essentially means that he wants the company logo to be displayed more prominently.

Since we had early discussions on the placement of the logo, I know that we anticipated this objection and that you have a series of alternatives in hand. Let's meet tomorrow and agree on the best alternative for giving Don what he wants. If you're available at 8:00 a.m., that's a good time for me. It also allows us time to schedule a meeting with Don later in the day.

I believe we can resolve this issue to everyone's satisfaction and still meet our deadline.

- Managers have to deal with last-minute changes, and explaining them to staff is difficult.

- Make your point directly and clearly.

Request for Employee Participation in Charity Drive (9-10)

Company Name
Address
City, State Zip

To: All Staff Members

From: James R. Powers

Date:

Subject: Community Campaign

We have always had a proud tradition of supporting the Community Campaign, that excellent organization that helps us to extend a helping hand to the needy in our community.

Soon, you will have the opportunity to share in this fine tradition, once again, through your support of our annual Community Campaign.

By giving just one hour's pay each month, through payroll deduction, you ensure that the health and human care needs of our communities are met the whole year.

I urge you to join me in contributing to the Community Campaign so that together we may help improve the quality of life for everyone.

- Usually, the organizing institution provides boilerplate letters. Try to personalize them if possible.

- Make it easy by offering payroll deductions.

Company Name
Address
City, State Zip

To: Senior Management

From: Hal Wellington

Date:

Subject: Mid-point Progress Report—Marmot River Plant

As I reported last month, changing the coating of the steam lines to a zinc base, while worthwhile in terms of reduced cost, has caused us to slip the schedule by two months. We have had additional problems in the last month. Because of an early freeze, we were not able to break ground for the laboratory addition. We estimate that this setback will cost us six months for that part of the project. Because of the increased time involved, we will incur additional labor costs. We will therefore be over budget by approximately $56,000.

Impact of the early freeze confined to laboratory addition. No one could have anticipated the severity of the October 20 freeze, the worst in 25 years. The schedule, as outlined in our original proposal and as revised last month, was predicated on more normal temperatures. Naturally, this affects only the laboratory addition. Renovations to the main plant itself, where we have already "closed the envelope," or made the building weather-tight, will progress on the schedule we set forth last month.

Renovations to main plant close to revised schedule. We have completed the new flooring and all major rewiring. We have also replaced all light fixtures. This month we will be testing the flooring's ability to bear the new equipment. (All equipment was delivered on schedule. It has been stored in the yard for the past month under weather-proof sheathing.)

- Executive summaries for progress reports may be in the form of transmittal letters, memos (like this one), or individual pages after the title page.

- Use action headings (statements of significance) rather than generic headings (work completed, cost, conclusion) to make your points. If you're not on schedule, say so, and say why, without assigning blame or whining.

Executive Summary

J. M. Finnerty Corporation has had a contractual agreement with the Leveland County Commission on Human Rights since 1986. This year's goal under the agreement was to fill 15% of the Corporation's middle-management positions with minorities and 35% with females, through either promotion or external search. Unfortunately, we have been unsuccessful thus far. Only 7% of our middle-management positions are held by minorities, 16% by women. If the corporation fails to meet these goals in the next 10-month period, the ensuing litigation could represent a cost of a minimum of $95,000, even if arbitration is possible in some instances.

We have contacted Herman K. Fanton, a consultant skilled in training management in minority recruiting practices, and he is willing to help us institute a new program that will:

- provide intensive training for each manager with hiring responsibility

- institute new skills training programs to encourage promotion from within

- evaluate progress at each step

Rationale and technical back-up (including consultant's proposal, graph detailing minority and female recruitment, and table of median legal costs in similar cases) are attached.

- Executive summaries for final reports come after the title page of the report and so require no heading but the title.

- State why the report is important and highlight its organization through the use of bullets. If the writer has high credibility, and if the reader finds the message convincing, agreement could be reached on the basis of the summary.

Company Name
Address
City, State Zip

To: Bob Pickett

From: Sylvia Presser

Date:

Subject: Lateness of Promotional Materials for Schweitzer's Soda

We've had a terrible time getting the printer to stick to the delivery schedule on the Schweitzer's Soda posters. I believe it is still possible to meet the deadline for delivery to the distributors, but it's going to be close.

There are two reasons for the delay. We were set back almost a full week when we discovered errors in the artwork. These mistakes should have been caught by my staff. We are going to change some procedures to prevent this from happening in the future.

The second problem is that we increased the printing order by over 50% at the client's request. The printer couldn't handle it, and it was too late to find another. We found another shop to augment the first, but we were already behind.

As I said, I think we will still make the deadline of June 5, but it's going to take some serious babysitting.

- Admit any errors or misjudgments on your part, but don't grovel. Take responsibility, and use straightforward, non-evasive language.

- Give the whole story. Often your boss must report to his boss, and he/she needs all the facts.

Recommendation to Purchase Equipment (9-14)

Company Name
Address
City, State Zip

To: Monica R. Tolman

From: Henry Dumont

Date:

Subject: System 10 Upgrade

I recommend we purchase an IBM 4420-H12 disk drive to address the storage capacity problem we now have with System 10.

Purchasing this unit will allow us to:

- add the storage capacity we need to complete projects now underway
- upgrade System 10 cost-effectively

Add Storage Capacity

The IBM 4420-H12 will provide 700 megabytes of auxiliary storage to System 10. It will eliminate our current critical capacity problem and allow us to move forward with our plan to provide additional system functions.

Upgrade Cost-effectively

The IBM 4420-H12, at $13,000, is the least expensive option for meeting our needs and avoids having to upgrade the entire system now. The two other units we have considered, the 3840-A12 and the 4420-H13, cost $41,000 and $26,000, respectively. Upgrading the entire System 10 now would cost over $50,000. Although the entire system will have to be upgraded eventually, I do not see sufficient reason to do so now.

The IBM 4420-H12 clearly suits our needs best. With your authorization, we can move ahead on purchasing and installing this unit.

- Lay out your specific recommendation up front and let the reader know why it's important.

- Clearly state the benefits of your recommendation.

- Be sure to end by restating your recommendation and telling the reader what needs to be done next.

Company Name
Address
City, State Zip

To: Investment Committee

From: John Lerue

Date:

Subject: Budget Finance Loan

At its next meeting, the Committee must decide whether to approve the purchase of $1.2 million of convertible debentures in Budget Finance Corporation, a financial services company, headed by George Ephram, that buys commercial paper from retailers in low-income neighborhoods. I recommend that we approve this purchase: It both meets our financial criteria and advances us toward our advertised goal of participating in the revitalization of low-income areas.

Financial Criteria

- Budget Finance should be able to make payments on schedule. The anticipated increase in business seems reasonable, given Budget's strong management and projected market growth.

  1. Budget's program should attract retailers and overcome the industry's traditional problems—shoddy merchandise, inadequate follow-up on defaults, and poor selection of potential customers.

  2. In addition, the bilingual partner and employees should attract new business in the Spanish-speaking community.

  3. Budget's experienced management, innovative systems, and training and computer programs, combined with a growing

John LeRue   -2-   Date

economy, should easily provide Budget with the cash flow
necessary to repay its debt to the bank.

Minority Community

- This loan will be a visible symbol of the bank's commitment to
  helping low-income areas.

    1. Budget is involved in almost every neighborhood in which we
       have a branch (see Exhibit 1).

    2. Joint advertising, both print and TV, will reinforce this tie.

    3. Acquisition of convertible debentures will demonstrate the
       bank's interest in participating in the ownership of local
       business.

    4. Budget's training programs and the loan will have a ripple
       effect: Budget will channel the bank's funds to retailers,
       indirectly contributing to their increased sales.

Attachments

- Memos recommending a course of action should have a very tight argument. Here the
  investment committee clearly cares about the financial issue—and about aiding the minority
  community.

- Use of bullets and numbered points help readers to absorb the major points quickly.

Company Name
Address
City, State Zip

To: Paul DePalma, Vice-President, Human Resources

From: Edward Nisenson, Human Resources Manager

Date:

Subject: Increasing Support for Work Art Programs

Attendance at the city-funded "Work Art" project at the South plant has been light. As we discussed last week, city involvement at the plant is an important and visible example of business and government cooperation that should receive strong support. My informal analysis suggests that poor scheduling is the primary reason for low attendance, and I have developed a strategy to solve that problem.

Low Attendance Follows Poor Scheduling. Poor scheduling has adversely influenced the possibility of getting a good turnout. For example, "art-break" activities have been planned for the cafeteria during the noon hour. Because the previous plant manager declared the cafeteria off-limits to production line workers during lunchtime, these workers are still reluctant to attend events there, even though the new manager has rescinded that rule. In addition, several events have been scheduled during the 10-minute morning breaks. Workers stationed at any distance from the sites of these events cannot possibly get to them.

New Scheduling Strategy Will Improve Chances of Success. Scheduling changes can directly improve worker participation. Future events should be located in "neutral" areas, preferably outside the plant. Programs should be scheduled during shift changes rather than during working hours, and all programs should be scheduled during daylight hours to allay fears of workers who do not live in the area.

Next Steps. I suggest we meet next week to discuss how to implement this strategy and to consider other informal ways to encourage attendance at art events.

- This memo provides a cogent strategy and the support for it.

- Headings highlight the main points.

Company Name
Address
City, State Zip

To: All Staff

From: Len Fireman, President

Date:

Subject: Media Policy

Our policy for dealing with the media is to respond quickly and politely. Do not refuse to speak to media representatives or fail to return their phone calls. News is only news for a very short time, and the media must print or broadcast something. It's better if that something comes directly from a spokesperson for our company.

In general, it is best to refer media calls to me. I'm trained to deal with the media, and individual reporters are likely to prefer dealing with me in any case. If I am not available, Nancy Anne Hart, my administrative assistant, will know whom to call.

If no one is available and you must talk with a media representative, be sure that you do not give him or her misleading or incomplete information. Do not provide any information that could be construed as proprietary or personal. Do not give opinions—only factual information. If you do not know the answer to a question, say so. Never speculate. Your speculation is likely to be printed as a fact.

• Dealing with the media can be very stressful for people. Give the staff the names of company spokespersons to call, plus guidelines for dealing with media representatives that will ensure minimum strain.

Clarification of Existing Policy (9-18)

Company Name
Address
City, State Zip

To: All Staff

From: Vera Byers

Date:

Subject: Long-Term Salary Continuance Insurance Policy

Because we're a new firm, we've only recently started to provide formal, written notices of our policies and procedures. As some of you know, Joe Drabnik and I are working on a booklet describing these policies. We hope to have it ready by January 1.

In the meantime, though, many of you have asked about the long-term salary continuance plan. An employee becomes eligible after completing two years of continuous employment with the company, provided the employee works at least an average of 30 hours a week.

Once you are eligible, you are automatically enrolled in the plan. The plan pays you monthly benefits if you become totally disabled. The payments start 90 days after the disability, and continue until age 65. Payments are 60% of your base monthly salary up to a maximum benefit of $3,000 a month. "Base monthly salary" means your monthly rate of earnings immediately prior to becoming disabled. It does not include overtime or bonuses. Benefits will be reduced by any income you are entitled to receive from Workers' Compensation, Social Security or any retirement plan sponsored by the company.

If you have any questions before we issue the policy booklet, please don't hesitate to call me.

- When you're clarifying an existing policy, be sure to include all the relevant points.

- When dealing with employee benefits, keep an open door policy. Issues can be confusing and employees may need help in understanding the details.

Company Name
Address
City, State Zip

To: Clara Winstead

From: Bowman Steele

Date:

Subject: Changing Holiday Policy

We recommend changing the firm's holiday policy from 10 fixed
holidays to 7 fixed holidays (those indicated with an asterisk) and 3
"floaters":

> Day before New Year's
> New Year's*
> Good Friday
> Memorial Day*
> July Fourth*
> Labor Day*
> Thanksgiving*
> Day after Thanksgiving*
> Day before Christmas
> Christmas*

Our employees have asked for this change because the days before
New Year's and Christmas sometimes fall on a Saturday or Sunday
and because Good Friday has no significance for some of them.

We feel we should respond positively to their request as long as there is
adequate coverage assured in the office on "floating holidays." If you
agree with this change, please initial on the bottom and return this
memo to me. I'll take care of the rest.

- Make the nature of the change clear by stating what exists as well as what you recommend.

- Make it easy for the decision-maker to respond by giving your reasons and saying "initial this." The easier you make it, the more likely you'll be to get what you want.

Company Name
Address
City, State Zip

To: All Staff

From: Paul Pleasant

Date:

Subject: New File Back-up Procedures

For several years, we've survived quite nicely with a rather haphazard procedure for backing up our file disks. As the company has grown, however, we have been having problems. For example, people take the disks home to work on them, and other members of the staff cannot find copies. Furthermore, our insurance representative has pointed out that should we have a fire, our mailing lists and other proprietary data disks would be lost, and we would find it extremely difficult to reconstruct them.

As a result, we have instituted a new policy:

- Anyone using a disk must make a back-up copy. Back-up copies should be updated every Friday afternoon.

- Anyone who takes a data disk home must leave a copy in the office.

- Every two weeks, Hilary Newsome will take the essential data disks to the company's safe-deposit box. At that time, she will retrieve the old copies of the data disks for reuse. Program disks are already in the safe-deposit box. If any new programs are purchased, they must be taken to the safe deposit box on the next trip. If there should be any problem with initiating this policy, please contact me.

- Make sure everyone knows why the procedures are being implemented.

- Be very specific about *who*, *what*, *where*, and *when*. Assigning tasks and responsibilities by name is very helpful.

Company Name
Address
City, State Zip

To: All Staff

From: Jan Rockwell

Date:

Subject: Expense Account Procedures

Our accountant has told us that we must be very stringent about our records for expense account reimbursements. According to IRS rules, we must have written documentation (in the form of a bill or receipt) for any expense over $25.00. I understand how hard it is to remember to keep documentation, especially when you've been on the road for an extended period, but we (and you) do not want to violate any IRS dictates. As a result, we'll have to insist on written documentation (copies are fine) before we can reimburse you.

- Anything that constrains people, especially people who travel, will be greeted with a distinct lack of enthusiasm. Point out the reasons for the action and the consequences if they don't comply.

- Be understanding about the burdens of a policy, but never indicate that policy exceptions are possible.

Company Name
Address
City, State Zip

To: All Staff

From: Eugene Robards

Date:

Subject: Lloyd Reed

I'm pleased to announce that Lloyd Reed has been made a principal in our firm. Lloyd has been with Robards, Robards, and Tolsory for five years. Previously he was Director, Human Resources, for Weaver Industries, with responsibilities encompassing diverse manufacturing operations, including international operations in the Far East.

A broadly experienced personnel executive, Lloyd spent ten years with Wellfleet, Inc. in a variety of personnel positions with emphasis in organization planning, executive selection, management development, and labor relations.

Lloyd is currently President of the Arthritis Foundation of Whittier, and a member of the Executive Committee of the Human Resources Research Association. Previously he served as a Director for the Whittier United Way.

• Business career information, both in the company and elsewhere, reinforces the individual's professional expertise.

• Non-business background information on the individual provides the human touch.

Company Name
Address
City, State Zip

To: All Staff

From: John Elliott

Date:

Subject: New Travel Expense Policy

With the growth of our firm, expenses for business related travel have increased significantly. As a result, we've worked out a new travel policy based on a very favorable agreement we've reached with Thompson Travel. This policy should ensure we keep our costs in line with the competition's.

All travel arrangements will be made through Thompson to ensure that we obtain the most advantageous rates for airline tickets, hotel bookings, car rentals, and transportation to and from the airport. Please follow these guidelines:

- Book accommodations only in mid-range hotels (for example, Ramada Inns, Best Western).

- Choose the least expensive transportation option available,(i.e., taxis and hotel and airport courtesy cars rather than rental cars).

- Rent cars only from carriers with whom we have a corporate discount.

- Please make every effort to keep meal expenses under $35 per day. The company will not reimburse for bar bills.

We'll discuss this new policy at the regular Monday staff meeting, but if you have questions in the meantime, please call me.

- When dealing with something that could conceivably inconvenience people (in this case, limit their travel options), always say why. Make sure there is always some forum for discussing a new policy.

- Bullet format helps readability—and you do want this read and absorbed.

Announcement of New Company Policy, No Smoking (9-24)

Company Name
Address
City, State Zip

To: All Employees

From: Virginia L. Koop, Office Manager

Date:

Subject: Smoking in the Office

As of March 1, employees are not allowed to smoke anywhere in the office, including the restrooms. This policy is mandated by state law, and there can be absolutely no exceptions.

We understand this represents a serious inconvenience for the smokers in the office, so we have expanded the morning and afternoon coffee break period from 10 minutes to 15 minutes to allow time to go outside or to the nearby coffee shop.

- Writing a memo like this is called for only if you are truly creating a new policy. Even then, you may well have to speak to people individually.

- Accommodating employees in some way (here, by extending breaks) is a conciliatory gesture, encouraging cooperation.

Company Name
Address
City, State Zip

To: All Staff

From: Winston Marlowe

Date:

Subject: Fiona Maxwell Wins Annual Super Saver Award

We are very pleased to announce that Fiona Maxwell, our office manager, is the winner of the annual Super Saver Award for her suggestion to reuse and refurbish laser printer cartridges rather than buying new ones. Ms. Maxwell's suggestion has saved the company over $2,000 during the past six months.

As in the past, winners of the Super Saver Award and their guests receive a weekend at the Crystal Palace Resort Hotel in the Ozarks.

Keep those suggestions coming. Send a short description of your suggestion to John Theodore, our Personnel Manager. A brief (four to six sentence) rationale may also be included.

- To be effective, motivational awards should be meaningful (as this one is), and employees should believe that they are capable of achieving them.

- Giving public recognition to the winner of the award and describing the suggestion itself gives employees confidence that they, too, can be rewarded for making a difference.

Announcement of Resignation of Employee (9-26)

Company Name
Address
City, State Zip

To: All Staff

From: T. R. Kellogg

Date: Sam Griffith's Departure

Sam Griffith, Vice-President of Product Marketing, has resigned to start his own marketing consulting firm, Griffith & Associates, in Phoenix. We are sorry to see Sam leave and will miss his sharp, incisive wit, but wish him the best in his new venture.

Those who wish to give Sam a proper send-off are invited for wine and cheese in the 3rd floor conference room on Friday the 23rd at 4 p.m.

- Say what the departing employee will be doing (if he's joining a competitor, you can merely say he's "leaving to join another firm").

- Mention some positive aspect of the person that you will miss.

Company Name
Address
City, State Zip

To: All Staff

From: T. G. Kellogg

Date:

Subject: Loss of Business

I am very sorry to announce that Southeastern Telecommunications, Inc., our largest customer, has decided not to renew its contract with us to supply computer maintenance services. More than 30% of our business was with Southeastern, so the loss of the contract will substantially diminish our operating revenues.

We expect to know the full impact of the contract loss within 30 days. Within that period we will learn whether contract negotiations with several potential customers, which would replace half of the Southeastern revenues, have been successful. I will keep everyone informed as events develop.

Because of the problems we will experience over the next few months, the company has furloughed six service technicians and three home office personnel. Jack Wiggins, Marketing Vice President, has left the company. No further reductions in staff are anticipated.

Our company has grown fast and established an enviable record in its 12-year history. I know that everyone will pull together in the next few months to help us get back on track.

- Be direct about bad news and state plainly its impact—on the company and employees.

- Outline what the company is doing to solve the problems and appeal for cooperation.

- Promise to keep the staff informed—and do so.

Company Name
Address
City, State Zip

To: All Staff

From: Bob Lee

Date:

Subject: Office Move

As you all know, we recently lost the Hechlind Lawn Maintenance and Landscaping account. Hechlind represented over 28% of our annual business, and we're doing everything we can to replace their account by soliciting new clients. In the meantime, however, we'll need to cut overhead costs in every way possible.

Our move to 46 Quinnipiac Place has been postponed indefinitely, and we'll have to endure our overcrowded conditions for a longer period of time. We hope we can make this situation more bearable by adjusting sales representatives' schedules. Clearly, however, we need to discuss contingency plans. I've called a staff meeting for next Monday, to discuss everyone's concerns and answer questions. In the meantime, please call me if you have any questions.

- Make sure people learn the bad news (that you lost the contract) from a company representative, not outside suppliers.

- Set up a meeting to discuss the implications as soon as possible.

- Make any explanation straightforward. Skip convoluted phrasing. People will think they are being conned.

Company Name
Address
City, State Zip

To: All Staff

From: Michelle Voss, Public Affairs

Date:

Subject: Policy Regarding Contacts with News Media

Because of the recent gas leak and explosion at our plant in
Marlborough, some of you have been approached by the local press to
talk about working conditions. I felt it was a good time to reiterate our
policy regarding such matters.

Our policy is simple. All contacts and queries will be referred either
to my office or to the office of the President. No one is to speak for the
company, or speak as an employee of United Manufacturing, except for
myself or Mr. Greenberg. This includes all "off the record" inquiries.

We want to emphasize that we do not wish to cover anything up. But
it is important, especially when there is the threat of lawsuits, that the
company speak with a single voice. We will continue to cooperate with
the authorities on this matter, and we feel that it is important that we all
do our jobs as effectively as we can. We believe that this policy makes
everyone's life easier.

If you have any questions, you may reach me at ext. 500.

- The policy stated in this memo is pretty standard. While it is quite restrictive, it's important not to come on too strong. Be forceful and to the point. Avoid spelling out sanctions.

- Be sure to say that this policy is for everyone's benefit, state the reason for your concern, and give people an opportunity to ask you questions.

Community Service 10

Businesses and their managements play an important role in every community, large or small, that extends far beyond creating products, offering services, or providing employment. Business owners and leaders are frequently called upon to play key roles in community activities. These include local boards, service organizations, and community charities. Whether or not you participate, your responses to these types of requests will be a primary factor in shaping your community image. Therefore, your role (and that of your business) in your community should always be on your mind when writing letters in this area.

Requests, acceptances, and refusals. When writing a request for someone to serve on a board, head up an organization's program or join in a charitable venture, it is tempting to yank hard on the heartstrings. Certainly, stressing the value of an organization's goals, appealing to a sense of obligation, or using images of the downtrodden and unfortunate can be effective, but a little of this goes a long way. You want to write an appeal that gets a response, but sounding self-righteous or maudlin runs the risk of turning people off. The best tack is not to tell people how important, enormous or painful the situation is, but to impress upon them how much of a difference they can make by lending a hand.

Acceptances are the easiest letters to write. Remember to state clearly the amount of effort you are willing to contribute, or the subject of the speech or the content of the article you will write, so as to head off any future misunderstandings. Also, give some reasons why this activity is important to you.

Give reasons why you are refusing something, too. "I don't have enough time" isn't a reason, it's a given. Be more explicit about the demands on your time, leave things open for future contacts, and above all be human. A formal, curt refusal borders on rudeness. Keep in mind that the best reason of all is that you are donating your time to another community activity or service organization.

Fundraising letters. The guidelines set up for requests also apply to fundraising. Don't overdo it. More importantly, don't apologize because you're asking for a donation. Describe briefly the cause for which you are raising money, establishing why it is worthy of support. In asking for a donation of cash, give a range of contributions from a modest amount (relative to those you are soliciting) to a large amount, and let the contributors choose the amount with which they are comfortable.

Follow-up letters are particularly important in fundraising. Every donation must be acknowledged—just as you would send thanks for any gift, but also because people who feel appreciated are likely to give even more generously the next time. For large gifts, a handwritten, personal note is best.

Company Name
Address
City, State Zip

Date

Mr. Ernest Jacobs
42 National Parkway
Litchfield, MI 49252

Dear Mr. Jacobs:

Jack Cimarron has told me that you have been a staunch supporter of
Great Lakes Museum for many years, and I should very much like to
thank you in person. Do you still spend summers in Mackinac Island?
If so, perhaps we could find a time to have lunch when you arrive for the
season in July.

Alternately, you might like to come to the Museum for the opening of the
Voyageurs exhibit in May. Joni and I would be pleased to have you for
dinner first at 31 Glendale Avenue, and we could attend the opening
together. Do let me know.

With best regards,

Cyrus Goya
Chairman of the Board

- This doesn't sound like an "approach" letter, but that's what it is—and everyone concerned knows it.

- Since most major donors are extremely busy, a letter is a polite way to get their attention.

Direct Solicitation, Cash Donation (10-02)

Organization Name
Address
City, State Zip

Date

Mr. and Mrs. Bennett K. Merrill
57 Labrador Street
San Diego, CA 92118

Dear Mr. and Mrs. Merrill,

Our school has been presented with an exciting opportunity. An anonymous donor has offered us a one for two matching grant, based on our ability to raise new dollars.

Since you were willing to stand behind the school when it was in crisis last year, we are turning to you now in hopes of enlisting your support. For every $20 you give, the donor will provide $10 from his grant.

With your help, we have brought the school to a solvent state, and we have greatly broadened our donor base so that we no longer depend on a few benefactors. But much remains to be done—teachers' salaries are still low, the library still needs to add to its collection, and the playing fields require renovation.

Won't you help us take advantage of the donor's challenge and send your check for $20, $50, or $100 today?

Sincerely,

Velda Klein
President
Board of Trustees

• Form letters like these are sometimes unavoidable, but adding a handwritten postscript would personalize it and attract attention.

Organization Name
Address
City, State Zip

Date

Mr. Nick Edmunds
Pilots Unlimited
Cedarbrook Airfield, Building 23
Rahway NJ 07065

Dear Mr. Edmunds:

The Wickwire Tennis Tournament has benefited needy students in our community for the past 10 years, raising an average of $55,000 per year. This year, United Community Bank has once again agreed to be our primary sponsor.

Ronald F. Wickwire, our Superintendent of Schools, has again requested that I, along with Roy Thorpe from United Community Bank, co-chair the Tournament. Last year, as you probably recall, Pilots Unlimited gave the Tournament $500. At the time, you mentioned that you could probably do better than that this year, so we would like to ask you to consider a gift of $1,000. As we have done in previous years, we'll be happy to recognize your contribution in the program and to announce your participation during the Tournament itself.

We hope you will once again help us help our deserving high school graduates. Please make your check payable to the Wickwire Tennis Tournament and send it to the address at the top of this letter.

We look forward to seeing you in May at the Tournament.

Sincerely,

Bethany Stone
Roy Thorpe
Co-chairpersons

- If there are co-chairpersons, both should sign the letter.

- Remind the donor what he/she gave last year. Mention an increased amount. You (almost) never get more than you ask for.

Sender's Name
Address
City, State Zip

Date

Mr. James Glazer
Glazer, Glazer, and Sloan, P.C.
40 Brockcrest Boulevard
Ann Arbor, MI 48103

Dear Jim:

Thank you for taking the time to meet with Rick Stoddard and me
Tuesday in Detroit. I enjoyed meeting you and want you to know how
much we appreciate your information about alumni and others who
might have an interest in supporting Boulder College.

We greatly appreciate your pledge of $1,000. In addition, your advice
and suggestions about potential supporters are very helpful, and I hope
you'll continue to keep us informed about others you may discover.

Many thanks again for your support.

Best wishes,

Greg Daniels

- Naturally, you'll turn all this information over to the professional staff (who may have actually written this letter for you).

- Since you're acting as a volunteer, use a personal letterhead.

Organization Name
Address
City, State Zip

Date

Ms. Beth Davis
2 Peace Canyon Road
Auburn, WA 98002

Dear Beth:

Thank you so much for pledging the two framed Calder posters for our silent auction on May 2. We'll price them to start at $200 each, with the hope that they'll generate so much interest that they'll ultimately go to $500-600.

As we discussed, if you don't find it convenient to bring the prints in by April 15, we'll be glad to pick them up. Let us know.

Again, thank you for supporting the Wolf's Head Day School.

Best wishes,

Susan Woods

- Make it easy for the donor to make good on his or her pledge.

- Express gratitude directly.

Organization Name
Address
City, State Zip

Date

Ms. Lois Baird
378 Conchos Canyon Road
San Bernardino, CA 92405

Dear Ms. Baird:

As Chairman of the Board of the School Volunteers of San Bernardino, I'd like to thank you for your generous gift of $125 toward our summer reading program fund-raising efforts.

Your gift will help make training possible for elementary school aides in the fourth and fifth grades. We appreciate your continued support, and we'll keep you updated on our progress.

Sincerely,

Kerry J. Arlington
Chairman of the Board

- It's important to keep people up-to-date on an organization they have helped. Doing so is an essential part of continuing the relationship. If possible, be specific about how the gift will be used.

- Even if your organization provides a form letter, try to customize it by changing the body or by adding a postscript.

Thank You for Item Donation (10-07)

Sender's Name
Address
City, State Zip

Date

Mr. Patrick Reynolds
67 Buck Deer Way
Billings, MT 59101

Dear Mr. Reynolds:

As chairman of the Frontier Church Lawn Sale, I'd like to thank you personally for your donation of the antique squirrel gun. We understand that the weapon dates back to 1867 and according to Milt Stone, our local appraiser, it is museum-quality. We have every hope that it will fetch close to the $450 appraisal at the sale. As you know, this money will be applied to the restoration of the steeple, which was damaged in the recent tornado.

Thanks so much for your help.

Sincerely,

Mark H. Camden

- Be very explicit in your thanks. Form letters put donors off and may adversely affect future donations.

- The organization will likely thank Mr. Reynolds as well.

Company Name
Address
City, State Zip

Date

Mr. Alfred Motherwell
16 Pawpaw Terrace
Fargo, ND 58102

Dear Al:

I certainly understand that circumstances don't permit your supporting
the Bootstrap Halfway House at this time. We all get solicited for a
great many worthy causes, and everyone must set his own priorities.

When we talked Wednesday, though, I thought I detected some feeling
that you might consider helping us out in six months or so, or at least
that you'd take another look at your circumstances in December. I'll put
it on my calendar and call you then.

Best to Millie,

Eustace C. Cole

- Be persistent, but not obnoxious. People have legitimate reasons for refusing to give—it serves no purpose to lay on the guilt.

- If you say you're going to follow up, make sure you do it, just as you do in business.

Sender's Name
Address
City, State Zip

Date

Mr. Will Baptista
Associate Director of Development
Evergreen Medical Center
1334 Salinas Road
Salinas, CA 93907

Dear Mr. Baptista:

I've enclosed my check #107 for $1,000.00 to be applied toward the Dr. Hernando Rojas Memorial Center. As we discussed on the phone, Dr. Rojas was not only a superb physician, but also a great personal friend, and I am delighted to be able to help in the effort to memorialize his name.

Sincerely,

Herbert Frawley

- When making contributions, always indicate the use to which you wish them put—unless you are supplying an unrestricted gift (which is always welcome from the organization's point of view).

- If this were a business contribution, you would naturally write this letter on a business letterhead.

Company Name
Address
City, State Zip

Date

Mr. Robert Rolfe
Patrolmen's Assistance Organization
227 44th Street
Paterson, NJ 07514

Dear Mr. Rolfe:

I am very sorry that we will not be able to make our usual contribution to the Patrolmen's Assistance Organization Annual Ball this year. As you can see from our letterhead, we have moved our offices to an adjoining town and we are sure we will be called upon to support the policemen's association here. We wish you good luck with your fund-raising efforts.

Best wishes,

Augustine Birch
President

- If you're turning someone down, keep it simple. Convoluted explanations sound defensive.

- Writing a letter like this may forestall a series of increasingly persistent phone calls.

Sender's Name
Address
City, State Zip

Date

Mr. Gordon Winks
34 Hunt Club Drive
Clearwater, FL 33515

Dear Gordy:

As you know from your long tenure as Recording Knight of the Knights of the Roundtable, one of the last tasks of the program manager is finding a replacement. I've had a great time organizing things this past year, and I'd like to ask you to be program manager next year. Naturally, I'll be glad to help you in any way possible. I have files galore—and a list of many people I have already approached who said they'd be glad to address our group but couldn't fit it into their schedule this year. They'd be ideal candidates for the coming year.

Please call me or drop me a note and let me know what you think.

Best,

Paul W. Wishman

- If you are asking someone to act as your replacement, always offer to help in any way possible. Make the offer attractive by being specific about how you can make the job easier.

Company Name
Address
City, State Zip

Date

Mr. Milton Ponesby
45 Old Houston Road
Waco, TX 76710

Dear Milt:

I'm happy to hear from Howard Bussey that you're considering serving as development chairman for the 100th Anniversary celebration of the founding of our hometown. As chairman, I just want to make our invitation official.

As Howard mentioned to you, he had already gotten the campaign largely organized before his bank told him they were transferring him to New Orleans. Of the $230,000 we're aiming for, Howard tells me we already have firm commitments for $100,000, and, of course, the campaign has not even been announced yet.

I'm not saying there isn't a great deal of effort ahead, but I'm convinced that your energy and leadership will put us quickly over the top. I look forward to hearing you say "yes" at lunch next Wednesday.

Best to Sally,

Errol Dartmouth
Chairman
100th Anniversary Committee

- Development chairpersons are crucial to any endeavor, and this letter represents part of a long courtship. It's likely that the chairperson has tried to reach the reader by phone but has been frustrated by telephone tag.

Asking Individual to Serve as Board Member (10-13)

Sender's Name
Address
City, State Zip

Date

Ms. Pat Riddle
101 White Oak Farms
Warren, OH 44400

Dear Pat:

I truly enjoyed our lunch Wednesday, and I'm very excited by the prospect of your joining the board of the Mianus Toy Museum. As we discussed, I'm setting up a luncheon with Harry Klein, Ralph Delieto, and Jane Brainherd so you can meet some of the key members of the committees in which you're most interested. I'll call you in a week or so, after I've talked to them.

Again, I hope you decide to join us. The Museum board needs people like you.

Best wishes,

Hilda Forrest
(Mrs. Holden Liddy)

- You should issue invitations of this sort in person, following up with a letter confirming the items discussed and stating the next steps to be taken.

- If a woman chooses to use her husband's name, she should use this form for the signature.

Company Name
Address
City, State Zip

Date

Mr. Leb Wiley
40 Lone Star Circle
Laredo, TX 78040

Dear Leb:

I'm absolutely delighted you'll be serving with me on the board of the Texas Ranger Collection. You'll find that the chairman, Joe Tewkes, runs productive meetings and that we really get things accomplished.

As I said when we met a month ago, we can really use someone with your legal background to guide us in some of the fine points of deferred giving.

Welcome,

Stephen Walton

- It's great to feel welcome in any new position. Don't forget to extend this rule to community service as well.

- Underscore the particular area in which the new member will be expected to contribute.

Company Name
Address
City, State Zip

Date

Ms. Hattie Winston
344 Ala Moana Place
Honolulu, HI 96818

Dear Hattie:

I'm honored that you've asked me to serve on the board of Walk Against Want. Unfortunately, I'm simply overcommitted this year. I'm sorry I misled you during our lunch last week. I greatly respect the work Walk Against Want does with the homeless. But I took a good look at my calendar, and decided that it simply wouldn't be fair to take on anything else.

I will be going off the Board of Deacons next year, and that will provide me with a block of time for other volunteer activities. I hope you'll think of me again.

Best wishes,

Leila G. Good
Executive Vice President

- If you must say no, do so gracefully. You don't have to list all the commitments that make it impossible for you to say yes—doing so sounds a bit too much like whining.

- If you do want to leave the door open, tell the reader when to ask you again.

Solicitation of Votes for Election to Board (10-16)

Organization Name
Address
City, State Zip

Date

Dear Association Member:

Our association has always prided itself on the proportion of members who vote in board elections. Last year, for example, over 75% of you cast ballots for candidates for the board of directors, and we hope to better that percentage this year.

Some of you have expressed concern that you could not make an informed choice on the basis of the information we have provided in the past. As a result, we have expanded our biographical coverage of each candidate in the enclosed election kit. We hope that this additional information will enable you to cast your vote with more confidence.

The nominating committee selected the nine candidates from names recommended by the membership. Please vote for three (and only three) of the candidates by marking the attached ballot and returning it in the enclosed envelope.

Your vote can make a difference.

Sincerely,

Gertrude S. Sweet
Chairman

Enclosures

- Make it easy for people to vote. Provide an envelope (with postage, if the association can afford it). Give people the assurance that even if they don't know the candidates, they can still make an informed choice.

- It doesn't hurt to appeal to people's competitive spirit or to indicate that you've responded to the members' comments by providing additional information.

Company Name
Address
City, State Zip

Date

Mr. Andrew Ortega
Santa Cruz Board of Realtors
1114 Bayside Avenue
Santa Cruz, CA 95060

Dear Mr. Ortega:

I would be very proud to serve as a member of the Santa Cruz Board of Realtors. I understand that members serve for two-year terms and that my tenure begins in two weeks, on September 2.

I also understand that there will be a swearing-in ceremony on September 2. My office would like to send a photographer, if that would be allowed. If you could call my office to confirm the details, I would appreciate it.

I look forward to our first meeting. If you need anything from me, just call.

Sincerely,

Sally Benson

- Put your acceptance and appreciation in the opening.

- Define the terms of your acceptance.

- Make sure that any requests on your part (the photographer) are clearly stated.

Company Name
Address
City, State Zip

Date

Mr. Peter Spender
Membership Chairperson
Local Industry Council
2600 Sarasota Road
Syracuse, NY 13204

Dear Pete:

I appreciate your thinking of me, but I won't be able to join the Local Industry Council this year. I understand all the advantages, especially the opportunity to talk with other business owners on a regular basis. That's something I've missed since leaving Mammoth Construction—the contact with peers.

So you've made a good pitch, but I'm heavily committed this year, as I believe I mentioned. Keep me in mind, though. I expect my schedule to free up considerably after the end of June.

Best wishes,

J. William Forrester

- Give a reason for turning down the offer.

- If you have an interest in being asked to join at a later date, indicate this.

Company Name
Address
City, State Zip

Date

Mrs. Judd Stevens
The Caring Society
89 Appleyard Street
Dallas, TX 75201

Dear Jill:

I regret that Tom and I will not be able to attend The Caring Society's Dinner Dance next month. We are planning a vacation and will be out of state.

We do, however, insist on purchasing two tickets for the dance. Enclosed is my check for $150.00.

We are sorry we won't be there. It's always such a wonderful evening, and for such a good cause.

Sincerely,

Cindy Harms

Enclosure

- Keep it brief and to the point. You want to stay on the guest list for future events, but there's no need to write a novel about it.

Company Name
Address
City, State Zip

Date

Mr. Louis Cabrisi
Managing Editor
The Orange County Bulletin
1102 Anaheim Boulevard
Santa Ana, CA 92701

Dear Mr. Cabrisi:

I would very much like to contribute to The Bulletin's upcoming special report on the housing crisis in Orange County. I understand from our phone conversation that the deadline for submissions is November 16.

As a real-estate professional, I feel I have an important perspective to explore. There is a lot that developers in Orange County can be doing to relieve the crunch in affordable housing, but first perceptions must be changed. Too many people hear the term "affordable housing" and have visions of poorly constructed apartment houses slowly turning to slums. But what "affordable housing" really means is being able to afford living in the town in which you work. Diversity is good for our towns. There is room for everyone.

These are the issues I want to write about. I will submit an article of approximately 1,500 words.

If there is anything else you expect from your contributors, please contact me at my office.

Sincerely,

Michele Grimbell

- Tell them in your letter what you intend to write about, even if you've discussed it already. Some things look a lot different on paper than in conversation, and you don't want to do all that work and not get published.

- Always confirm the deadline and length of the article.

Company Name
Address
City, State Zip

Date

Mr. Anthony L. Feinstein
Community Relations Director
Mystic Utilities
255 Fifth Street
San Francisco, CA 94123

Dear Mr. Feinstein:

Our bimonthly luncheon group, Businessperson's Nosh (BPN), would very much like to have someone from your company address our group on the use of alternative energy sources in the Bay Area. As you may be aware, BPN prides itself on its socially responsible approach to all business decisions. Our members are especially interested in the steps Mystic Utilities is taking to reduce dependence on fossil fuels and nuclear energy.

We are currently scheduling programs for the fall season, and we have meetings on the first and third Wednesday of every month. I'll call you in a week to see who from your company would be willing to speak to us. We appreciate your help.

Sincerely yours,

Hap Forrest
Program Chairman
Businessperson's Nosh

- It's only fair to tell a potential speaker what kind of group you're asking him or her to address. In this case, that information will help the community relations director pick the right person.

- Follow up with a phone call.

Company Name
Address
City, State Zip

Date

Mr. Albert Lithgow
Center for Financial Studies
18 Old Bank Road
Amherst, MA 01002

Dear Mr. Lithgow:

I gladly accept your invitation to speak at the upcoming Western Massachusetts Business Seminar. I understand my speech will be at 2:30 p.m. on June 14, to be followed by a reception.

My speech will be on the topic "State Sources for Small Business Financing." I will be prepared to talk for 45 minutes and answer questions from the audience. There will also be some printed materials to be distributed and a chart that I will refer to in my speech. If you could provide an easel for the chart, that would be helpful.

Thank you again for the invitation. See you on the 14th!

Very truly yours,

Julia Ethier

- The acceptance, when, and where, go in the first paragraph.

- Be sure the topic is established, as well as the length of the talk. Any special needs you have, such as a slide projector or blackboard, should be in the letter.

Confirmation of Individual's Agreement to Speak (10-23)

Company Name
Address
City, State Zip

Date

Mr. George Sorensen
Torrence, Dale, and Booker
50 Everitt Street
Norwalk, CT 06854

Dear Mr. Sorensen:

I'm delighted you'll be addressing the New Businesses in the 1990s Conference on May 25 at the Orange Roof Hotel in Norwalk. As we discussed, you'll talk about "Investments for Entrepreneurs" at the luncheon meeting. The luncheon starts at 12 noon, and you'll be speaking from 12:30 to 1:00, with an additional 15 minutes allocated for questions.

I am particularly interested in what equipment (for example, an overhead projector, 35-mm slide projector, or chart easels) you'll need. If you'll let me know your requirements by April 29, I'll have plenty of time to ensure that the hotel provides you with what you need. If you are providing your own equipment and will need help bringing it into the ballroom, please let me know and I'll arrange for assistance.

I will call you the second week in April to make sure everything is in order. Again, thank you for agreeing to speak. Everyone is looking forward to hearing your views.

Sincerely yours,

Lowell Whiffen
Program Chairman

- Ask an individual to speak in person or on the phone—confirm the details in writing as soon as possible.

- Always stipulate a time limit for the speech and the Q-and-A session. Also, give a deadline for requesting equipment. Make the deadline at the month's end, not the beginning—people always assume they have the full month, whatever the actual date.

Company Name
Address
City, State Zip

Date

Ms. Marina K. Loundsberry
Executive Editor
Executive Communications, Inc.
2346 Pinewood Avenue
Madison, WI 53704

Dear Ms. Loundsberry:

I enjoyed talking with you last week and very much appreciate your invitation to participate next month in Executive Communications' workshop as the speaker on "Utilizing Facsimile Machines and Electronic Mail." As you know, I am a great believer, and user, of these new advances in telecommunications.

Unfortunately, I will be on my annual tour of the company's domestic offices during the seminar and cannot break away even for a day, so I will have to decline the invitation.

If you have other workshops in the future that will feature the same subject, I would be glad to speak, schedule permitting.

Sincerely,

John Greene
Vice President

- Whether declining or accepting, clearly identify the subject matter for the letter's recipient— who is probably trying to schedule many speakers.

- Leave the door open for future contact.

Sender's Name
Address
City, State Zip

Date

Mr. Rand Ingram
President, Boulder Board of Realtors
c/o Ingram and McDonald Realty
42 Baseline Drive
Boulder, CO 80302

Dear Rand:

I am extremely honored to have been chosen Realtor of the Year by the Boulder Board of Realtors. As you are aware, I have lived and worked in Boulder all my life (not a mean feat in these days of mobility), and it's always especially gratifying to be recognized in one's home town.

I understand from your letter that the banquet is at the Boulderado Hotel at 7 p.m. on September 30. My husband and I would be pleased to attend. Do I need to prepare any remarks, or is a simple "thank you" all that's required?

As you requested, I've enclosed a biography and a 5x7 glossy photograph for you to use for publicity purposes. Please be sure to credit the photographer, Michael Snow, whose name and address are printed on the back.

Thank you again for the honor.

Best wishes,

Sarah L. Perkins

Enclosures

- When accepting an honor, warm appreciation should shine through your letter.

- Make sure you help the person coordinating the event by providing photographs, bios, and other publicity materials.

Sender's Name
Address
City, State Zip

Date

Mr. Henry Stone
Chairman, Board of Directors
The Slater-Neville Nursery School
40 Mesquite Drive
Tucson, AZ 86700

Dear Henry:

I'm sorry to have to tell you that I will be resigning from the Board as of June 30, the last day of the spring semester. As you know, Samantha will be entering a pre-K program in the fall, and I feel that I should be expending my energy in helping her new institution.

You know you can count on me for continued financial support and advice, and I will be pleased to counsel you about fund-raising matters as I have in the past. I have greatly enjoyed working with you and all the other members of the Board, and I gained a great deal from your wisdom and sane approach to problem-solving under difficult conditions.

All the best,

Matthew Rowe

- Relationships are everything in business and community service. You may be leaving the Board, but you want to make sure that the relationship continues.

- If you have a legitimate excuse for leaving, mention it. If you have some other issue—a personality conflict, perhaps—this letter is definitely not the place to air it. If you want to get it off your chest, do so in person.

The pleasure of your company

is cordially requested at the

TENTH ANNIVERSARY CELEBRATION

of the

Permanent Commission

on Small Business Advancement

Wednesday, May 25

7:00 p.m.

Statler Inn
56 Wildwoode Courtyard
Greenville, South Carolina

Donation: $35 per person   Dinner
R.S.V.P. before May 22nd to 562-3441

- This invitation provides all the necessary information, but it should be accompanied by a self-addressed stamped envelope and response card for maximum return.

Please make _____ reservation(s) at $35 per person for the 10th Anniversary Celebration of the Permanent Commission on Business Advancement, May 25 at the Statler Inn, Greenville.

*NAME:*_____

*ADDRESS:*_____

*CITY:*_____ *STATE:*_____ *ZIP:*_____

*PHONE:*_____

Please find my check enclosed payable to the Permanent Commission on Business Advancement for the amount of $_____.
(Please list guests on reverse side)

Tickets will not be mailed to you.
Reservations will be held at the door.

- Make it easy for people to let you know they'll attend by providing a response card like this one and a stamped reply envelope.

Organization Name
Address
City, State Zip

Date

Ms. Linda Glickson
Coordinator, Community Programs
Arrowhead Mechanical, Inc.
4023 Merrill Drive
Madison, WI 53704

Dear Ms. Glickson:

Please thank everyone at Arrowhead Mechanical for the hospitality they extended to our high school physics teachers last Friday. We had a "debriefing" Monday, and our teachers had unanimous praise for the way your engineers explained the basic principles behind your newest designs. They felt, for example, that your main speakers, Drs. Kaplan, Williams, and York, geared their remarks precisely to the level of the teachers' experience and education.

They also expressed appreciation for the patience and enthusiasm of Mr. Andrews and Ms. Coburn, the technicians who led them through the laboratory.

Thank you again for all the help you've given us in our continuing education program. Once again, your people have surpassed themselves. The photograph we took will be featured in our April newsletter. I'll send you several copies to distribute and post.

Best wishes,

Stanley Bossner

- After showering the company with general gratitude, be specific about who deserves the thanks.

- Since the company hopes for good PR from these outings, be sure to note that their help will be recognized in print, if you can.

Job Search 11

Often, job seekers focus on a successful interview as the most important part of their search. However, getting the right job can also depend on well-written correspondence sent before and after the job offer. Because a prospective employer is likely to "meet" you on paper before he or she meets you in person, your written communication can work for or against you.

Before the job search begins. Clear communication results from clear thinking. In order to express who you are, what you have to offer, and what you need, be sure you have done your homework first. Identify your competencies and be able to articulate them verbally and on the written page.

Your resume should express relevant experience, achievements, and skills. While resumes vary in type and format, as the examples in this section do, their function is to communicate the best possible match between your skills and the employer's needs.

You may be interested in a certain profession without knowing much about it. Arrange an appointment to talk with someone working in that field. Ask him or her specific questions in order to learn as much about the job as you can. This is called conducting an information interview.

Although some information interviews result from contacting people you don't know, most are arranged on the recommendation of a mutual acquaintance. In your letter requesting an appointment, mention the source of your referral. Enclose a resume to provide more information about yourself to the interviewee. Always send thank-you letters to the mutual acquaintance and the person you interviewed. If a person is significant in helping you get the job you want, send an updating letter expressing further appreciation.

Learning about job openings. If the job you seek is advertised, your main task is to persuade the employer to interview you. Both your resume and your cover letter should be designed to motivate the reader to learn more about you. The same applies if you are writing to an executive search firm or making an unsolicited contact in a company. As always, follow up requests for information with appropriate thank-you letters.

Quite often, knowledge about job openings is shared through personal contacts, either written or verbal. The key is to develop and maintain a network of people who can pass along helpful information. You can build your job search network the same way you locate a good auto mechanic when you're new in town—ask people who are likely to know.

When writing to people you want in your network, send a brief letter explaining what you are looking for and how they can help. Ask them to refer you to a person or place. Follow up with a cordial letter thanking them for the referral.

Pursuing job leads. When you have pinpointed a job opening that you want to pursue or a company that you want to work for, write a request for an interview. Of course, follow up with a thank-you letter after the interview. If, after the interview, you know you're not interested in the position, be appreciative and complimentary and leave it at that. If you are interested, tell them why and reiterate what you have to offer the firm.

When you are offered the job. If you do not want the position at all, send a cordial and polite rejection letter. Thank them and give a brief reason for your decision. If the offer is acceptable, send an acceptance letter with attention to the details.

If you are interested in the position but have further questions, thank the prospective employer for the offer and ask for an appointment to discuss your concerns. You may then choose to accept the job outright, or to express further interest but with conditions and explanations for them. At this point, you can negotiate the revised job offer in a clearly stated letter, or accept or reject the restated offer.

Throughout the job search process. Double and triple check your correspondence and resume for mistakes in word usage, grammar, typing, etc. Make sure you have the proper spelling of names. A slip-up in this area can doom your chances for the job.

Sender's Name
Address
City, State Zip

Date

Mr. Ralph Tweed
Tweed and Sons
404 East Packer Highway
Evanston, IL 60201

Dear Ralph:

Please accept my resignation from Tweed and Sons, effective April 1. I have recently been offered an opportunity to move into sales management at Textrex, Inc. and have decided that this position best suits my professional goals.

Leaving Tweed and Sons was not an easy decision. My four years with the company have been both personally and professionally rewarding, and I appreciate the interest you have shown in my career since I joined the company. I wish the company only the best for the future. I will always be proud to say I started my career in sales with Tweed and Sons.

Thank you again.

Best regards,

Sarah P. Stanton

- Even if your experience in your current job has been an unending nightmare, try to leave on a positive, cordial note. It is never wise to burn your bridges behind you.

- Let your employer know where you are moving and why. Express sincere thanks for something the company has done for you, and wish your employer well.

Company Name
Address
City, State Zip

Date

Mr. Mark Coburn
Coburn Allen Associates
3000 Wheeler Street
Stamford, CT 06906

Dear Mr. Coburn:

I understand that you are attempting to recruit a vice-president, marketing, for a small family-owned trucking firm in the Midwest. I have enclosed my resume. We should talk because:

- I have 10 years of successively more responsible positions in marketing in the transportation industry. My achievements in each position were substantial.

- My family lives in Michigan, and I am eager to relocate to that area.

I will call you in a week to see if we can find a mutually convenient time to meet.

Sincerely,

Fabian T. Lorimer

Enclosure

- Executive search firms usually ignore unsolicited resumes. Don't waste your time unless you know that they're looking for someone with your credentials (it pays to network) and you can offer them something special or unique (your willingness to relocate to the Midwest, for example).

Company Name
Address
City, State Zip

Date

Mr. Paul K. Curry
Curry & Associates
175 Starr Avenue, Suite 26
Melbourne, FL 32919

Dear Mr. Curry:

I enjoyed our interview Friday, and I wanted to get back to you as soon as possible. As you know, Co-Ark Chemical has given me a choice of two outplacement firms, and I do want to have a basis of comparison.

We agreed that:

- Curry & Associates will provide secretarial support for a 500-letter direct-mail campaign, with each letter personalized and proofread.

- I will dictate an unlimited number of individual letters.

- I have full and unencumbered use of an office.

I need to know:

- Is there any limit on phone calls? Local? Long-distance? As you know, verifying names sometimes requires a great many brief calls.

I'll call you next week to discuss these items.

Sincerely,

Stephen M. Forrester

- Outplacement firms offer a great many services, but it's good to pin them down to specifics.

- Just because you've been fired or layed off doesn't mean that you don't have a right to be assertive.

Tamara Paul
21 Schmidt Avenue
New Haven, CT 06514
(203) 787-5210

Education

1986-1988   Yale School of Management, New Haven, CT
Candidate for Master's degree in Public and Private Management,
May 1988. Emphasis in marketing and strategic planning.

1980-1984   Oberlin College, Oberlin, OH
BA in Economics
Comfort Starr Fellowship
Appointed student member of President's Advisory Committee on
Budgetary Affairs. Member of Student Organization Funding
Committee.

Experience

Summer 1987   American Consumer Products, Westport, CT
Corporate Market Analysis and Planning
Developed and evaluated forecasts by market sectors. Analyzed
sensitivity of demand to cannibalization, economic scenarios, and
technological change. Presented findings to top management.

1985-1986   Data Management Corporation, New York, NY
Project Director
Directed marketing research projects from study design through
analysis of data and report-writing.

Provided manufacturers/advertising agencies with primary research
data used to:
- develop marketing strategies
- forecast new product potential
- optimize product growth and penetration
- identify sales opportunities

Tamara Paul   -2-

1984	Thomas Marketing Research, New York, NY Junior Project Director Designed questionnaires, analyzed data, and wrote reports. Account responsibility included Chesebrough-Ponds and Gillette.
Summer 1982-1983	Brewington Associates, Summit, NJ Market Research Field Assistant Acted as liaison between project directors and field force. Aided in the direction and supervision of data-gathering staff of 60 supervisors and 200 interviewers.

Professional Affiliations

American Marketing Association 1984-present
Junior Achievement Counselor 1985-present

- If your most recent educational credential is vastly more impressive than your work experience, you should highlight it by giving it star billing, providing it bears directly on the job you want.

- The job descriptions are functional and give the employer a "hook" so that he or she can think, "This woman can do what I need to have done—forecasts and market research reports—and her presentation skills must be first-rate."

BRIAN B. POTTER
28 Trumbull Street
New Britain, Connecticut 06050
(203) 777-2943

1988-Present **LEGISLATIVE AIDE,** Connecticut General Assembly, Hartford, CT. Clerk for the Substance Abuse Prevention Committee. Review proposed legislation, organize public hearings and meetings. Prepare statements and letters for State Representative.

1987 **FLOOR DIRECTOR,** Tom McDonough Show. WTBV-TV, New Haven, CT. Directed all communications between talent and crew. Managed all aspects of studio while taping, ran camera. Show seen in 104 markets nationwide.

1984-87 **PUBLIC ACCESS COORDINATOR and PRODUCTION MANAGER.** Cable Times, Norwalk, CT. Responsible for creating community programming using community volunteers. Worked with the local governments and school systems in lower Fairfield County to produce programs.

1983-84 **NEWS and FEATURE ASSISTANT.** WCBC-TV, New York. Collected and organized facts on developing news for producers and reporters. Premium placed on interview skills, accuracy, and ability to work under a daily deadline.

1983 **VIDEO WRITER/DIRECTOR,** Training Center, Metro Railroad, New York. Produced training and promotional tapes for internal use.

BRIAN B. POTTER   -2-

EDUCATION

GRADUATE SCHOOL OF CORPORATE AND POLITICAL COMMUNICATIONS, FAIRLEE UNIVERSITY, Fairlee, CT. M.A. Thesis in progress. Media, Organizational Communications.

COLGATE UNIVERSITY, Hamilton, NY. B.A. 1982. Graduated with Honors in English. Emphasis on writing.

- Be thorough and clear. Put yourself in the best light but don't inflate or lie. If you get caught, you definitely ruin your chances for landing a job. Don't be ashamed of blank spots in your resume. Many people have had periods of unemployment.

- Work experience is the most important category, so put it first. If you want to include an objective, that should go before work experience.

Thomas Kitter
23 North High Street
East Haven, CT 06512
(203) 555-1813 (Home)

Business
Experience

1978-Present   CARLETON ASSOCIATES   Boston, MA
Consulting assignments for many clients, including development
of comprehensive business plan for publishing venture;
management control system and functional reorganization of
newly spun-off company; financial projections and cash flow
planning for entrepreneur.

1970-1978   TRIAD CORPORATION   New York, NY
Sales and Marketing Consultant for this OTC-traded company.
Responsibilities included identification of new markets for
company's "Dial Us" information retrieval and order-taking
services; cost analysis and development of pricing policy; creation
of new sales materials. Sold firm's services to major prospects.
Recommendations resulted in creation of new direct marketing
division, now making substantial contribution to Triad's bottom
line.

1969-1970   AMERICAN HOMES QUARTERLY   Springfield, MA
Assistant Director of Marketing. Responsible for devising and
implementing marketing strategies for this 150,000-circulation
magazine and executive relocation service. Created advertiser-
sponsored "welcome to Springfield" kit; developed relocation
business through direct mail campaign and personal contact with
personnel directors. Sold long-term advertising contracts to major
manufacturing firms.

1968-1969   WILSON TOYS   Providence, RI
Management training. Worked first as apprentice on assembly
line to acquire "feel" for how production really works. Then
completed training programs in Sales, Marketing, and Finance
divisions.

Thomas Kitter
Page 2

Education
1964-1968   BROWN UNIVERSITY
BA with concentration in urban and American studies. Feature
writer for *The Brown Daily Herald*.

References available upon request.

- Mid-career resumes may or may not have a "career objective" at the top. The writer clearly felt that including such an objective would be limiting, especially since there is no obvious "next step."

BRIAN B. POTTER
28 Trumbull Street
New Britain, Connecticut 06050
(203) 777-2943

Proven Abilities to:

- Develop effective communications using a variety of media, including written and video communications.

- Work within the structures of public policy and government and anticipate the needs of public policy makers.

- Work with community leaders and public officials and enhance the image of the company within the community.

- Collect, organize, and analyze information clearly and effectively.

Achievements:

- Prepared testimony for State Representative. Handled sensitive constituent contact. Analyzed impact of proposed legislation.

- Participated in daily production of popular daytime talk show seen in 104 markets nationwide. Fluent in all aspects of video production: camera, directing, editing.

- Worked on the assignment desk in local news in New York City television. Set up interviews, investigated and created story ideas.

- Managed production crews for a variety of community television programs. Worked with community leaders to produce educational and informational programs.

BRIAN B. POTTER   -2-

Career Summary:

CONNECTICUT GENERAL ASSEMBLY, Legislative Aide, 1988-Present
TOM McDONOUGH SHOW, Floor Director, 1987
CABLE TIMES, Public Access Coordinator and Production Manager, 1984-87
WCBC-TV, New York, News and Feature Assistant, 1983-1984
METRO RAILROAD, Video Writer and Director, 1983

- This type of resume requires some tough editing. You must constantly ask yourself if information must be included and if it is being presented fairly and accurately. Don't over-inflate yourself, and don't be ambiguous. If you accomplished something, include it—don't dance around what was a group effort.

George F. Shepherd
1209 Dixworth Avenue
Marietta, Georgia 30060
(404) 953-4096 (home)

OBJECTIVE: Entry into Commercial Development via position as Construction Representative.

EMPLOYMENT: HARTWELL CONSTRUCTION COMPANY, Atlanta, GA
Project Engineer/Manager, June 1984 - present

- Project experience includes:
600,000-square-foot, class A office building for major U.S. corporation ($45 million).
Structural steel retail building located downtown Atlanta on air rights ($2 million).
Ten-story state educational facility ($10 million).
New 60,000-square-foot country club facility with elaborate interior work. Also demolition of existing facility ($3 million).
Several urban office building renovations, including extensive base-building and tenant fit-up construction ($1-2 million each).
- Oversee all phases of project estimating, bid, proposal, start-up, contract negotiation, extensive drawing and specification review, change orders, coordination, scheduling, and close-out.
- Inherited one project running at a loss and brought to completion at substantial profit.
- Played a major role in successful negotiation for project with first-time client. Subsequent performance as Project Manager assured further business with client.
- Successfully and profitably managed complex project built over railroad air rights. Project had been declined by other contractors due to technical difficulty.
- Brought projects within budget by working closely with owners/ architects on value engineering.

George F. Shepherd
Page 2

CHASE MANHATTAN BANK N.A., New York, NY
Trade Finance Department Officer, June 1979 - August 1983

- Acted as liaison between marketing and operations.
- Performed market studies to assess competition, pricing, areas for new product development, and other market characteristics.
- Assisted lending officers in problem-solving and developing marketing strategies and presentation for clients.

EDUCATION: GEORGIA INSTITUTE OF TECHNOLOGY, Atlanta, GA
Master of Science in Construction Management, School of Civil Engineering, 1984. GPA 3.6

- Intensive study of all aspects of construction management with a blend of academic and practical application. Heavy engineering and computer course format.
- Courses in Land Use Planning, Project Feasibility
- Analysis, Construction Accounting, Engineering Economics and Scheduling.
- Received research grant for work on computer programming of the CYCLONE scheduling model.

UNIVERSITY OF NEVADA-RENO, Reno, NV
Bachelor of Arts in Economics, 1979. GPA 3.7

- Graduated with distinction.

REFERENCES: Furnished upon request.

- This is an achievement-oriented resume with a chronological arrangement.

- The "objective" provides the needed focus.

JESSICA MARIE COLLINS
29 Fairgrounds Road
Durham, California 95928
(916) 435-7483

CAREER OBJECTIVE
A responsible position in the management and operations of a community service agency.

EDUCATION

Holmes School of Theology, Asuncion, New Mexico
Master of Divinity 1987

St. Dymphna College, North River, Minnesota
Bachelor of Arts in Religion and Social Services 1983

WORK EXPERIENCE

1983-Present

Archives Assistant
Holmes School of Theology Library, Asuncion, California
• Organized and processed archival papers of missionaries to China.
• Assisted patrons with research.
• Research Assistant for Asian Missionaries Indexing Project.

1985

Intern
California Food Bank, Chico, California
• Coordinated a four-month long, state-wide food drive in cooperation with the Governor's office.
• Recruited and trained food-drive volunteers throughout the state.
• Wrote instructional pamphlet for local food drive organizers.

JESSICA MARIE COLLINS   -2-

1981-83   Director of Children's Education
                           Grace Community Church, North River, California
                           • Directed the Sunday School of 75 children and 9
                             teachers.
                           • Administrated all church activities involving children.
                           • Initiated and implemented numerous seasonal and
                             liturgical celebrations and events.
                           • Recruited, trained, and supervised over 25 volunteers.

RELATED EXPERIENCE
                           • Board member on Publicity and Budget Committees of
                             Asuncion Area United Way Board of Directors.
                           • Attended three-day conference on "The Challenge of
                             Hometown Hunger" 1983. Taught a workshop on
                             "Training Volunteers in Food Banks" at same event.
                             Have taken numerous workshops on community
                             service topics such as housing, daycare, and
                             fundraising.
                           • Researched and wrote a 40-page Senior Thesis
                             entitled "Conflict and Cooperation among Social
                             Service Agencies in the Greater North River Area."
                             Received Honors with Distinction.

References available on request.

• A combination chronological and functional resume is often a good choice for the entry-level
  applicant. It communicates recent career preparation and relevant experience.

• Note the careful choice of verbs to communicate skills in organizing, training,
  administrating, and working with the public. The more specific the verb, the better.

PETER A. HASKINS
1741 Lancaster Drive
Othello, Washington 98902
(403) 483-8784

Innovative <u>Human Resources Director</u> with in-depth fifteen years of experience in personnel development. Analytical, research-oriented, and persuasive with strong skills in teaching and writing. Highly motivated and enthusiastic about sharing both private and public sector expertise with graduate students in business or public administration.

PERSONNEL ADMINISTRATION

Director of Personnel and Employee Relations, 1980-Present
Freedland Mining Company, Reno, Nevada
> Reporting to the Division President, managed five assistants and coordinated functions in support of Division operations.
> - Initiated and managed a cost reduction campaign that resulted in 27% reduction in controlled operating expenses.
> - Identified division-wide training needs and priorities to improve existing program. Impact: reduced turnover in staff and notable improvement in services, productivity, and morale.

Manager of Personnel Services, 1972-80
West Coast Gas and Electric Company, Fresno, California
> Chief Officer for staffing, compensation, training, benefits, and labor relations. Was invited to implement a Management Development program. This resulted in:
> - Initiation of customized management training program that became a model for the West Coast region.
> - Expansion of college relations program with target MBA schools.

PETER A. HASKINS   -2-

TEACHING AND TRAINING

Job-Related
- Designed and conducted numerous training events ranging from half-day seminars to five-day off-site events. Topics ranged from organizational behavior theory to recent legislative changes.

Private
- Taught night division course in Public Administration at University of Nevada at Reno, 1981-Present.
- Taught two courses in Personnel Development at Fresno Community College, 1975-77.

PUBLICATIONS

Training and Development Journal, May 1985. "The Role of the Personnel Director in a Downsizing Organization."

Personnel Journal, Winter 1981. "Does Your Company Know the Law?"

EDUCATION

Master of Public Administration. Rice University, Houston, Texas. 1972

Bachelor of Arts in Political Science, Cooper College, Ames, Iowa. 1969

- When you've got solid experience, focus your resume on your achievements and credentials. Stress the data that match the needs of the prospective employer and can lead to an interview.

- Be as specific as space allows when describing the impact of your work. Quantify the results when appropriate; for example, the percentage of costs that were reduced.

CURRICULUM VITAE
RICHARD RUNDLETT
677 Vista Road
Virginia Beach, VA 29483
(407) 374-2938

Richard Rundlett is an attorney in private practice in Virginia Beach, Virginia. He specializes in litigation on behalf of organizations dedicated to ecological protection and social justice. Since earning his J.D. from the University of Virginia in 1970, his clients have ranged from small, local organizations to nationally recognized movements. Greenpeace, People against Acid Rain, Citizens for a Nuclear Free Future, The Crusade Against Hunger, and Mothers Against Drunk Drivers are among his clients.

Prior to his law career, Richard served parishes in New England and the Midwest as a clergyman in the United Church of Christ for 12 years. Following his graduation from Andover-Newton School of Theology, in Massachusetts, he pastored both urban and rural congregations. These included a "three-point parish" in northern Montana where he traveled to three churches in a 150-mile radius to conduct services every week.

Richard's deep commitment to social justice and ecological concerns grows out of his experiences in high school and college. During that time, he lived on Whidby Island in the Puget Sound near Seattle, Washington. He saw the consequences of marine and air pollution, oil spills, and inadequate planning for environmental impact. He also became active in protecting the fishing rights of Native Americans in the Pacific Northwest. While completing a Bachelor's degree in Political Science at Washington State University, he "tested the legal waters" by working as a paralegal in a community service agency.

Richard lives near Virginia Beach with his wife and has two grown children. He spends his free time gardening and doing amateur photography. He is a popular speaker on ecological and justice issues and the author of several articles on these topics.

- Curriculum vitae, or CV, is Latin for "course of one's life." It is a short account of your career and qualifications within your profession. It can serve as an elaboration of your resume and can give the reader a more three-dimensional picture of who you are.

- Write it factually and in reverse chronological order. Some CV's omit information about personal life in the last paragraph.

Sender's Name
Address
City, State Zip

Date

Mr. Robert M. Stewart
Director, Sales
Systems Paper Company
31 Hillhouse Street
Seattle, WA 98102

Dear Mr. Stewart:

I believe my experience and solid record of achievement make me an ideal candidate for an industrial sales and marketing position in your firm.

I have over 13 years of professional sales and marketing experience, with a four-year career base established with General Products. As my enclosed resume indicates, I have successfully managed sales programs in the pulp and paper industry. My experience includes distribution channel organization and training, product promotion and development in both the international and domestic markets, and advertising and collateral promotional materials origination.

Please call me at (804) 322-4168 after 6 p.m. if you need further information about my experience.

Sincerely,

Daniel J. Murphy

Enclosure

- Generally, these letters are sent to so many people that individual follow-up is impossible. Providing a phone number and "best time to call" is the next best strategy.

Company Name
Address
City, State Zip

Date

Mr. Robert Barthman
President
Omega, Inc.
200 Broadway
Alma, MI 48801

Dear Mr. Barthman:

Since Riley and Santilli is merging with Mutual Corporation, I am
discreetly exploring career alternatives. I understand from Jon Pritchard
that Omega is seeking a potential partner, and I would welcome an
opportunity to talk to you about that possibility. My resume is enclosed.

My experience with Riley and Santilli, first in operations and then in real
estate development and finance, qualifies me to manage the growth of a
major regional real estate company. Furthermore, I am eager to
participate in the ownership of a growing firm while helping that firm
build its net worth.

I will call you next week to see if we can find a mutually convenient time
to talk.

Sincerely,

Wilson Dudley

Enclosure

- Explain, early on, why you are seeking employment and the position you seek.

- State, as crisply as you can, what qualifies you for that position.

- Ask for an appointment.

Sender's Name
Address
City, State Zip

Date

Mr. Philip Beckwith
Torrey/Phelps Associates
10 Twisting Pines Plaza
Dallas, TX 75200

Dear Phil:

Thank you for putting me in touch with Tom Stanley at Roth, Roche and Stern. We spoke on the phone at length on Tuesday, and I received a very favorable impression of both the company and Tom.

Tom has set up appointments for me with two managers who have openings in their departments, and he has been quite encouraging about my prospects at Roth, Roche and Stern. I look forward to pursuing my options there.

I'll keep you posted as things develop further. Thanks again for your help.

Best,

Mark Canter

- Referrals are the life's blood of a job search. Thanks should be immediate and specific but not drawn out.

- Always offer to keep the person informed about the results of his or her efforts to refer you (and then do it).

Sender's Name
Address
City, State Zip

Date

Ms. Rachel Cohen
Director of Marketing
Axiom Securities
111 Abington Avenue
Philadelphia, PA 19101

Dear Ms. Cohen:

I am a recent college graduate interested in finding a position in a securities firm. I understand that Axiom Securities has an excellent marketing trainee program, and I am writing you to find out more about it.

Among the questions I have are: When does the program begin and how long does the training take? What qualifications make for a successful applicant? And, of course, I would like to know what the application procedures are.

I hope you can help me with this information. I look forward to meeting with you to discuss career opportunities at Axiom Securities.

Sincerely,

Clara Marie Williams

- Be clear and concise. Don't try to bowl them over; just get the information. There will be other chances to impress.

- Unless they have some prepared information—and most small and medium-sized companies will not—you will do better to ask specific questions. And always, if possible, ask for information about particular jobs. Don't go on a fishing expedition.

Sender's Name
Address
City, State Zip

Date

Ms. Gail Thompson
Texmat, Inc.
280 Foxon Road
Rockville, MD 20800

Dear Ms. Thompson:

Thank you for sending me the information I requested on Texmat's hazardous waste control services. Your brochure and the annual report give me a much clearer picture of the range of services Texmat offers and the nature of its clientele.

I enjoyed talking with you on the phone last week, and appreciate the effort you took in getting the materials to me quickly.

Sincerely,

Ronald Vender

- Follow up with written thanks whenever anyone helps you further your job search.

- Be sure to mention how you benefited from receiving the information.

- Close with thanks and some reference to your request.

Sender's Name
Address
City, State Zip

Date

Mr. Walter Brooks
Managing Editor
The Portland News
81 Center Street
Portland, ME 04101

Dear Mr. Brooks:

I saw your advertisement for a news reporter, and I wish to apply for the job. Enclosed is my resume and some clips for your consideration.

Although I have made my living in banking, writing and news have always been my first love. I have been writing features for a couple of local newspapers while working at First Security Bank. I majored in journalism at Northeastern University and did an internship at *The Boston Globe* in my junior year. While I may not have all the hard news experience you are looking for, I certainly know how to write.

I look forward to an interview and hope to hear from you soon.

Sincerely,

Paul Northrop

Enclosures

- Do a little selling without overdoing it. Use the cover letter to refer to the resume by bringing out certain experiences or educational background. You do want them to read your resume the right way—as someone who is eminently qualified for the job.

- Make it clear that you are looking for an interview. Be positive!

Sender's Name
Address
City, State Zip

Date

Mr. Peter Morrissey
Holloway Development Corporation
2200 Corley Boulevard
Atlanta, GA 30300

Dear Mr. Morrissey:

It was a pleasure meeting you yesterday. I enjoyed learning more about the projects your company has underway and hearing about Holloway's ambitious plans for growth.

I came away from our meeting with a strong vision of how I might be a part of that growth. My skills and background dovetail closely with your company's growing need for experienced construction managers, and I believe I possess the talent, commitment, and energy you are looking for in prospective members of the "Holloway team."

Please keep me in mind as your plans to add staff take shape. I understand it will be a few weeks before you begin to schedule interviews for specific positions, and I look forward to hearing from you then.

Thank you again for meeting with me yesterday.

Sincerely,

George V. McNab

- Following up each interview in writing is crucial in showing you are a serious job applicant. This is your opportunity to make a more lasting impression on your interviewer, and to remind him or her of your strengths.

- Refer specifically to what you discussed and comment on what *you* took away from the interview.

Thank You for Interview, Not Interested in Job (11-19)

Sender's Name
Address
City, State Zip

Date

Mr. Richard Feyerherm
Golden Valley Computers
4291 Whittington Boulevard
St. Louis, MO 34778

Dear Mr. Feyerherm:

I want to thank you again for interviewing me for the Sales
Representative position with Golden Valley Computers. It was good to
learn about the nature and operations of your business.

As you explained, the person chosen for the job must be prepared to
travel one week out of three. After talking it over with my wife and
children, I have decided to withdraw my application from further
consideration. While our kids are still in school, my wife and I feel it is
important for me to work near home.

Again, Mr. Feyerherm, I appreciated the opportunity to meet with you. I
wish you and Golden Valley Computers all the best as your company
continues to grow.

Sincerely,

Tim Amundsen

• Make it short and sincere. Express your appreciation for the interview and explain briefly
why you no longer want to be a candidate for the job.

• Finish the letter with personal good wishes.

Sender's Name
Address
City, State Zip

Date

Mr. Jules Smeakins
Vice President, Human Resources
International Data Systems
123 Financial Plaza
Albany, NY 12211

Dear Mr. Smeakins:

Thank you for the opportunity to interview with you for the position of
Senior Analyst in the Finance Department. I enjoyed talking with you,
and with Charles Madden the day before. I've always had great respect
for IDS's innovative product line and strong support network.

The position seems challenging and interesting. The responsibilities as
you detailed them are a good match with my background, and although
every new job requires learning a new system, I feel confident I could be
up to speed quickly.

I look forward to our next interview. One last personal note—you
mentioned that you were a big Yankees fan, and I told you I supported
the Red Sox. I went home last night and watched your Yankees crush
my Sox 10-4. I just wanted you to know that I harbor no ill feelings!

I look forward to hearing from you soon.

Sincerely,

Martin W. Stewart

- This is an attempt to make a more personal contact with those doing the hiring and to get
  them to remember you. So, while you include a thank-you, look forward to the next time,
  and reiterate how qualified you are, the real meat of the letter is to make a personal comment
  to the interviewer.

Acceptance of Job Offer (11-21)

Sender's Name
Address
City, State Zip

Date

Mr. Alexander Heitner
Heldon Industries, Inc.
259 North Spring Road
Whittington, IL 62897

Dear Mr. Heitner:

Thank you for your offer to join Heldon Industries as a sales associate. I'm delighted to accept at the salary of $28,000 with the standard benefits package that we discussed on Thursday. I am looking forward to working with all the talented and committed people I met while interviewing at Heldon, and to representing such a fine company and a high quality line of products.

I will call you on Friday to give you whatever information you need prior to my starting work June 1. I look forward to seeing you again soon.

Sincerely,

Sarah P. Stanton

- First, express appreciation for the offer and state your acceptance. If salary has been an issue, reiterate the figure you finally agreed upon.

- Mention *why* you look forward to joining the company.

- State exactly *when* you will call again to clear up any details.

Sender's Name
Address
City, State Zip

Date

Mr. Alexander Heitner
Heldon Industries, Inc.
259 North Spring Road
Whittington, IL 62897

Dear Mr. Heitner:

Thank you for your offer to join Heldon Industries as a sales associate.
The salary and benefits package you propose is quite attractive, and I'm
sure I would find the job challenging and enjoyable.

Before I make a final decision, I would like to discuss with you further
your policy for reassigning sales associates to other locations after six
months. Are you free to discuss this one day next week? I will call you
on Friday to make an appointment, and look forward to talking with you
again soon.

Sincerely,

Sarah P. Stanton

- Express appreciation for the job offer and mention what you found attractive in it.

- State specifically what you want to know before making a decision.

- Make an appointment to discuss your concerns.

Sender's Name
Address
City, State Zip

Date

Mr. Alexander Heitner
Heldon Industries, Inc.
259 North Spring Road
Whittington, IL 62897

Dear Mr. Heitner:

Thank you for your offer to join Heldon Industries as a sales associate.
I'm sure I will find working with such a committed sales team both
challenging and enjoyable. Heldon Industries is a company I can feel
proud to work for.

The salary and benefits package you offer is quite attractive and well
within the range I've been seeking. I would, however, like to make my
starting date June 9 to accommodate commitments I have already
made for May. I will call you on Thursday to confirm this date and make
final arrangements for joining Heldon Industries.

I look forward to talking with you then.

Sincerely,

Sarah P. Stanton

- Express appreciation for the offer and say *why* you find it appealing.

- State the conditions of your acceptance.

- Make an appointment to confirm acceptance of these conditions.

Sender's Name
Address
City, State Zip

Date

Ms. Elaine Drile
Vice-President
Kidsworks
2 Toy Drive
Tallahassee, FL 32301

Dear Ms. Drile:

I have received your revised job offer, and I agree that the details to be worked out are not insurmountable. They do, however, require further discussion.

Since I will have the same job title and responsibilities at Kidsworks as I presently have, my motivation for this move is primarily financial. But the base salary you have offered is only slightly better than what I currently earn. The 15% performance bonus is more along the lines of what I was hoping to receive. It is important that the criteria of the performance review, upon which the bonus will be based, be established at the outset, so there is no confusion later. It must be decided what sales targets I must meet, what managerial changes and improvements you desire, etc. I can't meet your performance expectations unless I know what they are, and the more explicitly, the better.

Secondly, at my present job I have a company car. Since replacing it at my own expense dilutes the financial motivation for making this move, I would like Kidsworks to provide me with a car for my own use.

I would like to meet with you and Mr. Weiss to discuss these matters. I will call you to set a date.

Sincerely,

Richard Pearle

- Be tough and sure of what you want, but don't be obstinate. Remember that you are going to be working with these people soon. State your counter offer, explain your motivations (if that's appropriate), and keep communications open.

Sender's Name
Address
City, State Zip

Date

Mr. Alexander Heitner
Heldon Industries, Inc.
259 North Spring Road
Whittington, IL 62897

Dear Mr. Heitner:

Thank you for your offer to join Heldon Industries as a sales associate. Although the prospect of joining the Heldon team was quite tempting, I've accepted an offer from Fultrex, Inc. that would allow me to stay in the Chicago area.

I appreciate the time and effort everyone at Heldon took to answer my questions and make me feel welcome. My favorable impression of Heldon made my decision especially difficult.

Sincerely,

Sarah P. Stanton

- Despite your first impulse, never brag about your new job offer or demean a company when you turn down a job offer. Give a specific, preferably neutral reason for rejecting the offer (in this case, your reluctance to relocate).

- Always express appreciation for the time and effort expended by the people involved.

Sender's Name
Address
City, State Zip

Date

Ms. Susan R. Myren-Walker
Crestwood Communities, Inc.
314 6th Avenue, Suite 111
Aurora, KS 41556

Dear Ms. Myren-Walker:

I'm writing you on the recommendation of Matt Newman. Matt has told me about your work and recent promotion within Crestwood Communities. I am very interested in a career in the administration of retirement communities, especially those that offer full-service health care. Would it be possible for you to meet with me to share some information about your profession?

My training is in social work with an emphasis on gerontology. After six years as a case worker with senior citizens, I returned to school to pursue a Master's degree in Business Administration. I graduated last month, and I'm excited about pursuing my goal of combining my experience and training in a management position on behalf of the elderly. I have enclosed my resume for your information and convenience.

I will call you next week to arrange an appointment, if possible. I will be in your area during the second week of March—perhaps we can meet then.

Sincerely,

Jason Clarides

Enclosure

- State your purpose for writing and your source of referral in the first paragraph.

- Help your interviewee learn about your interests and how you've prepared for this, or a related career, by offering brief biographical information and your resume.

Sender's Name
Address
City, State Zip

Date

Ms. Susan R. Myren-Walker
Crestwood Communities, Inc.
314 6th Avenue, Suite 111
Aurora, KS 41556

Dear Susan:

I want to express my thanks to you again for meeting with me last week. The information you gave me about your work at Crestwood Communities was very helpful. I appreciated your willingness to speak openly and to offer useful advice.

I have already contacted Jean Simsbury and Ed Hernandez for additional information interviews, on your recommendation. Both of them were able to fit me into their busy schedules, and both were pleased to hear about your promotion.

Again, Susan, thank you for your time. I will keep you updated as my job search continues.

Best wishes in your new position!

Sincerely,

Jason Clarides

- Though this is still business correspondence, this letter can be more personal than your original contact. Let your interviewee know that you appreciated the time and information.

- Acknowledge the names of additional referrals.

Sender's Name
Address
City, State Zip

Date

Ms. Susan R. Myren-Walker
Crestwood Communities, Inc.
314 6th Avenue, Suite 111
Aurora, KS 41556

Dear Susan:

I'm writing to share my good news with you. I have accepted a position
as Director of Health Services with Casa del Sol, a retirement
community in Phoenix, Arizona. I will be moving there within the month.

You were an important part of my getting this job, and I want to thank
you for it. My interview at Casa del Sol resulted from my meeting with
your colleague Jean Simsbury. Your referral was a key link in the chain.

I'm very excited about the work I will be doing. It calls for someone who
has my experience in social service agencies, direct contact with the
elderly, and training in business administration. It's a good match!
Thank you again for your help, Susan.

Best regards,

Jason Clarides

- This kind of letter is appropriate for people who were especially helpful in your job search.
  Information interviewees often appreciate knowing how your search turned out. This letter
  not only updates them but maintains a professional network.

Sender's Name
Address
City, State Zip

Date

Dear Linda,

Thank you for dinner last night. It was a pleasure to reconnect after so long.

I was very glad to hear that your business continues to prosper, and I appreciate your offer to pass along my resume to Ron McMullin at Technology Park. I'm planning to call him when I'm in town.

I'll keep you posted on my job search. I look forward to seeing you at the Ancient China Exhibition next month.

Kind regards,

Thomas Luft

- This is a hybrid letter—a cross between a friendly note and a job-search letter. Because it's directed to a friend, it should be handwritten on personal letterhead.

Request for Reference, to Business Associate (11-30)

Sender's Name
Address
City, State Zip

Date

Mr. Joel Beamon
Alliance Business Systems
Fair Park Road
Carmel, CA 93921

Dear Joel:

It was great to see you at the Financial Networking Conference last week. As I mentioned, I am thinking about moving on and have been putting out some feelers in the San Francisco area. One name that came up was Allied Bank, which is undergoing a major restructuring of its Bonds and Acquisitions Department.

I am writing to you because I want to follow up on it, and I was wondering if you knew anything about their plans for the future. I also know that you are a friend of Al Goodspell. I was hoping you could give me a good reference. It's always hard going into these things cold, and having my name mentioned to the Senior V.P. would be a big help. Since you had an opportunity to see me work in our five years together at WestBank, your reference would really mean something.

If you know of any other good leads, please let me know. I really appreciate any help you can give me. I hope that someday I can return the favor.

Thanks again.

Very truly yours,

Justin R. Spellman

- Don't beg, plead, or wheedle. Just ask. Everybody understands the importance of connections, and it's inherently complimentary to ask somebody to use theirs to help you.

- If you are asking for a reference from somebody who doesn't know your work history well, send them a resume.

Personal Letters 12

Personal letters cover a broad range of topics—from the pleasant-to-write "thank yous" and "congratulations" to the more difficult "sympathy" letters. Letters to public officials are also challenging to compose because you want to get your point of view across in a responsible and reasonable tone.

If you know someone in both a business and a more personal context, the problem of how to treat such delicate matters as sympathy notes and congratulations letters is bound to arise. Here are two rules that will help you write those kinds of letters.

Keep it simple. In circumstances in which a gift is warranted, for example when a colleague gets married or has a child, you need not write at all. Simply enclose a small card that says "congratulations" and sign your name (if it's a personal friend and business associate) or your company's name (if it's a client or the relative of a client, and many people in your firm know him or her). Similarly, if you are sending flowers to a funeral home or making a contribution in memory of someone who has died, enclosing a card will suffice. If you choose not to send a gift, many commercial greeting and/or sympathy cards have tasteful messages that can substitute for a letter. (Do, however, check to make sure. Some cards today are masterpieces of bad taste, and you cannot always tell from the cover.)

Keep your comments to a minimum of socially acceptable phrases if you do not know the person in any other capacity than as a business associate or as a client or customer. Presuming on a familiarity that doesn't exist is worse than writing nothing at all. If you do know the person, relating a brief, personal anecdote provides human warmth.

Send handwritten notes when appropriate. The key here is hand–written. Don't expect to dictate a note to your secretary or to dash off a letter on your word processor and expect it to have the same effect as your having taken the time to write it by hand. (The only exception to this rule is if your handwriting is totally illegible.)

The examples in this section provide good models for a variety of situations, but if you are unsure about the impact of anything you write, have someone else read it for tone and aptness. Otherwise, send a present, flowers, or a card. Remember, don't pretend a friendship exists when it doesn't.

Letters to public officials. Be objective and dispassionate when writing to public officials such as town or city employees, legislators at any level, or editors of newspapers or magazines. Your major objective is to win someone over to your way of thinking—not to demonstrate that you're smarter or have found a flaw. Ranting and raving—excesses in any form—will only convince the recipient of the letter that the writer is irrational.

Sender's Name
Address
City, State Zip

Date

Dear Joe,

I was very sorry to hear that you weren't well. I'm sure that someone with your energy is very frustrated by the forced inactivity, but it's only for a short time.

Suzie tells me that you can have visitors in a couple of weeks. I'll be sure to come see you then.

Best,

Lloyd

- This kind of letter must be handwritten, unless your handwriting is indecipherable. A get-well card is also acceptable.

- Don't go on and on. Be positive but not maudlin. If you say you'll do something—visit, call, whatever—note it on your calendar and then do it.

Sender's Name
Address
City, State Zip

Date

Dear Pete,

I was devastated to hear of Joy's death. We shared so many good times together—on our Sierra Club hikes, for example—and we were always part of the team "that made it happen" here at work.

There's never anything that can be said that will make it better, but Joe and I hope you will count on us for help—with the kids, for example, or for anything else you need. We'll call you.

With my deepest sympathy,

Lorna

- Handwrite any sympathy note. Refer briefly to your association and friendship with the person who died.

- Offer to help, but don't expect an immediate response from the grieving person. It may be better to wait awhile and then call him or her and make a very specific offer—for example, "Can we take you and the kids to dinner Wednesday?"

Sympathy to Business Associate's Family (12-03)

Sender's Name
Address
City, State Zip

Date

Dear Mr. Markham,

I was very sorry to hear of Joy's death. We will miss her very much. Joy was a kind person you could always depend on—for a smile, for a humorous "lighten up, guys" when we needed it most, for doing more than her share, and more.

My deepest sympathy,

Lorna Whitehead

- Sympathy notes must be handwritten. They should never include comments like "I know how you feel" or anything else that presumes on a nonexistent intimacy.

- If the person was a business associate, refer to something that made him or her a good person to work with.

Sympathy to Employee's Family (12-04)

Company Name
Address
City, State Zip

Date

Dear Mrs. Brightwell,

Everyone here was very sad to hear about Mason's death. We counted
on him—he was always here to open up and greet our first customers.
People said it was a pleasure to do business in a place where
"customer service" wasn't just a phrase. Mason always put the
customer first—and the customers knew it.

We'll miss him very much.

Our sympathy,

Charles Tampa

- If you're the boss, you handwrite the letter and refer to the rest of your staff's sadness.

- If you have business details, like benefits or distributions to discuss, write another letter at a later date. Don't include such issues in a sympathy letter.

Sympathy to Employee (12-05)

Sender's Name
Address
City, State Zip

Date

Dear Tim,

I was very sorry to hear of your mother's death. It must be very hard to lose a parent.

I'm sorry I was out of town and unable to attend the funeral. You were in my thoughts.

My deepest sympathy,

Rob Marwick

- If you didn't get to the funeral, apologize. Sending flowers or a plant to the house or making a contribution in the person's name might be called for, depending on the relationship.

- If you didn't know the deceased, keep your handwritten note short. You can usually safely say it's hard to lose a parent.

Company Name
Address
City, State Zip

Date

Dear Winnie and John,

We were all delighted to hear of the arrival of John, Jr., on May 1.
We're looking forward to seeing pictures and perhaps the baby himself
at the annual Fourth-of-July picnic.

Best,

Carl Nuveen

- Like all personal notes, this should be handwritten. Use personal stationery with your company's letterhead if writing in an official capacity. Otherwise, use personal stationery or send a conservative card. Use your discretion about sending a gift.

- You don't need to be effusive. Simply acknowledge the birth and the parents' joy.

Company Name
Address
City, State Zip

Date

Mr. and Mrs. Jacob Hudson
365 Lombardy Street
Eugene, OR 97403

Dear Sarah and Jake,

We were delighted to hear about the new addition to your family. It must thrill Lindy to have a new sister. We're looking forward to seeing all of you at the company Holiday party so we can greet Carol Cynthia Hudson in person.

All the best,

Martin Liggett

- Another obvious opportunity for a handwritten note, in which case you would not need the inside address.

- "The new addition to your family" is a much better phrase than "adoption," since the manner in which the child arrived is not important.

Sender's Name
Address
City, State Zip

Date

Dear George,

Mary and I wanted to send our very best wishes to you and Lonnie on the occasion of your wedding.

I understand you're honeymooning in Cancun and will return on the 20th. I hope we can all get together for dinner when you get settled.

Best,

Tom

- If you don't know both spouses, address the one you do know and mention the other one in the body of the handwritten letter. If you refer to your spouse, you must use personal letterhead.

- It's pleasant, but optional, to suggest a dinner after the newlyweds get settled. If you send a gift, you can write a brief note on the card and skip the letter.

Company Name
Address
City, State Zip

Date

Dear Marie,

I was delighted to read that Josephine had been cited as a National Merit Semifinalist. It must make you very proud.

The paper also mentioned that Josephine would be going to my old college in the fall. If she would like some (relatively dated) information on what it's like, please have her call me. Since I'm active in the alumnae association, I may also be able to put her in touch with more recent graduates.

Again, my congratulations.

Best wishes,

Arletta

- People are always glad to have their children's accomplishments noted. Offering to help in some way—through talking about the college, by offering a summer job—is a good way to sustain a relationship.

- If you know the award recipient personally, you should write to her as well.

Thank You for Hospitality (12-10)

Company Name
Address
City, State Zip

Date

Mr. Charles Long
Optimum Resources, Inc.
45 Broadway
New York, NY 10003

Dear Charles:

I want to thank you and Charlotte for making my first business trip to the New York area a pleasant one. To be shown around by two "native New Yorkers" gave me a view of the city I would never have gotten by seeing New York on my own.

I expect to reciprocate when the sales convention is in my home town of San Francisco next fall.

Please give my best to Charlotte, and thanks again to both of you for a most pleasant two days.

Kindest regards,

Martin Unger

- Be sure to thank both host and hostess, if it applies.

- Because this is a business relationship, the letter is typed on company letterhead.

Thank You for Gift (12-11)

Company Name
Address
City, State Zip

Date

Mr. Len Bookbinder
President
Bookbinder Printing
1027 West Gardenia Boulevard
Burbank, CA 91503

Dear Len,

Thanks so much for the crystal book-shaped paperweight. I have admired these beautiful paperweights in the magazine ads, and I very much appreciate your thoughtfulness.

Let's have lunch soon.

Best wishes,

Edward Curry

- Any gift should be acknowledged, in writing, as promptly as possible.

- Use your company stationery or write the note by hand on personal letterhead.

Thank You for Flowers (12-12)

Company Name
Address
City, State Zip

Date

Mr. Kit Dailey
Accounting Temps, Inc.
650 Laramie Avenue
Overland Park, KS 66204

Dear Kit,

Thanks so much for the beautiful flower arrangement. It brightened our new office for over a week and fit in perfectly with our color scheme. We're sorry you missed the open house but hope you will stop by the next time you're in the area. You ought to see where your people are working. The coffee pot is always on.

Best,

Sybil Drexel

- It's always a good idea to end a thank-you with some kind of informal invitation.

Company Name
Address
City, State Zip

Date

Mr. Jerry Bowman
Broadway Realty
10 Broadway, 7th floor
New York, NY 10004

Dear Jerry:

I tried to catch you before you went on vacation, but I was too late.
Thank you so much for keeping an eye out for Super Delivery while I
was away last week. One of the disadvantages of a one-person outfit is
the inability to be all places at once, and the checks you collected from
Super Delivery were very important to me. I wouldn't have had time to
chase them down.

I'll do the same for you—anytime.

Best,

Howard Lambert

- Thank people for any out-of-the-ordinary favor in person, if possible. In this particular case,
  writing a note is preferable to waiting until you see the person, thereby risking forgetting
  entirely.

Sender's Name
Address
City, State Zip

Date

Jane Harrigan
Director of Admissions
Harley College
179 Congress Avenue
Brooklyn, NY 11201

Dear Mrs. Harrigan:

I'm pleased to tell you about Lillian Heath, whom I have known since she was a child. Lillian is the daughter of a close friend, and I have had the opportunity to observe her in a variety of settings.

Lillian has substantial "people" skills. I have seen her converse with senior members of government and the gardener with equal ease and charm. As she once said to me, "You don't learn anything while you're talking." I feel that her empathy with other people and her desire to learn from them may be interpreted by some as shyness, but I can assure you that there is a core strength in Lillian that any employer would find valuable.

As you already know, Lillian has done an admirable job preparing herself for life, winning honors in high school and college. Her extensive summer work with college-bound inner city youths, which she has reported to me with great enthusiasm, has given her a good sense of what it would be like to work for the Admissions Department.

In short, I heartily recommend Lillian Heath to you—for her ability to deal with people, her record of achievement, and her energetic approach to dealing with life's vagaries.

Sincerely,

Veva A. Miller

- Character references, like other reference letters, should be confined to the specifics of what you actually know. Whatever you do, don't resort to artificial phrasing and exaggeration—it will prejudice your reader against the applicant.

Letter to the Editor (12-15)

Company Name
Address
City, State Zip

Date

Mr. Robert L. W. James
Editor
The Haystack Observer
212 Main Street
Southbridge, MA 01550

Dear Mr. James:

I am sorry to have to bring this matter to your attention, but my calls to reporter Ann-Marie Newhardt have been to no avail. The article headlined "Small Potatoes — The City Coalition's Inner-City Garden Program" gave an inaccurate account of our group's efforts to establish a community self-help program. Specifically, it is not true that administrative costs consume 55% of our budget. As you can see from the attached annual report, our administrative costs are only 22% of our budget, well within the range of similar organizations. Ms. Newhardt may have been relying on verbal information from outside sources.

We would greatly appreciate it if you would print this letter and/or a correction in your next issue. We would not want a fine program damaged by an inaccurate impression.

Sincerely,

Joan L. Koobley
Chairman of the Board

- Write *only* if you have already tried to talk to the reporter and if the error is major. Chances are, a greater number of people will notice the inaccurate charge when the paper retracts it than did the first time around. If you are refuting information, be sure to document your position.

Sender's Name
Address
City, State Zip

Date

Representative Adele Curran
State Capitol
Dover, DE 19901

Dear Representative Curran:

I wish to express my support for the Adams Street Men's Shelter in downtown Wilmington. I think the state should assume some of the burden for running this shelter for homeless men. The Lutheran Church should not be the only group to tackle what is surely a municipal problem.

I'm writing because I'm sure you are getting many letters attacking the establishment of a city-run men's shelter, and I wanted you to know that not everyone agrees with that view. I am a merchant in the downtown area, and I live within a half mile of the proposed site for the shelter. I reject the argument that this shelter will increase crime in our neighborhood, or lead to the concentration of bums in our city. These people already live here. Ignoring them is not going to make them invisible. I see them every day, and I don't think we are doing enough.

At least we can provide a bowl of soup and a safe place to sleep. At least we can know that some old, crippled man isn't going to starve on our streets while we sleep, or get beaten up by some kids who think it's amusing to prey on the helpless.

I believe we, the citizens, should do more. I think we should have the Adams Street Men's Shelter, and I hope you will join me in supporting it.

Sincerely,

Henry Parsons

- Never bully, never threaten; always make a reasoned argument. Make the most persuasive case you can. Think in terms of not only persuading the public official, but also giving them something *they* can use in making your argument as your representative. Remember that personal, self-interested arguments are not very persuasive to a public official—they must appeal to a broader constituency.

Faxes 13

Facsimile machines have changed the pace of business forever. Managers and customers who were once satisfied with reading something the next day or next week now insist on seeing something within hours, if not minutes.

Because of the speed of the medium, some writers equate faxes with phone calls and wrongly assume that their readers will not object to incorrect grammar and usage, just as they would not object to sentence fragments or the occasional slip of the tongue during a phone conversation. This assumption is dangerous, as anyone who has ever received a sloppy fax knows.

Faxes should be prepared with the same care you would use in writing a letter. As with a letter—but even more so with a fax—be as brief as possible. A long, involved fax diminishes its sense of urgency and immediacy.

Faxes are excellent vehicles for placing, receiving and confirming orders, keeping customers informed about new products and services, preparing people for meetings and following up with assignments, and for keeping in touch with salespeople, customers, and divisions outside the home office, to name just a few uses.

When using the faxes in this section as models, be guided by the following rules.

Always send a cover sheet. There are two kinds of cover sheets required for faxing. The first, which we'll refer to as the *master* cover sheet, shows the name of the recipient, their fax and phone numbers, the number of pages being sent, and a phone number to call in the event that there is trouble receiving the fax. In addition, when faxing a price list or other sales material, a resume or other informational documents, include what we'll call an *explanatory* cover sheet. This brief document permits you to explain the attachments and as well as gives you an opportunity to interject a personal touch. The cover sheet for a resume and response to request for information in this chapter are examples.

Use appropriate design. Both kinds of cover sheets should be designed with an attractive logo that reproduces clearly on fax paper, giving you another opportunity to reinforce the identity of your company. Don't use your regular letterhead if it has embossing or metallic type because it won't reproduce effectively by fax. Instead, create one just for faxes that will look crisp and attractive. Make sure the margins are wide enough (at least three-quarters of an inch) so that words will not get cut off. Use a type size of at least 12 points and a sans serif typeface such as Helvetica.

Confidentiality is a serious concern. Never fax anything you would not care to see on the front page of a newspaper. Many offices have their fax machines stationed in public locations where anyone passing by can read what is transmitted. If there is any sensitive material in your fax, call the recipient and tell them the fax is being sent so they can be there to receive it.

Proofreading is crucial. Faxes are legally binding documents. If you quote prices or send any other contractual information, make sure it is correct. Don't let the demand to "fax me something on that right away" hurry you into neglecting proofreading.

Don't handwrite your faxes. First, it's unprofessional. Second, documents are difficult enough to read when faxed. Faxing a handwritten note can make your message unreadable. Take the extra couple of minutes to type your fax.

Company Name
Address
City, State Zip
Phone number
Fax number

Date:

To:

Fax #:

From:

Number of pages (including cover sheet):

In case of transmittal problems, please call _____ at
(212) 555-_____.

- The cover sheet should include all information necessary for the fax to get to the intended recipient and for the recipient to reply to the sender.

- Use your company logo if it reproduces crisply. Using the logo is the equivalent of a mini-advertisement.

Cover Sheet for Resume (13-02)

Name
Address
City, State Zip

To: P. R. Jamison, Director of Human Resources, Philbrick Corp.

From: Jennifer Neale

Date:

Subject: Financial Analyst Opening

Thank you for taking time to talk with me about the financial analyst position. As you requested, here is my resume. I believe my experience as a financial assistant with Air Limited has been excellent preparation for your position.

I am excited about the possibility of working with a growing, innovative company like Philbrick. I look forward to meeting you in person and will call your office on Tuesday to set up an appointment.

- Sending a resume by fax is becoming common. Use the fax to sell yourself. Be brief, but show enthusiasm.

- Point out specific items you would like the recipient to notice. Tell why you are interested in their company.

- Say how you plan to follow up.

Company Name
Address
City, State Zip

To: Carmen Alonzo, Monroe & Associates

From: Phyllis Corbett, Customer Service

Date:

Subject: Catalog Request

At your request, I am faxing catalog sheets for our Carry Case #33-11
and Carry Case #33-15. Both are available for immediate shipment.

If you'd like to order, you can phone our sales line: (202) 555-6630
between 9 am and 6 pm eastern time. We accept all major credit cards.

- Mention availability of the product.

- Include ordering information.

Quotation (13-04)

Company Name
Address
City, State Zip

To: Wayne Babcock, Elyria Glass Co.

From: Carroll Peavey

Date:

Subject: Price Quotation: Carpenter Ant Control

Now that we have completed the inspection of your office and shop, we can confirm the price of the service you requested:

Type of Service: One-time service to control carpenter ants

Property to be Serviced: One-story commercial property with attic

Included in Service: Carpenter ants and other ants only

Application: Power-spray exterior with Empire M.E.;
                          spray cracks and crevices all rooms and attic;
                          dust attic soffits

Cost: Service $130.00
                         Tax   10.40
                         TOTAL $140.40   (payable at time
                                                of service)

As we discussed, we can schedule service for Sunday, August 20 (while you are closed), provided we make arrangements for access. We look forward to serving you.

- Make information clear and specific — even though it's a fax, you should include enough information to protect yourself. Since it is a written document, you can be held responsible for the information given, as with any contract.

- Don't miss an opportunity to include a human touch. People do business with people, not with organizations.

Company Name
Address
City, State Zip

To: Carlos Martinez, Prime Source Media

From: Edward Gruber, Sales Manager

Date:

Subject: Correction of Price Information

We regret that the price information sent to you on June 23 contained an error. The correct price for the Roto Literature Display Rack is $356.75. This price went into effect on June 1. We are sending you a catalog with the new pricing, which should arrive by Thursday.

We hope our error will not cause you any inconvenience. If you wish to change your order, please phone Jennie Tomkins (collect) at (203) 555-3985, and she will make any adjustments immediately.

- Acknowledge your error.

- Take corrective action immediately, and give the name of a contact to talk to.

Company Name
Address
City, State Zip

To: Spike Gerald, Head Coach, Pittsfield Tigers

From: Ed Brown, Northeastern Sales Manager

Date:

Subject: Confirmation of 8/13 Phone Order

Thank you for your August 13 order of :

Three (3) Ease-E hydroculators @ $29.95	$89.85
One case (12 bottles) of Ease-E muscle liniment	27.95
One box (10) Ace bandages	15.95
Sub Total	133.75
10% educational discount	(13.38)
State tax (6-1/2%)	7.82
Postage and handling	4.95
Total	$133.14

These items will be shipped on Monday, August 17, via UPS and should reach you by Friday, August 21. If your order has not arrived by Friday afternoon, please telephone Missy Curtis at (213) 555-2295.

- Itemize the order (include unit prices) as well as any other costs (shipping, tax).

- Include shipping details and the name and number of someone to contact if the order is not received on time.

Company Name
Address
City, State Zip

To: J. Termini, Genengineer, Ltd.

From: K. Bartlett

Date:

Subject: Shipping Date of Thermocycling Oven—
         Your Order #6667-552

We shipped your thermocycling oven (Model #345A) by air courier at
10:00 a.m. today. In the ten years we have been dealing with British
customs, this method of transport has averted major delays in delivering
products to our customers. If you do not receive your oven by 3 pm
your time on Friday, December 6, please fax or call me and I will
expedite its delivery.

- Letting customers know when to expect merchandise is especially important when dealing overseas. Giving them a contingency plan if the merchandise fails to arrive is equally crucial.

- Use the name of the item rather than model number in the Subject line. It's more meaningful than a bunch of numbers.

Apology for Shipment Error (13-08)

Company Name
Address
City, State Zip

To: Marion Hamilton, Equipment Unlimited, Inc.

From: Edward Thacker, Customer Service

Date:

Subject: Replacement of Incorrect Shipment (Order #LL-52-4597)

When we received your fax this morning, we checked with our shipping department, and we did indeed send you the 42" space organizers instead of the 52" organizers. We are very sorry for this error.

We will ship the correct items to you today, via Federal Express, at our expense. You will receive them tomorrow. Please return the 42" organizers in the original box, and we will credit your account for the purchase price and all shipping and handling charges. Please send the box by Federal Express and charge the shipment to our account (#8005-5555-0).

If you need any additional information, please call Tom Binder (collect) at (815) 443-0077. Please refer to your order number: LL-52-4597.

- Apologize for the error, but keep it simple and matter of fact (errors can happen to anyone and don't require abject apologies).

- Be clear about exactly what the customer needs to do and about exactly what costs you will cover (or reimburse).

438 *FAXES*

Company Name
Address
City, State Zip

To: Tom Johnson, Electronics of America

From: Cynthia Wallace, Purchasing Department

Date:

Subject: Price Quotation

We wish to purchase a personal computer and need written price quotes for the following equipment. You may use this form to respond.

1.   PC 10000X with $_____
     8 mb RAM
     300 mb Internal hard drive

2.   Quest 300 Super XGA $_____
     15" Monitor

3.   Scope 96HX modem $_____

3.   DataMost PS 90 printer $_____

Are there any price advantages if we order all of these items as a package at one time?

Please fax this information to me at the cover sheet number. (We will not respond to phone calls without a written quote.)

- Make it easy for the recipient to respond.

- It's easier to see items in a list than if you put the same information in paragraph form—and you're more likely to get all the information you want .

Company Name
Address
City, State Zip

To: Merry Mites Costume Company

From: George Gates, Production Manager

Date:

Subject: Costume Order — Urgent

Please send us the following by UPS 2nd Day or equivalent:

4 (four) child (#12M) frog costumes	@$22.00	$88.00
3 (three) child (#24M) reptile costumes	@$25.00	$75.00
Total		$163.00

Our tax-exempt number is: 4569078

Our address is:
            Whitfield Theater Company
            23 High Street
            Alma, MI 07984

We have always been very pleased by the quality of your costumes and the service you provide. We need these costumes by April 3 for dress rehearsal. Please notify us immediately by fax or phone if there is any problem filling this order by that date. Thanks for your help.

- If you have an urgent deadline, let your supplier know, both in the Subject line and in the body of the fax.

- Treating suppliers as partners rather than adversaries can help in getting orders filled on time. Mentioning that you've been pleased with past service seems trivial, but this kind of positive feedback can be very helpful in getting what you want.

Company Name
Address
City, State Zip

To: Pet Distributors, Inc.

From: Jerry MacDonald, Prairie Pet Lodge

Date:

Subject: Return of Damaged Shipment

Your September 4 shipment of vegetarian dog biscuits and cat croutons
(Order #6754A) arrived damaged. It appears that water penetrated the
packaging material at some time before we received it because mold is
apparent on portions of the cartons.

I'm certain you'll want to examine the shipment to ensure that this sort
of problem does not happen again. Please fax us how the shipment will
be picked up and when you can reship. We need to receive a
replacement no later than one week from today, since we have almost
no inventory left.

- A fax gives a sense of urgency when a deadline is involved.

- Be sure to give your original order number and your expectation of how the damaged
  shipment will be resolved.

Company Name
Address
City, State Zip

To: Mort Palmer, Broxo Manufacturing

From: Tom Knight, Purchasing Manager

Date:

Subject: Cancellation of PO #1908832

Mort, this fax is to advise you of our cancellation of our Purchase Order #1908832 for 500 serial cables. As we've discussed, our sales have slowed down this summer and we won't need the cables until October. You can expect a Purchase Order for the original 500 plus another 250 at that time.

Sorry for any inconvenience. We value your company as a key supplier and look forward to a continuing relationship.

- Canceling or changing orders by fax saves valuable time and is particularly critical if you need to get to the supplier before manufacturing begins.

- When dealing with suppliers, particularly in situations like this, be sure to remind them that they are important to your company.

Complaint to Supplier, Cannot Reach by Phone (13-13)

Company Name
Address
City, State Zip

To: Paul Freeman, Sales Manager, Elite Computer Products

From: Anna West, Fulfillment Manager

Date:

Subject: Delay in Order

We have been trying to reach you by phone since Tuesday, but you
have not been available and no one has returned our calls.

We are very concerned about the delay in our order for three Elite
Display Adapters (EM 12-4668). We placed the order with you three
weeks ago, on August 12, and were assured by Ted Simms that we
would have the adapters by last Friday at the latest.

These delays have caused us to miss deadlines with our customers,
which has put us in an awkward position. We have had a good working
relationship with your company until now. But unless we hear from
someone by tomorrow noon, we will be obliged to place our orders with
another supplier. I certainly hope this will not be necessary.

- Keep your language direct and firm, but leave an opening to resolve the problem amicably.

- Give enough information so that someone can track the problem.

- Be specific about any deadlines and what action you plan to take.

Company Name
Address
City, State Zip

To: Jerome White, Account Executive, Midway Enterprises

From: Alyssa Montenegro

Date:

Subject: Clark Technical Financials for Steinman Meeting

Here are the numbers you need on Clark Technical for your meeting tomorrow afternoon:

Revenue	$130,114,000.00
Operating expenses	112,320,000.00
Operating income	17,794,000.00
Interest expense	463,000.00
Net income	17,331,000.00
Earnings per share	.64
No. of shares outstanding	27,079,687

I will send the full report on the company by overnight courier tonight; you should have it by 10:00 a.m. tomorrow. I will be in my office until 4:00 p.m. today (212-555-5672) if you need any additional information.

• Since this is urgent data, give the recipient a contact (in this case, the sender) who can answer questions or provide additional information.

Company Name
Address
City, State Zip

To: Elliott Newsome

From: Charles White

Date:

Subject: QualityCare, Inc. Presentation

As you know, we've been trying to land the QualityCare account for more than a year. I've just been advised that they have begun interviewing new agencies. I want your approval to call Ed Bascomb, president of QualityCare, to set up a presentation for one week from today. If we wait any longer, I'm afraid they will have already made their decision.

Please fax or phone me as soon as you arrive at your hotel so I can proceed.

- Faxing someone at their hotel is better than leaving a phone message at the desk, since you can be sure they'll get the entire message in a clear, ungarbled way.

- A fax to a guest who has not yet arrived at the hotel should be clearly marked on the cover sheet "Hold for Arriving Guest."

Company Name
Address
City, State Zip

To: Edward Heath, VP Marketing

From: Benson Aronot

Date:

Subject: Immediate Approval Required

Ed, I've attached copy and layout for the new trade ad which has to be shipped to Hardware Buyer magazine by Friday. If it's okay, please initial the cover sheet and fax it back to me.

If you have changes, please call me right away so we can implement them in time to make the closing date.

Thanks for your quick response.

- Faxes are ideal for getting written approvals. Specify when the approval is needed and why it is urgent.

- Allow for the possibility of not getting the approval, and what steps will be necessary as a result.

Company Name
Address
City, State Zip

To: Grace Antonio

From: Susan Royce

Date:

Subject: Alyce Carson, Potential Customer

Ted Cochran tells me that you will be in San Francisco on Monday and Tuesday to meet with the Dickson Company. While you are in San Francisco, I thought you might want to get in touch with a former colleague of mine, Alyce Carson, who has just been promoted to head buyer for Tigress Cosmetics: (415) 555-6800.

Tigress is developing a new line of all-natural cosmetics; they are looking for suppliers. I think they would be particularly interested in our aloe and collagen products.

Alyce is a graduate of Oberlin (art history) and spent three years in Albuquerque with Macon Department Stores (she was assistant buyer for ladies wear and cosmetics when I headed purchasing there). She joined Tigress in January of last year, transferred to the West Coast in April, and was promoted to her present position on October 1. She lives in Tiburon with her husband, Walt, and two children. Alyce enjoys sailing, antique toys, and Impressionist painters. You can reach her through Tigress or at her home: (415) 555-4825.

She is a very bright lady — I think you will enjoy each other's company. Relay my greetings, and tell her I'm still looking for the tin wind-up Scottie to add to her collection.

- Tell the person why he or she should meet the contact.

- Provide nonsensitive personal information, so your colleague will have something to talk about.

Company Name
Address
City, State Zip

To: Robert Andres, Flags of the World, Inc.

From: Michael Durst

Date:

Subject: Confirmation of Phone Conversation 9/22

I thought it would be helpful to confirm our phone conversation of this morning to be sure we cover all points.

You advised that payment for Invoice #667332 will be mailed by the end of the week. Your order #12234-5 will be shipped no later than January 22.

In addition, you asked me to provide you a quotation for the following items:

      1,000 2" diameter x 3' poles
      2,500 gold tassels, 2"
      2,000 bronze wall mounts

As I said, you'll have my quote within 7 days. If you'd like to add to this request, please let me know by Monday and I will incorporate the additional items in the quote.

We appreciate your business.

- Confirming phone conversations avoids misunderstandings and gives you another opportunity to maintain a strong relationship with customers.

- Thanking a customer for business is always appreciated.

Company Name
Address
City, State Zip

To: Keiko Nakagawa, Ichi-ban Imports, Tokyo

From: Jerrold Hammacher

Date:

Subject: Final Arrangements for Convention Logistics

I have just spoken to Tom McCaw and Sarah Greenlee, who were able to answer all our questions about the convention logistics.

It is important that you and I talk to confirm the final arrangements before you leave Tokyo on Wednesday. I will call your office Monday about 10:00 a.m. your time; if that is not convenient, you may call me at (201) 555-6688 Monday, between 9:00 a.m. and 11:00 a.m. Tokyo time.

It will be a pleasure finally to meet you at the convention.

- Be clear about whose time zone you are referring to.

- Allow a second option — a way for the other party to reach you — since you cannot be sure of his or her availability.

Networking 14

The saying, "The best things in life are free" doesn't apply to most aspects of business, but when it comes to networking, nothing could be truer. By spending just a small amount of time investing in business relationships you can produce bountiful rewards. Work toward building positive relationships today with the knowledge that you'll be able to ask for assistance, if you should need it, tomorrow.

Be appreciative. Most people are flattered when you turn to them for their expertise or assistance and are eager to help (unless you become a nuisance). But if and when you do need help, remember to ask for it as a favor, rather than as something to which you're entitled. Take nothing for granted, and always express your gratitude. And if you can offer to return the favor, do so. Be gracious but don't grovel.

Be specific. Have a clear idea of what you're seeking and be as specific as possible. Generally, those people you want to network with are the most successful and busiest. Don't waste their time with broad, unfocused requests.

Be realistic. Recognize that access to other people is one of the most valuable assets a business person has. Don't expect, for example, that your network contact will call the CEO of his company to arrange an informational interview for you just because you ask. Give a reason why the CEO might find talking to you of interest — perhaps you can provide competitive intelligence based on recent research in the industry. If you make unreasonable requests, you may not get a second chance.

Be honest. If you are in the early stages of a job search, product development, or market research, be very open about your need to "pick someone's brain" so that the person will not expect too much structure in your request—and will understand your objective.

Don't be greedy. If you are describing a new product or service to members of your network, don't attempt to "sell" them at the same time. If you truly believe network members might have a need for your product or service, you can always pursue sales, on a very non-aggressive basis, a bit later on. Remember that maintaining your network is more important than making a sale.

Company Name
Address
City, State Zip

Date

Lucy Martinez
International Partnership, Inc.
2066 Glendale Avenue
Camden, NJ 08103

Dear Lucy:

It's a pleasure to announce the formation of Global Prospects, Inc. I wanted you to be one of the first to know, since we were all in Taos together the night we first discussed the idea. We've gotten the backing we needed from a group of private investors who are extremely enthusiastic and supportive. I think you know Joseph Timm, who has been instrumental in putting the deal together.

We'll be sending you our promotional material as soon as we get it. In the meantime, thanks for all your support and good wishes and, most of all, for providing an example of success and quality in a challenging market. Your company is the best in your industry. I hope we can be half as successful in ours.

Sincerely,

Jesse Potter
President

- Providing news about your endeavors gives your network something to talk about, and the ability to spread the word about you at the same time.

- A flattering comment will be remembered and will cast a favorable light on you as well.

Request for Feedback on New Product (14-02)

Company Name
Address
City, State Zip

Date

Diana Marley
Vice President, Human Resources
Partners Insurance
700 Pratt Street
Meriden, CT 06450

Dear Diana:

You've always offered useful advice when I was pondering new markets for our training programs. What do you think about this idea? A Curriculum Advisor from Ames Secretarial School has come to us with a proposal to create and teach a program for administrative assistants tentatively titled, "Interpersonal Skills for Support Staff." (I've attached the preliminary schedule.)

I know that service has always been your watchword at Partners Insurance. Do you think that other major insurance companies like Partners would be interested in a program such as this? How much would you be willing to pay for such a program? Do you think your administrative assistants would be receptive to a program of this type?

I'll call you Tuesday to set up a lunch so I can hear your thoughts.

Best wishes,

Nick Viti
President

- Provide a series of thought-provoking questions to start things going.

- You'll get the most helpful insights in person, so try to set up a face-to-face meeting. The offer of a meal is a good incentive to the party whose help you're seeking.

Company Name
Address
City, State Zip

Date

Diana Marley
Vice President, Human Resources
Partners Insurance
700 Pratt Street
Meriden, CT 06450

Dear Diana:

Thanks for your encouragement concerning our "Interpersonal Skills for Administrative Assistants" workshop. As a direct result of your input, we've expanded the program from four hours to eight hours and have added a two-part exercise on "dealing with difficult people." As I mentioned, we field-tested the program in New Orleans a month ago, and participants in that workshop were so enthusiastic that we were able to book four programs at that company for next month.

Now that I feel confident the program is of the same high quality as our other offerings, I'd like to ask another favor. I know you have many associates in human resources within the insurance industry, and you did say that several of them had a need for this kind of workshop when we conducted our preliminary market research. Would you be willing to provide us with introductions to some of these people? I'd be more than happy to have one or two of our recent participants fill you in on their reactions to the program, if that would be helpful.

I'll call Thursday so we can talk further.

Yours truly,

Nick Vitti
President

- Anything regarding names and referrals is best discussed on the phone or in person, especially since you may be able to get additional marketing intelligence that way.

- Don't make members of your network guinea pigs for your untested ideas. Always field-test first. Maintaining the trust of the network is far more important than making the first sale.

Company Name
Address
City, State Zip

Date

Kyle Snow
Nova Consulting Group
1300 East Parham Road
Richmond, VA 23280

Dear Kyle:

I just finished speaking with Charles Stein. Thanks for referring him to me. I'm confident I can be of help to him in both his business and personal accounting needs.

As I discussed with you after the Rotary Club dinner last Thursday, I'll be happy to direct any clients to you who are in need of your marketing expertise. In fact, I'm seeing someone next week who I suspect is a perfect candidate for your services. I'll give you a call after the meeting.

Kindest regards,

Gerry Solomon

- One of the best uses of networking is exchanging referrals. Select business associates to refer to who you know are skilled in their professions as well as completely dependable. After all, your reputation is at stake.

- Keep in touch with those with whom you've agreed to exchange referrals, not only so they'll keep you in mind, but also to let them know *you* are thinking of *them*.

Request for Help with Employee Search (14-05)

Company Name
Address
City, State Zip

Date

Andrea Cummings
Dome Associates
500 Frontage Road
Pontiac, MI 48057

Dear Andrea:

I know you've just gone through the horrors of hiring people for your new location, and lived to tell the tale. Now I face a similar fate. Graham McNamara, our computer guru, is leaving us to relocate to Fiji (really!)

You mentioned that several candidates you interviewed for your company impressed you, but didn't quite suit your needs. Would you be good enough to fax their resumes to me (after checking with them first, of course). That would be of tremendous assistance in my search for a qualified replacement for Graham.

Thanks for your help.

Sincerely yours,

Josie Board
VP Administration

- Personalize your request with a few details.

- Most people will respond positively to a request for help. Make it easy by stating exactly what you want.

Company Name
Address
City, State Zip

Date

Edwina Kelsey
Galaxy Search
604 South Cochran
Los Angeles, CA 90036

Dear Edie:

As you may have read in the trades, Yorke, Pardee, and Choate, the law firm that has represented us for ten years, is no longer operating. The breakup of the partnership was extremely messy, and there is no way that I would continue the relationship with any of the partners on an individual basis.

I know that many of your clients have relationships with the top firms in L.A. Could you let me know whether there is anyone that they could recommend? Of course, I'm also going to call Judwin, Lawrence and Chasen, but I understand they have a tendency to assign associates to accounts as small as mine, and I prefer to deal with a partner.

My priorities are excellent service, extensive knowledge of international licensing, and then, and only then, price.

Hope to hear from you soon.

Yours truly,

Rod Nemerson
Executive Vice President

- The best sources for recommendations of professionals are people in your industry.

- State why you are changing professionals without going into too much detail; then give your criteria so the reader can make useful recommendations.

Business Forms 15

How business documents look, particularly those sent outside the company, is as important to successful communications as their contents. This section provides styles for the major kinds of documents.

In addition to using the proper formatting, attention should be paid to the other physical aspects of business writing. You should use high-quality stationery and spelling should always be checked (particularly the name of the recipient).

Forms should be readable and simple to follow. The "plain English" movement has done a great deal to simplify forms, through appropriate use of white space (margins, space between paragraphs) and headings. Using a readable type face and resisting the temptation to mix fonts or to overuse italics or bold face also help ensure readability.

Company Name
Address
City, State Zip
1 to 12 blank lines depending on length of letter (for shorter letters leave more blank lines)
Date
1 to 12 blank lines depending on length of letter (for shorter letters leave more blank lines)
Person's name
Title
Company name
Street address
City, State Zip
 double space
Dear (salutation):
 double space
First paragraph, body of the letter begins. (This is always single spaced with the paragraphs starting at the left margin.)
 double space
Next paragraph
 double space
Last paragraph
 double space
Sincerely yours,
 quadruple space

Typed name
Title
 double space
Writer's initials (uppercase): typist's initials (lowercase)
 double space
Enclosure (if needed)

6 blank lines from top of page
Name of recipient
Page 2
Date
    triple space

This is how you set up the second page of a letter in Full Block Style.
All paragraphs begin at the left.
    double space
Next paragraph
    double space
Last paragraph
    double space
Sincerely yours,
    quadruple space

Typed name
Title
    double space
Writer's initials (uppercase): typist's initials (lowercase)
    double space
Enclosure (if needed)

Company Name
Address
City, State Zip
1 to 12 blank lines depending on length of letter (for shorter letters leave more blank lines)
Date
1 to 12 blank lines depending on length of letter (for shorter letters leave more blank lines)
Person's name
Title
Company name
Street address

City, State Zip
double space
Dear (salutation):
double space
First paragraph, body of the letter begins. (This is always single spaced with the paragraphs starting at the left margin or indented 5 spaces.)
double space
Next paragraph
double space
Last paragraph
double space

Sincerely yours,
quadruple space

Typed name
Title
double space
Writer's initials (uppercase): typist's initials (lowercase)
double space
Enclosure (if needed)

6 blank lines from top of page

Name of recipient   -2-   Date
                                    triple space

This is how you set up the second page of a letter in Modified Block
Style. Remember that you can start paragraphs at the left margin or
indent 5 spaces.
          double space

                                                    Sincerely yours,
                                                        quadruple space

                                                    Typed Name
                                                    Title
          double space
Writer's initials (uppercase): typist's initials (lowercase)
          double space
Enclosure (if needed)

Company Name
Address
City, State Zip

quadruple space

To:

double space

From:

double space

Date:

double space

Subject:

triple space

First paragraph, body of the memo begins. (This is always single spaced with the paragraphs starting at the left margin.)

double space

Next paragraph

double space

Last paragraph

double space.

Writer's initials (uppercase): typist's initials (lowercase)

CHAPTER TITLES

Chapter titles are set in all caps and centered on the page.

<u>Section Headings</u>

Section headings are also centered. They are upper case and lower case and underlined. You should have at least two heads at every level of subdivision.

<u>Section Subheadings</u>

Underlined subheadings, flush left, head each subdivision.

- If you are going to divide a subsection further, you may do so by using bullets or some similar mark of distinction. These sections should be indented.

- This is a popular format. You should also include an Executive Summary, a one-page summary of the entire report.

Outline (15-05)

Title
triple space

I. FIRST ORDER DIVISION—ALL CAPITALS
double space
  A. Second Order Division—First Letter Of Each Word Is Capitalized
    1. Third order division—Only first letter is capitalized
    2. Note that each division and subdivision is indented 4 spaces from the heading superior to it
      a. Fourth order division
      b. If you have an a, you must have a b
      double space
II. IF YOU HAVE A 1, YOU MUST HAVE A 2

A. _____
  1. _____
    a. _____
    b. _____
  2. _____
B. _____
  1. _____
  2. _____

Company Name
Address
City, State Zip

Date

Company Name
Address
City, State Zip

INVOICE

Basic fee .... $

Other itemized expenses .... $

Total: $

Invoice is payable upon receipt.

Please make check payable to: Company Name
Address
City, State Zip

- This form should satisfy accounting departments because it provides a description of the basic service and allows for extra expenses.

- There's no need to include the "Please make check payable to" unless it's different from the letterhead.

- Be sure to include when payment is due.

Company Name
Address
City, State Zip

INVOICE

Date   Number

Order #:
P.O. #:
Cust. #:
Terms:

SOLD TO: SHIP TO:

ITEM #   DESCRIPTION   QTY.   UNIT PRICE   EXT. PRICE

Sale Amount: $
Discount: $
Tax: $
Freight: $

Total Sale: $

Index by Subject

(**Boldface** numbers indicate chapter introductions. Numbers in parentheses are document numbers found at the top of each letter. They are followed by page numbers.)

A

Acceptance letters, **339**
    to attend function to receive award (10-25), 365
    to donate (10-09), 349
    of job offer, **372,** (11-21), 400
    of request for interview (2-18), 90
    to serve in trade association (10-17), 357
    to speak (10-22), 362
Accounting services
    inquiring about (8-05), 265
    inquiring about temporary help (8-26), 286
Address, change of (2-09), 81
Advertising, goals of, **71** (*see also* Advertising agency; Advertising campaign; Advertising rates; Public relations)
Advertising agency
    hiring of (2-01), 73
    notifying of impending review of (2-03), 75
    requesting information from (2-02), 74
Advertising campaign
    announcing (1-23, 1-24), 25, 26
Advertising rates, requesting
    from magazine (2-06), 78
    from newspaper (2-05), 77
    from radio and television (2-07), 79
Agendas, **305**
    for background meeting (9-03), 309
    for meeting (9-02), 308
    to revise policy (9-02), 308
Announcements, **71, 306** (*see also* Memos; Press releases)
    of advertising campaigns (1-23, 1-24), 25, 26
    of annual meeting (8-36), 296
    of bad news (9-27), 335
    of board meeting (8-37), 297
    of change in administrative procedures or arrangements (3-07), 109
    of change in sales territory assignment (1-29), 31
    of change of address (2-09), 81
    of employee promotion (9-22), 330
    of job opening (7-01), 229
    of merger (2-24), 96
    of new branch, office, or store (1-19, 2-11, 2-15), 21, 83, 87
    of new business (14-01), 453
    of new business name (2-14), 86
    of new personnel (1-28, 2-12, 2-21), 30, 84, 93
    of new policy (9-23, 9-24), 331, 332
    of new product or product line (1-25, 2-13, 2-19), 27, 85, 91
    of new salesperson, to client (3-06), 108
    of new subsidiary (2-10), 82
    of price change, to sales force (1-26), 28
    of sales programs (1-21, 1-22), 23, 24
Apologies
    for billing error (4-02), 146
    for computer error (4-03), 147
    for damaged goods, with refund (3-39), 141
    for damaged shipment (4-06), 150
    for delayed shipment (1-39, 1-43, 4-04), 44, 48, 148
    for employee rudeness (4-07), 151
    for incorrect payment (6-28), 214
    for late payment (6-29, 6-30), 215, 216
    for missed meeting (3-23, 3-24), 125, 126
    for missing documentation or instructions (4-08), 152
    for shipment error (4-05, 13-08), 149, 438
Applications
    credit, inquiry to bank regarding (8-02), 262
    job, response to (7-05), 233
Appointments (*see also* Meetings)
    confirming (3-20), 122
    setting up (3-19), 121
Appraisals, job performance (7-24, 7-25), 252-253, 254-255
Appreciation letters (*see also* Thank-you letters)
    for answering questionnaire (1-33), 35
    for article (3-13), 115
    for award (10-25), 365
    to customers
        for complimentary letter or phone call (3-15), 117
        for meeting (3-21), 123
        for opportunity to quote (1-48), 53
        for order (1-37, 1-38), 42, 43
        for payment, with information regarding other products or services (3-29), 131
        for suggestion (3-14), 116

for helpful advice (8-34), 294
for help in job search, **372**
to hotel/facility for service (8-41), 301
for job application (7-05), 233
for permission to use name as reference
  (1-11), 13
for printing article (2-28), 100
for setting up sales call (3-22), 124
to supplier, during difficult project (6-22), 208
Approach letter (10-01), 341
Approval letter
  of drawings (1-63), 68
Article
  offer to write (10-20), 360
Assignments
  follow up to meeting (9-04), 310
Authorization letter
  to transfer funds (6-27), 213

B

Background information
  use of, in longer press release (2-27), 99
Backorders
  letter notifying of shipment (1-43), 48
Banking services
  inquiring about (8-16), 276
Benefits, employee
  clarifying (9-18), 326
  description of (7-21), 249
Bids (*see* Quotations)
Billing (*see also* Invoices)
  arranging terms of (6-02), 188
  clarifying (4-01), 145
  error in (4-02), 146
  sending duplicate, per request (3-36), 138
  under consignment terms (1-61), 66
Bonus program
  explaining (1-30), 32
Broadcast advertising (*see also* Media)
  requesting rates for (2-07), 79
Brochures, use of (*see also* Catalogs)
  in announcing new product (3-01), 103
  in promoting workshop (1-20), 22
  in requesting appointment with potential
    customer (3-19), 121
  in requesting opportunity to quote (1-47), 52
  in welcome letter (1-01, 1-03), 3, 5
Bullets
  in announcements (9-23), 331
  in recommendations (9-15), 322-323
  in reports (9-12), 319
  in resume (11-07, 11-08), 382, 384-385
Business association
  inquiry to (8-18), 278

Business forms, **459**
  invoices (15-06, 15-07), 467-468
  letters (15-01, 15-02), 460-464
  memos (15-03), 464
  outlines (15-05), 466
  reports (15-04), 465
Business plans
  cover letter for (8-32), 292
  executive summary (8-31), 291

C

Cancellation of order (6-18, 13-12), 204, 442
Career summary (*see also* Curriculum vitae)
  including, in resume (11-07), 383
Car leasing
  inquiring about (8-07), 267
Cash flow problems (3-31), 133
Catalogs, enclosing (*see also* Brochures)
  when acknowledging return (3-37, 3-38,
    3-39), 139, 140, 141
  when issuing duplicate invoice (3-36), 138
  when merchandise ordered is unavailable (1-
    41), 46
  when responding to request for information (1-
    09), 11
  when welcoming new customer (1-04), 6
Check has been sent (6-32), 218
Check missing
  new check issued (6-31), 217
Client list
  use of, in requesting opportunity to quote (1-
    47), 52
Collection agency (*see also* Collection letters)
  as ultimate threat, **166**
  warning customer of using, to collect on
    returned checks (3-27), 129
Collection letters (*see also* Collection agency)
  avoiding, **165-166**
  moderate tone (5-08, 5-09, 5-10, 5-11), 174,
    175, 176, 177
  sequence of, **166**
  stern tone (5-12, 5-13, 5-14, 5-15, 5-16), 178,
    179, 180, 181, 182
Commission program
  explaining (1-30), 32
Community service, **339-340** (*see also*
  Fundraising)
Company not responsible letters (4-09, 4-10, 4-
  11), 153, 154, 155
Complaints from customers (*see* Apologies;
  Company not responsible; Customer
  dissatisfaction; Customer
  misunderstanding)
Complaints to suppliers, 143-144

faxed to supplier unable to reach by phone (13-13), 443
  to hotel/facility for service (8-42), 302
  regarding service company (6-20), 206
  regarding temporary office help (6-19), 205
Complimentary letters (*see also* Congratulatory letters)
  purpose of, **101**
  to supplier (6-24), 210
  for supplier's employee (6-25), 211
Computer error
  apology for (4-03), 147
Confirmation letters and faxes
  accepting changed specifications in (1-60), 65
  accepting terms (1-56), 61
  accepting terms, with invoice (1-57), 62
  of agreement to speak (10-23), 363
  changing specifications in (1-59), 64
  with exception to original terms (1-58), 63
  of order (13-06), 436
Congratulatory letters (*see also* Appreciation letters)
  on adoption (12-07), 419
  on being quoted in media (3-10), 112
  on a birth (12-06), 418
  on child's achievement (12-09), 421
  on expanding business (3-12), 114
  on marriage (12-08), 420
  on new job (3-09), 111
  on opening new office (3-11), 113
  on promotion (3-08), 110
Consignment terms (1-61), 66
Consulting service
  inquiring about (8-08), 268
Consumer goods
  announcing sales program of (1-21), 23
Consumer services
  generating leads for (1-12), 14
Contact person, identifying
  in letter announcing sales program (1-21), 23
  prior to meeting to discuss fees (2-02), 74
Contracts
  arranging details for, with public relations firm (2-16), 88
  cover letter for (1-62), 67
  for freelancer (2-08), 80
Cover letters
  for business plan, executive summary (8-32), 292
  for contract (1-62), 67
  for payment (6-26), 212
  for proposal (1-52), 57
  for quotation (1-49), 54
  for resume, **372**, (11-12, 11-13, 11-17, 11-26), 391, 392, 396, 405

Credit
  approving retail (5-05), 171
  inquiry to bank regarding status of application for (8-02), 262
  refusing commercial (5-06), 172
  refusing retail (5-07), 173
  requesting, with terms (6-02), 188
  requesting terms of (6-03), 189
  request to customer for application (5-01), 167
  request to customer for financial data (5-02), 168
  requirements for (5-07), 173
Credit cards
  inquiry regarding business (8-03), 263
  using, to make paying easier, **165-166**
Credit reports
  requesting, on individual (5-03), 169
  requesting, on company (5-04), 170
  responding to, with clarification (5-17), 183
  responding to false (5-18), 184
Curriculum vitae (11-11), 390 (*see also* Summary, career)
Customer complaints (*see* Apologies; Customer dissatisfaction; Customer misunderstanding)
Customer dissatisfaction (*see also* Company not responsible letters; Customer goodwill; Customer relations)
  following up on (1-06), 8
  right to payment despite (4-13), 157
  soliciting business following (1-08), 10
  and threat of legal action (4-19), 163
Customer goodwill
  and billing (3-33), 135
  maintaining, during sales representative changes (1-29), 31
Customer misunderstanding
  of delivery terms (4-18), 162
  of delivery time (4-12), 156
  of product specifications (4-15, 4-16, 4-17), 159, 160, 161
  of terms of sale (4-13, 4-14), 157, 158
Customer relations, **101-102** (*see also* Company not responsible letters; Customer dissatisfaction; Customer goodwill)
  and credit and collection matters, 165-166
  and handling complaints, **143-144**
  in soliciting new business from former customer (1-08), 10
  thank-you for good suggestions (3-14), 116

D

Data sheet
  use of, in updating product specifications

(1-27), 29

Deadlines (*see also* Lead time)
for approvals (1-63), 68
confirming extension of (1-55), 60
for discount on early payment (3-30), 132
for quotation (6-05), 191
requesting extension of, for quotation
(1-54), 59
specifying, on cover letter for questionnaire
(1-32), 34
for submission of material for publication (10-20), 360
for verification of compliance with regulatory
agency (1-64), 69

Declining (*see also* Regrets)
to accept job, **372**
to join organization (10-18), 358
to speak (10-24), 364

Delays (*see also* Lateness)
apology for, in shipping (4-04), 148

Delivery
misunderstanding regarding (4-12), 156

Discount offers
for cash orders (5-06), 172
inquiring about (6-04, 8-14), 190, 274
in prepayment option (1-16), 18
in sales program (1-22), 24
in store opening (1-19), 21
in thank-you for permission to use name as
reference (1-11), 13
for timely payment, **165,** (3-28, 3-30), 130,
132

Distribution
of sales flyer (1-14), 16

Documentation
apology for missing (4-08), 152
request for missing (6-17), 203

Donation letters (*see also* Solicitations; Thank-you letters)
acceptance (10-09), 349
refusal (10-10), 350

E

EEOC compliance
request for verification of (1-64), 69

Elected representative
requesting help from (8-22), 282

Employees (*see also* Personnel relations)
apology for rudeness of (4-07), 151
complimenting supplier's (6-25), 211
motivating (7-28, 9-25), 258, 333
press release announcing achievement of (2-23), 95

Employment agency

requesting information from (8-24), 284
requesting information from temporary
(8-26), 286

Employment verifications
providing (7-20), 248
request for (7-19), 247

Enclosures
invoice as (1-57), 62
with questionnaire (1-32), 34
in response to request for information
(1-09), 11
for signature (1-62), 67

Equipment
confirming rental of (8-40), 300
inquiring about office (8-06), 266
recommending purchase of (9-14), 321

Estimates (*see also* Quotations)
offering free, in soliciting new business
(1-12), 14

Evaluations (*see* Appraisals, job performance; Job
performance)

Event planning services
inquiring about (8-13), 273

Executive search firm
approaching (11-02), 374
requesting information from (8-25), 285

Executive summaries
of business plan (8-31), 291
of business report, **306**
of final report (9-12), 319
of progress report (9-11), 318

F

Faxes
apologizing for shipment error (13-08), 438
to associate about client (13-17), 447
canceling order (13-12), 442
confirming order (13-06), 436
confirming phone conversation (13-18), 448
correcting prices (13-05), 435
cover sheet
master (13-01), 431
for resume (13-02), 432
notifying of shipment (13-07), 437
to order (13-10), 440
for quotation (13-04), 434
requesting approval (13-16), 446
requesting decision (13-15), 445
requesting permission to return shipment (13-11), 441
requesting quotation (13-09), 439
responding to request for information
(13-03), 433
setting time for phone call (13-19), 449

to supplier who does not return phone calls (13-13), 443

uses of (1-54), 59, **429**

with urgent data (13-14), 444

Feedback

in advertising campaigns (1-23), 25

and customer dissatisfaction, **143**

and questionnaires (1-34), 37

soliciting, in proposal cover letter (1-52), 57

in updates of products (1-27), 29

Flyer (1-14), 16

Follow-up letters

for booked speaker (10-23), 363

in fundraising, **340,** (10-08), 348

to meeting (9-04), 310

to proposal (1-51), 56

to questions regarding request to bid (1-53), 58

recommending other products or services to current customer (3-29), 131

regarding an order (1-37), 42

to resume (7-04), 232

in sales, **2**

Forms, business (*see* Business Forms)

Franchising

inquiring about (8-09), 269

Freelancer

work agreement with (2-08), 80

Funding

inquiring about, from venture capital firm (8-19), 279

Fundraising letters, **340** (*see also* Acceptance letters; Solicitations; Thank-you letters)

G

Get well letter (12-01), 413

Gifts, **411**

thank-you for (12-11), 423

Government

dealing with local (8-27), 287

inquiry to federal (8-20), 280

inquiry to state (8-21), 281

request for action to local town (8-23), 283

"Grabber," uses of, **1**

H

Help

requesting (8-33), 293

Hiring process (*see also* Job approaches)

necessity for putting things in writing in, **227-228**

Hotels

appreciation to, for help/good service

(8-41), 301

complaining, about service (8-42), 302

requesting rates (8-38), 298

reserving meeting facilities (8-39), 299

I

Incentives

in announcing opening of new branch store or office (2-15), 87

in questionnaire cover letter (1-32), 34

in welcome letter, (1-01), 3

Industrial products

generating leads for sales of (1-13), 15

Inquiries, **259**

accounting services (8-05), 265

car leasing (8-07), 267

consulting services (8-08), 268

credit card (8-03), 263

event planning services (8-13), 273

to franchisor (8-09), 269

insurance (8-04), 264

medical plans (8-15), 275

office equipment (8-06), 266

office lease (8-01), 261

to Planning and Zoning Commission (8-12), 272

supplier discounts (8-14), 274

telephone (8-10), 270

Insurance coverage

inquiring about (8-04), 264

Internal communications, **305-306** (*see also* Agendas; Memos; Recommendations; Reports)

Interviews

accepting request for (2-18), 90

follow-up to, rejection (7-10), 238

information, **371-372**, (11-26, 11-27, 11-28), 405, 406, 407

invitation to (7-06), 234

laying groundwork for, **371**

outline of, **228**, (7-07), 235

requesting, **372**, (11-17), 396

thank-you for, **372**

Introductions (*see also* Announcements; Press releases)

of new employee (2-21), 93

of new salesperson (3-06), 108

of new subsidiary (2-10), 82

Invitation to dinner/luncheon (10-27), 367

response card accompanying (10-28), 368

Invoices (*see also* Billing; Statements)

duplicate, per customer request (3-36), 138

as enclosure with confirmation letter (1-57), 62

formats for (15-06, 15-07), 467, 468
notifying of incorrect charge on (6-16), 202
Itemizing
    in letter acknowledging order (1-37), 42
    on statement for goods delivered (1-46), 51

J

Job approaches (*see also* Job search; Job offers;
        Job openings; Resumes)
    cold (11-12), 391
    with referral (11-13, 11-30), 392, 409
Job descriptions
    entry level (7-22), 250
    middle level (7-23), 251
    writing, **228**
Job offers
    accepting (11-21), 400
    confirming, **228**, (7-08), 236
    expressing interest in, with conditions
        (11-23), 402
    expressing interest in, with questions
        (11-22), 401
    negotiating (11-24), 403
    rejecting (11-25), 404
    revising (7-09), 237
    terminating (7-11), 239
Job openings
    announcing, **228**, (7-01), 229
    discovering, **372**
Job performance (*see also* Appraisals, job
        performance)
    memos regarding (7-12, 7-13), 240, 241
    written evaluation of (7-24, 7-25),
        252-253, 254-255
Job search, **371-372** (*see also* Job approach; Job
        offers; Job openings; Resumes)
Job skills
    outlined in job description (7-22, 7-23), 250,
        251
Jury duty
    requesting employee be excused from
        (8-30), 290

L

Landlord
    dealing with (8-29), 289
Lateness (*see also* Delays)
    explaining (9-11, 9-13), 318, 320
Leads
    letters generating (1-12, 1-13, 1-24), 14, 15, 26
Lead time
    for submission of ads (2-06), 78
Leasing agreements (8-28, 8-29), 288, 289

Legal action
    notifying customer of, for nonpayment
        (5-16), 182
    responding to customer's threat of (4-19), 163
Legal implications
    in personnel matters, **228**
Legal services
    inquiring about (8-17), 277
Letterheads
    for community service letter (10-04), 344
    for personal letters (12-06, 12-10, 12-11), 418,
        422, 423
Letters
    full block (15-01), 460-461
    modified block (15-02), 462-463
Letter to the editor (12-15), 427
Limited time offers
    use of, in store opening (1-19), 21

M

Magazine advertising
    requesting rates for (2-06), 78
Managing your business **259-260** (*see also*
        Inquiries; Requests)
Maps
    use of, in trade show announcement
        (1-18), 20
Marketing, **1-2** (*see also* Advertising, goals of;
        Advertising campaign)
    role of sales letter in, **1**
    use of questionnaires in (1-33), 35
Media (*see also* Broadcast advertising; Letter to
        the editor)
    procedures for dealing with (9-17, 9-29), 325,
        337
Medical plans
    inquiring about (8-15), 275
Meetings, **101** (*see also* Appointments)
    confirming (3-17), 119
    to discuss employee problem (7-13), 241
    to discuss program development and cost (3-
        16), 118
    to discuss services and fees (2-02, 2-17), 74,
        89
    follow-up to (3-21), 123
    notifying of (8-36, 8-37, 9-01), 296, 297, 307
    recap of (9-06), 312-313
    requesting associate attend (3-18), 120
    rescheduling (3-23), 125
    to review sales performance (1-31), 33
    to submit quote (1-47), 52
Memos, **228**, **305** (*see also* Reports)
    announcing assignments (9-04), 310
    announcing job opening (7-01), 229

announcing motivational award (9-25), 333
bad news (9-27), 335
format for (15-03), 464
planning (9-05), 311
policy (9-18, 9-19, 9-23, 9-24), 326, 327, 331, 332
procedure (9-17, 9-20), 325, 328
recommendation (9-14, 9-15, 9-16), 321, 322-323, 324
regarding benefits (7-21), 249
regarding performance (7-12, 7-13), 240, 241
requesting change in project (9-09), 316
requesting employee participation in charity drive (9-10), 317
resignation (9-26), 334
thanking employee for suggestion (9-07, 9-08), 314, 315
Merchandise
being shipped (1-42), 47
ready for pick-up (1-44), 49
unavailable (1-40), 45
Motivation letter (7-28), 258 (*see also* Personnel relations)

N

Negotiation
of job offer, **372**, (11-24), 403
Newspaper advertising
requesting rates for (2-05), 77

O

Opening sentence, **1**
Orders, **2**
acknowledging (1-37, 1-38, 1-39, 1-40, 1-41), 42, 43, 44, 45, 46
canceling (6-18), 204
received, unable to process (1-41), 46
rejecting proposed substitution of (6-21), 207
sent by fax (13-10), 440
special, customer misunderstood terms of (4-14), 158
Outline, format for (15-05), 466
Outplacement firm
requesting information from (11-03), 375
Overnight service
uses of (1-54), 59
Overpayment
rectifying with refund check (3-35), 137

P

Payments
cover letter for (6-26), 212

crediting for (3-32), 134
and customer dissatisfaction (4-13), 157
debiting account, in lieu of (3-33), 135
explaining delay in (6-30), 216
inquiring about terms of (6-05), 191
notifying policy change regarding (6-15), 201
offering discounts for timely, **165**
requesting additional, due to overlooked charges (3-34), 136
withholding, until work or order is complete (6-14, 6-15), 200, 201
Payment due, **102** (*see also* Collection letters)
for goods received (1-46), 51
on services rendered (1-45), 50
Performance (*see also* Warning memos to employees)
complaining of unsatisfactory, to service company (6-20), 206
complaining of unsatisfactory, to temporary employment agency (6-19), 205
regarding sales (1-31), 33
Personal letters, **411-412**, (*see also* Congratulatory letters; Sympathy letters)
Personnel file (6-25), 211
Personnel relations, **227-228** (*see also* Benefits, employee; Employees; Job descriptions; Job offers; Job openings; Job performance)
and business reverses (9-27, 9-28), 335, 336
policies affecting (9-24), 332
Planning and Zoning Commission
inquiry to (8-12), 272
Policies
announcing changes in (3-05, 6-15, 9-20, 9-21, 9-23, 9-24), 107, 201, 328, 329, 331, 332
clarifying, in memo (9-18), 326
recommending changes in (9-19), 327
Postscript
use of, to generate response (1-32), 34
Premium
use of, as incentive to new customer (1-17), 19
Prepayments
as discount option (1-16), 18
requiring, after repeated delays in payment (3-31), 133
Press releases, **71-72**
for anniversary celebration (2-26, 2-27), 98, 99
announcing employee achievement (2-23), 95
announcing merger (2-24), 96
announcing new employee (2-22), 94
announcing new partner (2-25), 97
announcing new product or product line (2-19, 2-20), 91, 92

long version (2-27), 99
short version (2-26), 98
Pricing
correcting of (13-05), 435
explaining change in, to sales force (1-26), 28
notifying dealer of changes in (3-02, 3-03),
104, 105
Probationary period, confirming, **228**
Procedures (*see also* Policy)
announcement of new (9-20, 9-21), 328, 329
Products
announcing new (1-25, 2-13, 2-19), 27, 85, 91
dealing with customer misunderstanding of (4-
15), 159
explaining, in sales letter (1-13, 1-25), 15, 27
inquiring about, to supplier (6-01), 187
requesting change in (9-09), 316
updating specifications of (1-27), 29
Promotions
and relationship with ad agency (2-03), 75
of sales program (1-21, 1-22), 23, 24
use of, in announcing opening of new branch
or office (2-15), 87
use of contest for (1-15), 17
use of testimonials in (1-17), 19
Promotions, job
announcing, **306,** (2-22, 9-22), 94, 330
notifying of (7-26), 256
Proposals, **2** (*see also* Quotations)
enclosed in thank-you for opportunity to quote
(1-48), 53
follow-up to (1-51), 56
rejecting (6-08), 194
sample of (1-50), 55
Public officials
expressing point of view to (12-16), 428
Public relations
goals of, **71**
hiring, firm (2-16), 88

Q

Questionnaires
consumer expo (1-36), 40-41
cover letter for (1-32), 34
to inactive client (1-35), 38-39
about salespeople (1-34), 36-37
Quotations, **2** (*see also* Proposal)
confirming (8-40), 300
cover letter for (1-49), 54
fax containing (13-04), 444
in flyer (1-14), 16
rejecting (6-06), 192
requesting (6-05), 191
requesting opportunity to submit (1-47), 52

responding to request for, with questions (1-
53), 58

R

Recommendations, **305**
to adopt a course of action (9-15), 322-323
to adopt a strategy (9-16), 324
to purchase equipment (9-14), 321
Recruitment letters
of board member (10-13), 353
of development chairperson (10-12), 352
of program chairperson (10-11), 351
References, **228**
character (12-14), 426
checking, for credit approval (5-03, 5-04), 169,
170
for employee who is leaving (7-15, 7-16), 243,
244
for former employee (17-17), 245
placing, in resume (11-08, 11-09), 385, 387
requesting (7-18, 11-30), 246, 409
soliciting (1-10), 12
thank-you for (1-11, 11-29), 13, 408
Referrals, 451-452
requests for (14-03, 14-04), 455, 456
role of, in arranging interview, **371**
Refund
for damaged goods (3-39), 141
Refusing (*see* Declining)
Regrets
inability to attend function (10-19), 359
Rejection letter (*see also* Declining)
of job offer, **372**
Rejecting proposed substitution in order
(6-21), 207
Repairs
confirming agreement to make, under warranty
(6-12), 198
requesting, of product under warranty
(6-10), 196
Reports, **305-306**
final (9-12), 319
format for (15-04), 465
progress (9-11), 318
Requests
for approval (13-16), 446
for decision (13-15), 445
for feedback on new product (14-02), 454
for help (8-33), 293
for help with employee search (14-05), 457
for information regarding job (11-15), 394
for list of attendees at meeting (3-22), 124
for missing documentation (6-17), 203
for names of professionals (14-06), 458

for opportunity to quote another's speech or article (1-47), 52
for payment covering returned check (3-25, 3-26, 3-27), 127, 128, 129
for permission to return shipment (13-11), 441
for quotation (13-09), 439
for speaker (10-21), 361
to use name as reference (1-10), 12
Resignations
  announcing, **306,** (9-26), 334
  from current job (11-01), 373
  from organization (10-26), 366
Responses
  to request to bid (1-53), 58
  to request for information (1-09, 13-03), 11, 433
  to resume, with recommendation (7-04), 232
  to unsolicited resume (7-03), 231
Resumes
  career change (11-10), 388-389
  curriculum vitae (cv) (11-11), 390
  early career: achievement (11-07), 382-383
  early career: chronological (11-05), 378-379
  entry level: chronological (11-04), 376-377
  entry level: functional (11-09), 386-387
  fax cover sheet (13-02), 432
  mid-career: achievement (11-08), 384-385
  mid-career: chronological (11-06), 380
  response to, with referral (7-04), 232
  response to unsolicited (7-03), 231
Returned check
  requesting payment for (3-25, 3-26, 3-27), 127, 128, 129
Returns, **102**
  acknowledging, for credit (3-38), 140
  acknowledging, for exchange (3-37), 139
  when customer misunderstands how to use product (4-15, 4-16, 4-17), 159, 160, 161
  of damaged goods (3-39), 141
  explaining changed policy regarding (3-05), 107
  of incorrect item (6-36), 222
  of item damaged in shipment (6-34), 220
  of item mistakenly included in shipment (6-35), 221
  of non-returnable item (4-14), 158
  of shipment that is no longer needed (6-39), 225
  tracing lost (3-40), 142
  after trial period (6-09), 195
  of unused merchandise, for credit or return (6-33), 219

S

Salary
  notification of increase (7-27), 257
Sales, **1-2** (*see also* Sales letters)
  use of contests in (1-15), 17
  use of flyers in (1-14), 16
  relationship of, to credit and collections, **165**
Sales calls
  arranging (1-12), 14
  follow-up to (1-05, 1-06), 7, 8
Sales campaign
  determining effectiveness of (1-19), 21
Sales force
  introducing addition to (1-28), 30
Sales letters, **1-2** (*see also* Sales)
  to follow up on sales call (1-05, 1-06), 7, 8
  to generate leads (1-12, 1-13), 14, 15
  to welcome new business (1-02), 4
  to welcome new client (1-03), 5
  to welcome new customer (1-04), 6
  to welcome new resident (1-01), 3
Salespeople
  communicating with, **2**
Sales territory
  explaining changed assignments in (1-29), 31
Samples
  use of, in letter to generate leads (1-13), 15
  use of, when requesting to quote (1-47), 52
Services
  explaining (1-12, 3-04), 14, 106
  requesting, under product warranty (6-11), 197
  role of questionnaire in improving (1-34, 1-35), 36-37, 38-39
Shipments, damaged
  apologizing for (4-06), 150
  returning item (6-34, 6-38), 220, 224
Shipment refused for quality reasons (6-13), 199
Shipping, **2**
  apologizing for delay in (4-04), 148
  errors in (1-06, 4-05), 8, 149
  explaining delay in (4-10), 154
  notifying of delay in (1-39), 44
Small Business Administration
  application cover letter (8-35), 295
Smoking policy
  announcing (9-24), 332
Solicitations (*see also* Thank-you letters)
  for cash donation (10-02), 342
  to current customer, to increase business (1-07), 9
  to former customer (1-08), 10
  for fundraiser (10-03), 343
  offering free estimates in (1-12), 14
  of votes to elect to board (10-16), 356

Speakers
    accepting request (10-22), 362
    refusal by (10-24), 364
    request for company/organization to provide (10-21), 361
Specifications
    accepting changes in, in confirmation letter (1-60), 65
    changing, in confirmation letter (1-59), 64
Stop payment
    because of replacement of missing check (6-31), 217
Subsidiary
    announcing new (2-10), 82
Suggestions
    awarding employee's (9-25), 333
    to supplier (6-23), 209
    thank you to employee for (9-07, 9-08), 314, 315
Suppliers, **185-186**
    complimenting (6-24, 6-25), 210, 211
    declining to do business with (6-07), 193
    inquiring about discounts from (8-14), 274
    making suggestions to (6-23), 209
    reaching by fax, to complain (13-13), 443
Sympathy letters
    to business associate and friend (12-02), 414
    to business associate's family (12-03), 415
    to employee (12-05), 417
    to employee's family (12-04), 416

T

Telephones
    inquiring about equipment (8-10), 270
    setting time for, with fax (13-19), 449
    use of, in handling customer complaints, **143**
Tenant
    dealing with (8-28), 288
Termination
    of employee (7-14), 242
    of relationship with ad agency (2-04), 76
Terms
    accepting, in confirmation letters (1-56, 1-57, 1-58), 61, 62, 63
    dealing with customer misunderstanding of (4-13, 4-14), 157, 158
Testimonials
    use of, in promotional materials (1-17), 19
    use of, in requesting opportunity to quote (1-47), 52
Thank-you letters (*see also* Appreciation letters)
    for company hospitality (10-29), 369
    for donation (10-06, 10-07), 346, 347

    for employee suggestion (9-07, 9-08), 314, 315
    for favor (12-13), 425
    for flowers (12-12), 424
    for gift (12-11), 423
    for help in arranging interview, **371-372**
    for hospitality (12-10), 422
    for information helpful in job search (11-16, 11-27, 11-28), 395, 406, 407
    for input (14-03), 455
    for job interview, **372**, (11-18, 11-19, 11-20), 397, 398, 399
    for pledge (10-04, 10-05), 344, 345
    for referral (11-14, 11-27, 11-28, 11-29), 393, 406, 407, 408
Tone, **260**
Transfer of funds letter (6-27), 213
Travel
    advising of special requirements for (8-43), 303
    changing procedures in (9-21, 9-23), 329, 331
    requesting hotel rates (8-38), 298

U

Utilities service
    inquiring about (8-11), 271

V

Venture capital firms
    inquiry to (8-19), 279
    writing executive summary for (8-31), 291
Verification, employment
    providing (7-20), 248
    requesting (7-19), 247
Volunteer service
    refusing (10-15), 355
    requesting (10-11), 351
    welcoming to (10-14), 354

W

Warning memos to employees (7-12, 7-13), 240, 241 (*see also* Appraisals; Job performance)
Welcome letters
    to new board member (10-14), 354
    to new business, from supplier (1-02), 4
    to new client (1-03), 5
    to new customer (1-04), 6
    to new resident (1-01), 3
Workshop promotion letter (1-20), 22